Empowering Settings and Voices
for Social Change

Empowering Settings and Voices for Social Change

Edited by Mark S. Aber, Kenneth I. Maton, and Edward Seidman

OXFORD
UNIVERSITY PRESS
2011

PROPERTY OF ~~WCIARD~~DISCARD
SOCIAL WORK ~~LIBRARY~~

OXFORD
UNIVERSITY PRESS

Oxford University Press, Inc., publishes works that further
Oxford University's objective of excellence in research,
scholarship, and education.

Oxford   New York
Auckland   Cape Town   Dar es Salaam   Hong Kong   Karachi
Kuala Lumpur   Madrid   Melbourne   Mexico City   Nairobi
New Delhi   Shanghai   Taipei   Toronto

With offices in
Argentina   Austria   Brazil   Chile   Czech Republic   France   Greece
Guatemala   Hungary   Italy   Japan   Poland   Portugal   Singapore
South Korea   Switzerland   Thailand   Turkey   Ukraine   Vietnam

Copyright © 2011 by Oxford University Press, Inc.

Published by Oxford University Press, Inc.
198 Madison Avenue, New York, New York 10016

www.oup.com

Oxford is a registered trademark of Oxford University Press
All rights reserved. No part of this publication may be reproduced, stored in a retrieval system, or
transmitted, in any form or by any means, electronic, mechanical, photocopying, recording, or
otherwise, without the prior permission of Oxford University Press

Library of Congress Cataloging-in-Publication Data

Empowering settings and voices for social change / edited by
Mark S. Aber, Kenneth I. Maton, and Edward Seidman.
    p. cm.
Includes bibliographical references and index.
ISBN 978-0-19-538057-6 (alk. paper)
 1. Community psychology. 2. Social psychology. 3. Social change.
4. Power (Social sciences) I. Aber, Mark Stephen, 1958- II. Maton, Kenneth I.
III. Seidman, Edward.
RA790.55.E48 2010
302–dc22

                                                                                    2010012909

ISBN-13: 978-0-19-538057-6
ISBN-10: 0-19-538057-6

9 8 7 6 5 4 3 2 1
Printed in the United States of America on acid-free paper

We dedicate this volume to Julian Rappaport for his friendship, generosity, intellectual acumen, vision, commitment, and profound faith in the power of ordinary people to change the world.

Acknowledgments

We wish to express our appreciation to the American Psychological Association Science Directorate for a Festschrift Scientific Conference Grant to honor the career of Julian Rappaport. Initial drafts of a number of chapters in this volume were presented at the conference held at the University of Illinois in June, 2005.

CONTENTS

CONTRIBUTORS

Mark S. Aber
Associate Professor
Department of Psychology
University of Illinois at
Urbana-Champaign

Rachel M. Angus
Research assistant
Department of Human and
Community Development
University of Illinois at
Urbana-Champaign

Anne E. Brodsky
Associate Professor
Department of Psychology
University of Maryland
Baltimore County

Joseph P. Gone
Associate Professor
Department of Psychology and
Program in American Culture
University of Michigan

James G. Kelly
Professor Emeritus
Department of Psychology
University of Illinois at Chicago

Jessica Owen Kostelnik
Department of Psychology
University of Virginia

Reed W. Larson
Pampered Chef Endowed Chair
in Family Resiliency and
Professor in the Departments
of Human and Community
Development Psychology and
Educational Psychology
University of Illinois
at Urbana-Champaign

Kenneth I. Maton
Professor
Department of Psychology
University of Maryland
Baltimore County

Jessica R. Meyer
Department of Psychology
University of Virginia

Maria A. Ramos Olazagasti
Deparment of Psychology
New York University

Julian Rappaport
Professor Emeritus
Department of Psychology
University of Illinois at
  Urbana-Champaign

N. Dickon Reppucci
Professor
Department of Psychology
University of Virginia

Deborah Salem
TMI Research Associates
Ann Arbor, Michigan

Edward Seidman
Senior Vice President
Program William T. Grant
  Foundation and Professor
Department of Applied Psychology
Steinhardt School Culture
  Education and
  Human Development
New York University

Irma Serrano-García
Professor
Department of Psychology
University of Puerto Rico

J. Eric Stewart
Assistant Professor
Department of Interdisciplinary
  Arts & Sciences and Masters
  of Arts in Cultural
  Studies Program
University of Washington
Bothell

Edison J. Trickett
Professor
Department of Psychology
University of Illinois at Chicago

Vivian Tseng
Senior Program Officer
William T. Grant Foundation

Hirokazu Yoshikawa
Professor
Graduate School of Education
Harvard University

PREFACE

This book is a rich stimulating, inspiring tribute to the multiple and far-reaching contributions of Julian Rappaport.

The reader is invited to absorb the values, concepts, and analyses that represent Julian's vision of how community psychology can evolve as a unique field of psychology.

Three of his major concepts and points of view are noted in terms of their merit and influence on other scholars. These familiar contributions are: the place of narrative in empowering the narrator and their social networks and communities, the impact of settings as a crucible for the celebration of community, AND the concept of empowerment as a trenchant unifying idea that includes people, settings, and communities. The implications for how we think and how we carry out our work are far-reaching. These three orienting ideas are not simply there for empirical elaboration; they serve as an incisive challenge to notions of professional aspiration. These ideas, for example, challenge us not to accept the status quo but free us from any previous professional preciousness and dislodge us from a colonial attitude to those with whom we work and from whom we learn.

His vision is there for us to not only emulate but to absorb and make personal and explicit for ourselves. It is the spirit of Julian Rappaport that is his most enduring legacy.

If we can take in his ideas and adapt them for ourselves, we stand a chance to contribute to a community psychology that is not just another professional item but is a framework that is liberating and thoughtful and appreciative of the trust we engender with the people and communities with whom we collaborate.

His contributions challenge community psychology to embrace a plurality of methods and ways of working in communities that can assist our own inquiries to be substantial, provocative, and endearing. His work has been vigorous and courageous. He has challenged us to do our own work that is nonexploitive of the respondents we learn from, to be directly palpable to citizens as well as colleagues, and to be useful to those community members with whom we are working and from whom we learn.

Rappaport has resisted giving in to those premises of a psychology that do not give back directly to the community. His attention to the ways our working relationships with citizens can be discoveries both for them as well as us is a forthright, up-front value that knowledge and help is to be generated within a framework that dispels elitism, quaintness, and pat formulations. By his example, he has encouraged us to be discoverers, learners, and adventurers. Without sanctimony he has challenged us to do more than conduct a study or design an intervention. He asks us to be another kind of professional: to engage our topic with openness to method and to spend time understanding the complex issues (historical and political, expressed and implicit) that affect the current circumstances of community residents. He has modeled an antidote to elitism, one that values care, courage, intellectual openness, and reciprocity with communities.

As you dig into the individual chapters, along with the two integrative commentaries, you have an opportunity to reflect and ponder the unique qualities of Julian Rappaport that have helped all of us choose to live up to standards of curiosity and investment in multidisciplinary thinking that he has modeled for the field of community psychology.

In reading these contributions, I have been enriched to think anew about research methods, premises of science, and the potential role of inquiry that enlarged my view about what is possible. I was encouraged to keep at a mission that more fully understands the political and economic contexts that touch on our work—how awareness of social contexts and their interdependence with the lives of citizens we work with can both free us and serve as a catalyst to examine our premises and choices of method and vision for our work.

The thoughtful qualities of the chapters and commentaries validate Rappaport's keen, in-depth thinking, toughness of mind, and spirit to innovate. They motivate us to follow our values and to avoid conforming to orthodoxies—whether theories, methods, assumptions, or traditions.

This collection is testament to Julian Rappaport. His work is accessible for us to embrace. His contributions are clearly presented with no encouragement to proselytize. This is a commendable quality. Those who learn from respected mentors or respected colleagues may feel duty-bound to mimic or repeat without debate his or her ideas, assumptions, and visions. Not here.

You are invited to join a remarkable journey as you read and savor what each of the 10 far-ranging contributions and 2 integrative commentaries have shared. The total collection makes it easy and expectant to look forward to Julian Rappaport's next contributions.

My personal suggestion is to read Rappaport's own statement as a starting point before exploring the other rich contributions. You may be refreshed to see how the contributors have been stimulated and energized by his work and then have framed their own individual contributions to this volume and in their own careers.

James G. Kelly

1 Empowering Settings and Voices for Social Change: An Introduction

Kenneth I. Maton, Edward Seidman, and Mark S. Aber

The field of community psychology developed in the mid-1960s as a reaction against the limitations of traditional, reactive, and intrapsychological approaches to research and social problems (Bennett, Anderson, Cooper, Hassol, Klein, & Rosenblum, 1966; Rappaport & Chinsky, 1974). The developers of the field highlighted the importance of social contexts and environments in understanding behavior and social problems, envisioned a strengths-based rather than a deficits-based approach to research and action, and emphasized the importance of prevention of problems and larger community and social change. Although much progress has been made in contributing to the prevention of individual problems, less progress has been made with regard to fundamental social change. The broad range of issues that challenged society throughout the latter half of the 20th century persists today. These include the failure of urban schools, homelessness, domestic violence, intergroup conflict, substance abuse, teenage pregnancy, immigration, poverty, child abuse, youth violence, and racial and sexual discrimination, to name a few.

Disciplines vary greatly in their approaches to bringing about social change. Community psychology draws upon a distinct set of values that guides its research and action in this area. Key values include: individual wellness (physical, psychological, social, and spiritual health), sense of community, respect for human diversity, citizen participation, collaboration and community strengths (working together with citizens and groups in the community and building on their strengths), grounding in systematic empirical research, focus on social systems, and an overarching concern for social justice for marginalized individuals and groups (Dalton, Elias, & Wandersman, 2007; Levine, Perkins, & Perkins, 2005; Rappaport & Seidman, 2000).

Bridging a number of the above values is the concept of empowerment. According to Julian Rappaport, who first proposed empowerment as a guiding paradigm for the field of community psychology (Rappaport, 1981), empowerment is, "a process, a mechanism by which people, organizations, and communities gain mastery over their affairs" (Rappaport, 1987, p. 122). Rappaport intended the term to help ensure that citizens, not professionals, had the determining voice in designing solutions to the problems they face and also to place emphasis on the central role of lack of power—and the corresponding need to gain additional power and resources—for successful efforts toward social change. To further emphasize these aspects of empowerment, and to more fully situate the term in a setting-centered versus person-centered context, Rappaport (and others) has since endorsed a definition of the term proposed by the Cornell Empowerment group in 1989:

> An intentional, ongoing process centered in the local community, involving mutual respect, critical reflection, caring and group participation through which people lacking an equal share of valued resources gain greater access to and control over those resources
> (cited in Wiley & Rappaport, 2000, p. 62).

We view empowerment as central to any effort by researchers, community practitioners, or policymakers to bring about meaningful social change related to marginalized individuals and groups. It is invaluable as a guiding paradigm because it points both to a process of social change (citizen-based) and an outcome of such change (enhanced access to critical resources) for those lacking power in society (Zimmerman, 2000). The process of empowerment is participatory and developmental—occurring over time, involving active and sustained engagement, and resulting in growth in awareness and capacity (Freire, 1993; Hur, 2006; Kieffer, 1984). Various empowerment outcomes are critical, including political, economic, and psychological empowerment (i.e., enhanced control, influence, and capacity in each of these domains) and multiple levels of analysis (i.e., individual, collective). Many different aspects of empowerment as a process and as an outcome have implications for the work of social scientists interested in enduring social change. In the current volume, we limit attention to two: developing new empowering settings in the community and enhancing the influence of existing ones, and using research methods that seek to hear, understand, support, and amplify the voices of those individuals and groups in the community who are the focus of our efforts. In this introduction, we briefly discuss each of these, concluding with a description of the current volume.

EMPOWERING SETTINGS

For marginalized or oppressed individuals, the process of empowerment can be expected to take place over an extended period of time, in relevant community settings (Maton, 2008). To be considered empowering, a community setting must have both an empowering process (participatory, developmental) and an empowering outcome (enhanced control, capacity, and access to resources). Empowering settings exist in an array of community domains, including those that: *(1)* empower adults to overcome personal difficulties; *(2)* empower youth living in adverse circumstances to develop, achieve, and accomplish; *(3)* empower people in impoverished communities to take action to improve the locality in which they live; and *(4)* empower historically oppressed citizens to resist and challenge societal culture and institutions and take action to change them. The first two domains noted encompass empowerment at the individual level and the latter two at the collective level. Various types of settings inhabit these four community domains, including, but not limited, to mutual-help groups, congregations, youth development organizations, educational settings, civic engagement organizations, social action settings, and social movement organizations.

Empowering settings contribute to community betterment and social change through both direct and indirect pathways of influence (Maton, 2000; Maton, 2008). A direct path is through a setting's external activities in the community, such as public education, community services, resource mobilization, and policy advocacy (Davis, McAdam, Scott, & Zald, 2005; Humphreys, 2004; Peterson & Zimmerman, 2004; Wandersman & Florin, 2000). An indirect path of influence is through the radiating impact of empowered members, including their impact on family and social networks, institutional attitudes and program development in organizations, and state and national policy (Maton, 2008).

Seminal conceptual work on empowering settings in community psychology was provided by Rappaport in his classic 1977 volume, *Community Psychology: Values, Research, and Action*, and in two early articles focused on empowerment (Rappaport, 1981, 1987). In these works, he underscored small-group and organizational levels of analysis as central to community psychology's capacity to contribute to social change and emphasized the important role of "mediating structures"—those settings such as churches, neighborhoods, and voluntary associations that stand at the interface between individuals and the larger society (cf. Berger & Neuhaus, 1977). In the 1980s, Rappaport, his colleagues, and their students documented positive, empowering outcomes and processes for members of GROW, a mutual-help group for individuals with serious mental illness (cf. Rappaport, Reischl, & Zimmermann, 1992). In the late 1980s and early 1990s, Rappaport generated a conceptual framework linking the "community narratives" shared among members of settings to member empowerment (Rappaport, 1993; Rappaport & Simkins, 1991).

Recent work in the empowering settings area has built upon Rappaport's framework and other contributions. For example, the theory of empowerment, as it relates to organizational settings, was discussed by Zimmerman (2000), who distinguished between community settings that empower members (empowering settings) and those with the capacity to achieve change in the larger community (empowered organizations). Maton and Salem (1995) generated a set of organizational characteristics common to multiple types of settings that contributed to member empowerment. Bond and Keys (1993) described organizational development practices that involved a co-empowerment process within a formerly struggling community-based organization. Wandersman and Florin (2000) conducted an intervention program with neighborhood block associations that enhanced their capacity to empower members and influence the surrounding community. Perkins, Crim, Silberman, and Brown (2004) proposed an integrative framework to encompass multiple, strengths-based, empowering strategies in community development efforts to build capacity. Finally, Evans and Prilleltensky (2005); Janzen, Nelson, Hausfather, and Ochocka (2007); Maton (2008); Peterson and Zimmerman (2004); and Speer and Hughey (1995) elucidated various activities and pathways through which community settings contribute to external impact in the community and within the larger society. Overall, work to date provides a solid foundation for future research and action centered on the contribution of empowering community settings to community and social change.

PRIORITIZING VOICE AND NARRATIVE METHODS

Marginalized and oppressed individuals lack access to mainstream sources of power and communication; their voices and perspectives rarely are heard or used as a catalyst for action. This results in a range of issues, including prejudice and serious misunderstanding on the part of mainstream society, government officials, program developers, and social scientists about the life circumstances, culture, and strengths of such individuals. Quantitative field research methods can become part of the problem, when studies are limited to the individual level of analysis, researchers are focused on deficits rather than strengths, and comparative analyses of variables selected for study depict marginalized groups as inferior.

Given limited understanding of marginalized groups and their life circumstances, programs, services, and policies directed toward them can be ineffective and, at worst, victim-blaming, counterproductive, and disempowering. To remedy this lack of understanding, researchers with strong social justice orientations have increasingly stressed the need to prioritize the voices of marginalized groups in our research by using alternative approaches, including narrative and qualitative research methods and collaborative research processes. Consistent with an empowerment perspective, such efforts to amplify the voices of the "other" can be expected to contribute to larger social change efforts via enhanced understanding of the perspectives, strengths, culture, and life circumstances of marginalized groups by policymakers, program developers, and the general public. In addition, qualitative approaches—and narrative approaches in particular—that present nuanced, rich perspectives of individuals and communities have the potential to strengthen the sense of community and mutuality among members of marginalized and oppressed populations and potentially increase their influence and involvement in social change efforts (Bond, Belenky, & Weinstock, 2000). Although quantitative research methods applied to marginalized and oppressed populations can also be broadly collaborative, generative, ecologically and culturally sensitive, strengths-based, and accessible, it appears more likely that these qualities will emerge when qualitative and narrative methods are employed together with quantitative methods.

Within community psychology, Rappaport was one of the first to argue for the use of narrative methods as part of the empowerment agenda. Specifically in his 1990 paper "Research methods and the empowerment social agenda," he argued, "Research that asserts a strengths perspective and that seeks to give voice to the people of concern may benefit from data collection and analysis approaches that emphasize description, multiple perspectives and authentication of those voices that often are ignored" (p. 58). During the 1990s, Rappaport and his students conducted a number of studies that pioneered the use of narrative methods to amplify the voices of those studied; serve social change by helping to turn "tales of terror" into "tales of joy;" enhance collaboration and empowerment; and contribute to a better understanding of the connection among *(1)* dominant cultural narratives in society, *(2)* community narratives shared among members in grassroots settings, and *(3)* individuals' personal narratives in these settings (Mankowski & Rappaport; 2000; Rappaport, 1993, 1995, 2000).

There have been a growing number of studies in community psychology in the last decade focused on authenticating and amplifying the voices of those lacking power in society. These encompass studies of the community narratives and lives of a wide range of ethnic minority and non-mainstream cultural communities in the United States, including, for example, Mexican-Americans (Harper, Lardon, Rappaport, Bangi, Contreras, & Pedraza, 2004), African-Americans (e.g., Kelly, Azelton, Lardon, Mock, Tandon, & Thomas, 2004), and members of a Native Alaskan community (Mohatt et al., 2004). They also include qualitative investigations of rarely studied groups in international context, including members of the Revolutionary Association of the Women of Afghanistan (Brodsky, 2003), people living in Guatemala and South America (Lykes, Blanche, & Hamber, 2003), and members of a Nicaraguan agricultural cooperative (Kroeker, 1995). As part of this trend, there is also a focus on increasing collaboration with those being studied, including those taking part in social action-focused participatory action projects (Chataway, 1997; Jason, Keys, Suarez-Balcazar, Taylor, & Davis, 2004). Overall, the use of narrative and related qualitative methods to authenticate and amplify the voices of those lacking power in society has become much more accepted in the field in the past decade and has the potential, ideally when combined with quantitative methods in sophisticated mixed-methods designs, to become an important part of our efforts to contribute to citizen empowerment and social change.

THE CURRENT VOLUME

The current volume is an integrated collection of chapters that build upon papers presented at a conference honoring Julian Rappaport's career (June, 2005, University of Illinois), sponsored by the American Psychological Association. The volume is organized around recurring and interrelated themes in Rappaport's body of work, which continue to be important for community psychology and other social change-oriented disciplines. The goal of the volume is to expand on and further develop innovations in theory, research, and action as they pertain to social settings as well as the broader goals of social change. Two cross-cutting themes—empowering community settings and voices for social change—characterized Rappaport's thinking and writing and serve as integrating and foundational themes of the volume.

The chapters of the volume are organized into three major parts. Part I of the volume, *Empowering Settings*, consists of three chapters on empowering settings and a commentary chapter. Edward Seidman and Vivian Tseng address several salient questions related to the development of a theory of social setting intervention: What is the nature of current and future conceptualizations of social settings? What are the actionable features in social settings? Are different actionable features synergistic or antagonistic? How can settings be created or restructured so that they place a premium on empowerment and promotion? Kenneth Maton and Anne Brodsky review the current state of knowledge related to organizational characteristics of empowering community settings, and then extend focus to an examination of mediating mechanisms and pathways of influence in the larger community. Specific focus is placed on empowering settings in the domains of personal transformation, minority student achievement, and social action in an international context. Reed Larson and Rachel Angus examine youth programs as settings that foster youth development, voice, and both individual and community empowerment. They highlight setting processes through which youth develop strategic thinking for understanding and impacting the community, experience enhanced motivation, transcend an egocentric perspective, and develop abilities to work collaboratively and bridge the divide between youth and adult worlds. A fourth chapter by Edison Trickett provides commentary related to the three preceding chapters. He raises probing questions about the varied conceptualizations of empowerment applied across chapters and across types of settings, the importance of attending to "ripple" effects of setting processes and activities at multiple levels of analysis, the ecological influence of the researcher–setting relationship, and the complex challenges of intervention.

The chapters in Part II of the volume, *Giving Voice*, examine how action scientists have sought to understand and amplify the voices of those individuals and communities who serve as the focus of their research and social change actions. Deborah Salem explores the role of institutional beliefs, community narratives, and personal stories in recovery from serious mental illness. She addresses the understanding of recovery that comes from the voices of consumers, the role personal stories play in recovery, the influence of setting narratives on consumers' personal stories and institutional belief systems on setting narratives, and the inability of traditional settings to prioritize consumers' voices. Joseph Gone traces the cultural contours of "mental health" among the Gros Ventres of the Fort Belknap Indian reservation in north central Montana. This group configures wellness much differently than professional psychology, emphasizing respectful relationships instead of egonic individualism and the ritual circulation of sacred power instead of secular humanism. Gone examines the implications of his narrative analysis for community-based professional psychology. N. Dickon Reppucci examines youth voices in the juvenile justice system. Drawing on brief histories of zero-tolerance policies in our schools and an increasingly adversarial and punitive juvenile justice system, he illuminates the loss of focus on individualized justice and accountability to youth. Reppucci observes that by blaming and punishing youth, we avoid a focus on needed social change. Hirokazu Yoshikawa and Maria A. Ramos Olazagasti examine community narratives in the areas of prevention and public policy. Using examples from recent work on HIV prevention, welfare-to-work program evaluations, and immigrants' attitudes and use of government programs, they illustrate how community narratives challenge the assumptions of universality in scope and relevance that undergird these initiatives and help to inform culturally anchored prevention research and action. The concluding chapter in this section, by Eric Stewart, provides commentary focused on the four preceding chapters. Building on critical theory, he argues that a primary purpose of narratives is to expose and question the social ideologies that lead to the oppression of marginalized groups. Stewart addresses the strengths and limitations of narrative work to date, including the chapters in this section, to accomplish this purpose.

Chapters in Part III of the volume, *Retrospect and Prospect*, aim to situate the earlier chapters in the context of several decades of work on empowering settings, prioritizing individual voices and social change. Irma Serrano-Garcia examines consistencies and contradictions in Rappaport's work over the course of his career. She finds consistency in a number of areas, including his emphasis on collaboration, resource development, a focus on strength versus weakness, and the need for multilevel interventions and multidisciplinary understanding. Contradictions are reported in the definition of power, views on prevention, and the role of the profession vis-à-vis government. In the volume's final chapter, Julian Rappaport reflects on the evolution of his thinking on empowerment and narrative methods over the years and explicates his current thinking on the field's potential. In his words, "What matters is that we remain faithful to the underlying values, goals and intentions that have so often established us in settings as both insiders and outsiders, able to both advance and critique the many places where a progressive social and political agenda can benefit from a research-based scholarly analysis." (p. 237).

REFERENCES

Bennett, C., Anderson, L., Cooper, S., Hassol, L., Klein, D., & Rosenblum, G. (1966). *Community psychology: A report of the Boston Conference on the Education of Psychologists for Community Mental Health*. Boston: Boston University.

Berger, P., & Neuhaus, R. (1977). *To empower people*. Washington, DC: American Enterprise Institute.

Bond, L. A., Belenky, M. F., & Weinstock, J. (2000). The Listening Partners Program: An initiative toward feminist community psychology in action. *American Journal of Community Psychology, 28*, 697–730.

Bond, M. A., & Keys, C. B. (1993). Empowerment, diversity and collaboration: Promoting synergy on community boards. *American Journal of Community Psychology, 21,* 37–58.

Brodsky, A. E. (2003). *With all our strength: The Revolutionary Association of the Women of Afghanistan.* New York: Routledge.

Chataway, C. J. (1997). An examination of the constraints on mutual inquiry in a participatory action research project. *Journal of Social Issues, 53,* 747–765.

Dalton, J. H., Elias, M. J., & Wandersman, A. (2007). *Community psychology: Linking individuals and communites.* 2nd Edition. Belmont, CA: Thomson/ Wadsworth.

Davis, G. F., McAdam, D. Scott, W. R., & Zald, M. N. (2005) (Eds.). *Social movements and organization theory.* Cambridge, England: Cambridge University Press.

Evans, S., & Prilleltensky, I. (2005). Youth civic engagement: Promise and peril. In M. Ungar (Ed.), *Handbook of working with children and youth: Pathways to resilience across cultures and contexts* (pp. 405–415). Thousand Oaks, CA: Sage.

Freire, P. (1993). *Pedagogy of the oppressed* (2nd ed.). New York: Continuum.

Harper, G., Lardon, C., Rappaport, J., Bangi, A., Contreras, R., & Pedraza, A. (2004). Community narratives: The use of narrative ethnography in participatory community research. In L. A. Jason, C. Keys, Y. Suarez-Balcazar, R. Taylor, & M. Davis, (Eds.), *Participatory community research: Theories and methods in action* (pp. 199–217). Washington, DC: American Psychological Association.

Humphreys, K. (2004). *Circles of recovery: Self-help organizations for addictions.* Cambridge, England: Cambridge University Press.

Hur, M. H. (2006). Empowerment in terms of theoretical perspectives: Exploring a typology of the processes and components across disciplines. *Journal of Community Psychology, 34,* 523–540.

Janzen, R., Nelson, G., Hausfather, N., & Ochocka, J. (2007). Capturing system level activities and impacts of mental health consumer-run organizations. *American Journal of Community Psychology, 39,* 287–299.

Jason, L. A., Keys, C., Suarez-Balcazar, Y., Taylor, R., & Davis, M. (Eds.) (2004). *Participatory community research: Theories and methods in action* (pp. 199–217). Washington, DC: American Psychological Association.

Kelly, J., Azelton, L., Lardon, C., Mock, L., Tandon, S., & Thomas, M. (2004). On community leadership: Stories about collaboration in action research. *American Journal of Community Psychology, 33,* 205–216.

Kieffer, C. (1984). Citizen empowerment: A developmental perspective. In J. Rappaport, C. Swift, & R. Hess (Eds.), *Studies in empowerment: Steps toward understanding and action* (pp. 9–36). New York: Haworth.

Kroeker, C. J. (1995). Individual, organizational, and societal empowerment: A study of the processes in a Nicaraguan agricultural cooperation. *American Journal of Community Psychology, 23,* 749–764.

Levine, M., Perkins, D. D., & Perkins, D. V. (2005). *Principles of community psychology: Perspectives and applications.* 3rd Edition. New York: Oxford University Press.

Lykes, M. B., Blanche, M. T. & Hamber, B. (2003). Narrating survival and change in Guatemala and South Africa: The politics of representation and a liberatory community psychology. *American Journal of Community Psychology, 31*(1/2), 79–90.

Mankowski, E. S., & Rappaport, J. (2000). Narrative concepts and analysis in spiritually based communities. *Journal of Community Psychology, 28,* 479–493.

Maton, K. I. (2000). Making a difference: The social ecology of social transformation. *American Journal of Community Psychology, 28,* 25–57.

Maton, K. I. (2008). Empowering community settings: Agents of individual development, community betterment, and positive social change. *American Journal of Community Psychology, 41,* 4–21.

Maton, K. I., & Salem, D. (1995). Organizational characteristics of empowering community settings: A multiple case study approach. *American Journal of Community Psychology, 23,* 631–656.

Mohatt, G. V., Hazel, K. L., Allen, J., Stachelrodt, M., Hensel, C., & Fath, R. (2004). Unheard Alaska: Culturally anchored participatory action research on sobriety with Alaska natives. *American Journal of Community Psychology, 33,* 263–273.

Perkins, D. D., Crim, B., Silberman, P., & Brown, B. (2004). Community development as a response to community-level adversity: Ecological theory and strengths-based policy. In K. I. Maton, C. Schellenbach, B. Leadbeater, & A. Solarz (Eds.), *Investing in children, youth, families, and communities: Strengths-based research and policy* (pp. 321–340). Washington, DC: American Psychological Association.

Peterson, A., & Zimmerman, M. (2004). Beyond the individual: Toward a nomological network of organizational empowerment. *American Journal of Community Psychology, 34,* 129–146.

Rappaport, J. (1977). *Community psychology: Values, research and action.* New York: Holt, Rinehart, & Winston.

Rappaport, J. (1981). In praise of paradox: A social policy of empowerment over prevention. *American Journal of Community Psychology, 9,* 1–25.

Rappaport, J. (1987). Terms of empowerment/exemplars of prevention: Toward a theory for community psychology. *American Journal of Community Psychology, 15,* 121–148.

Rappaport, J. (1993). Narrative studies, personal stories, and identity transformation in the mutual help group context. *Journal of Applied Behavioral Science, 29,* 239–256.

Rappaport, J. (1995). Empowerment meets narrative: Listening to stories and creating settings. *American Journal of Community Psychology, 23,* 795–808.

Rappaport, J. (2000). Community narratives: Tales of terror and joy. *American Journal of Community Psychology, 28,* 1–24.

Rappaport, J., Reischl, T. M., & Zimmerman, M. A. (1992). Mutual help mechanisms in the empowerment of former mental patients. In D. Saleebey (Ed.), *The strengths perspective in social work practice* (pp. 84–97). New York: Longman.

Rappaport, J. & Chinsky, J. M. (1974). Models for delivery of service from a historical and conceptual perspective. *Professional Psychology, 5,* 42–50.

Rappaport, J. & Seidman, E. (Eds.) (2000). *Handbook of community psychology.* New York: Kluwer/Plenum Publishing.

Rappaport, J. & Simkins, R. (1991). Healing and empowerment through community narrative. *Prevention in Human Services, 10,* 29–50.

Speer, P. & Hughey, J. (1995). Community organizing: An ecological route to empowerment and power. *American Journal of Community Psychology, 23,* 729–748.

Wandersman, A., & Florin, P. (2000). Citizen participation and community organization. In J. Rappaport & E. Seidman (Eds.), *Handbook of community psychology* (pp. 247–272). New York: Plenum.

Wiley, A., & Rappaport, J. (2000). Empowerment, wellness, and the politics of development. In D. Cicchetti, J. Rappaport, I. Sandler, & R. Weissberg (Eds.), *The promotion of wellness in children and adolescents* (pp. 59–99). Washington, DC: CWLA Press.

Zimmerman, M. A. (2000). Empowerment theory: Psychological, organizational and community levels of analysis. In J. Rappaport & E. Seidman (Eds.), *Handbook of community psychology* (pp. 43–63). New York: Kluwer/Plenum Publishing.

2 Changing Social Settings: A Framework for Action

Edward Seidman and Vivian Tseng

In his classic 1977 volume, *Community Psychology: Theory, Research, and Action*, Julian Rappaport underscored the salience of small-group and organizational levels of analysis as "places to stand" for community psychologists and other action scientists. We refer to Rappaport's small groups and organizations as *social settings*, a term that encompasses classrooms, schools, community-based and human service organizations, workplaces, families, and peer groups. These social settings represent the immediate contexts of individual's daily experiences (Bronfenbrenner, 1979). Although on a practical basis, many community psychologists intervene in these social settings, few have gone on to define what constitutes a social setting or explicated how different strategies might dynamically alter different aspects of such settings. (For a noteworthy exception, *see* O'Donnell, Tharp, & Wetzel's [1993] description of activity settings and the corollary strategies of intervention.) In this chapter, we build on Rappaport's work by offering a framework for action to improve social settings.

Articulating a framework for understanding and changing social settings has been a goal for community psychologists since the field's beginnings (Bennett et al., 1966, Rappaport, 1977), but our understanding of social settings has been encumbered by an abiding focus on individuals as the unit of analysis (Seidman & Rappaport, 1986). In articulating our framework, we first offer a brief summary that explains how to understand the ways social settings function (Tseng & Seidman, 2007). The focus of this chapter is on several underlying approaches for social intervention, their accompanying strategies and tactics, and how they are targeted at one or more features and/or processes of a social setting. The goal of each intervention strategy is to improve social settings and to foster the development and well-being of those within the setting. We underscore how important amplifying the strengths and empowerment of the social setting are to each strategy. Strength-based and empowerment concepts are fundamental to our framework for action, as they were for Rappaport (1977, 1981, 1987).

Targeting settings for change is not controversial for community psychologists—we have largely agreed on that point for decades. Knowing how to create setting change has proven more elusive. What features of settings should be targeted for change? What are the action levers for creating change?

A SYSTEMS FRAMEWORK FOR UNDERSTANDING SOCIAL SETTINGS

We recently described a framework to understand the functioning of social settings (Tseng & Seidman, 2007). We drew heavily upon concepts from dynamic systems theory (e.g., Altman & Rogoff, 1987; Bronfenbrenner, 1977; Buckley, 1968; Kelly, Ryan, Altman, & Stelzner, 2000; Lewin, 1951; Maruyama, 1963; von Bertalanffy, 1957) and from the literature on activity settings (Gallimore, Goldenberg, & Weisner, 1993; O'Donnell, Tharp, & Wetzel, 1993; Weisner, 2002). Our discussion of social settings focuses largely on community-based organizations and schools[1], but the setting aspects in our framework could apply to other settings as well, particularly those that have a physical location and clear boundaries (although these boundaries may be permeable).

In Figure 2–1, we illustrate our framework for understanding social settings. We conceptualize social settings as dynamic systems that consist of three major aspects: social processes (i.e., patterns of transactions between two or more groups of people, including norms and practices), resources (i.e., human, economic, physical, and temporal resources), and organization of resources (i.e., how resources are arranged and allocated). We postulate that these setting elements are in dynamic transaction with one other.

---

1 In tandem with the development of our settings framework, several other teams proposed similar frameworks specifically for understanding how human service organizations (Foster-Fishman & Nowell, 2007) and classrooms operate (Ball & Forzani, 2007; Cohen, Raudenbush, & Ball, 2003; Pianta, 2006).

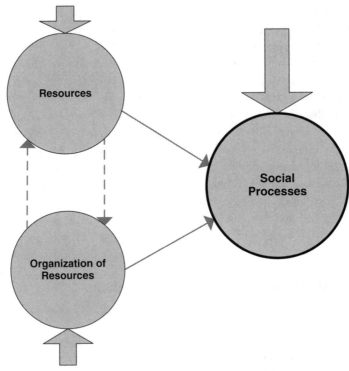

Figure 2.1   Framework for social setting action

Social Processes

Although each of the three setting components is essential, we begin by focusing on social processes, because they are the central way through which individuals (e.g., youth and adults, service deliverers, and recipients) experience settings. As such, they are critical for improving setting outcomes. By focusing on social processes, we follow the work of many scholars in developmental psychology and education. For example, developmental psychologists argue that proximal processes (i.e., interactions between people and their immediate environments) are the primary mechanisms influencing human development (Bronfenbrenner & Morris, 2006), and education scholars assert that in addition to altering setting resources, we must also alter social processes in a setting, such as instruction and role relationships, to trigger significant educational change (Fullan, 2001; Ball & Forzani, 2007; Cohen, Raudenbush, & Ball, 2003; Pianta, 2006). Fairweather (1972) argued that role relationships must be prioritized if social change is to be achieved. In a similar—but more inclusive—way, Sarason (1982) underscored the importance of behavioral regularities. Seidman (1988) subsequently reframed these concepts as social regularities to be more inclusive.

The conception of social processes is steeped in a transactional world-view (Altman & Rogoff, 1987). Social processes are relational units seen in the ongoing transactions between two or more groups in a setting (e.g., teachers and students, peer groups, and staff and youth). These transactions include the social interactions between groups, their communication and feedback channels, and contingencies associated with their interactions. Social processes are shaped by individuals' roles within the setting; there are dominant scripts. For example, the relationships between an adult and youth in a classroom are largely defined by the adult's role as a teacher and youths' roles as students. These processes have a temporal quality that involves a constant stream of action in which transactions are repeated, behaviors are recalibrated based on feedback, and patterns are reinforced over time. Finally, social processes are mediated psychologically: individuals interpret and make meaning of these processes. The concept of social processes overlaps with the concept of social regularities (Seidman, 1988, 1990) and with cultural anthropologists' conceptualizations of certain aspects of activity settings—specifically the daily interactions, routines, and scripts for behavior in settings (Gallimore, Goldenberg, & Weisner, 1993; Weisner, 2002).

Social processes are manifested in one or more of three major domains—norms, interactional patterns and practices, and participation. Each of these domains consists of many variables, and the domains mutually influence each other. For example, setting scripts or norms influence practices and vice versa. Norms reflect transactions between youth's beliefs and behaviors and those of others in the setting. They tap setting culture in terms of setting-level behavioral scripts, acceptability of aggressive behavior, or expectations of success. As Weinstein (2002) argues, such norms and expectations are reinforced over time and by other settings and larger social-ecological forces.

Interactions between members of a setting—particularly between teachers and students or peer groups—are central social processes. As Tyack and Cuban (1995) eloquently stated, "Change where it counts the most—*in the daily interactions of teachers and students*—is the hardest to achieve and the most important" (p. 10; italics added). Several reviews of the literature concluded that warm, supportive relationships have been consistently shown to foster youth's sense of belonging, importance, and engagement in settings (Eccles & Gootman, 2002; National Research Council [NRC] & Institute of Medicine [IOM], 2004). Reciprocal interactions between teachers and students and their communication and feedback channels have been held as the key to facilitating positive developmental outcomes, both at the setting level and for individual students (Pianta, 2006). These interactions focus on the social and instructional dimensions. Beyond dyadic relationships is an important, larger web of social network relationships that unfold within and outside the setting. For example, programs that help youth establish a stronger social network, connecting youth with nonfamilial adults who can provide an array of resources and encouragement, are viewed as successful (Jarrett, Sullivan, & Watkins, 2005). School reform efforts sometimes seek to build professional learning communities wherein teachers jointly examine how students are doing and collaboratively plan their lessons (Fullan, 2001). Power relationships offer another window into relationships in which, for example, youth might collectively decide on the issues they will address, critically analyze those issues, and develop and carry out political campaigns.

Resources

The availability and quality of human, economic, physical, and temporal resources matter for setting outcomes, but we and others have postulated that they alone are not sufficient for creating meaningful outcomes. The key is whether they precipitate changes in social processes. *Human resources* refers to individuals who inhabit the settings and the characteristics of these individuals (e.g., staff's education, training, skills, cultural values, and beliefs). *Physical resources* refers to the availability and quality of curricular materials, technology, space, facilities, and buildings. However, the best curricula or nicest space is only important to the degree that it can be used effectively in the setting. *Economic resources* refers to financial expenses such as per pupil expenditure or staff salaries. *Temporal resources* refers to the amount of available time, such as the length of school days.

Organization of Resources

The term *organization of resources* refers to the ways in which people, space, and time are arranged and money is allocated in a setting. Like resources, the organization of resources matters for setting outcomes but only as they condition the everyday experiences of the setting inhabitants. The organization of resources may be more relevant to their daily experiences than resources to conditioning social processes. *Social organization* refers to how people are grouped in a setting (e.g., single-sex vs. co-educational schools, tracked vs. mixed ability classrooms). *Organization of time* refers to how time is scheduled (e.g., block scheduling, year-round school). *Physical organization* refers to different types of spatial arrangements, such as desks in rows versus a circle versus no desks.

A FRAMEWORK FOR ACTION

Most intervention strategies are guided by a fundamental approach. Underlying each approach is a particular set of assumptions based on ideology, values, and/or empirical data. These approaches have been classified according to a variety of schemas (*see*, for example, Bennis, Benne, & Chin, 1976; Crowfoot & Chesler, 1974; Rothman, 1974). Building, in part, off some of these schemas and our own thinking, we view most social intervention strategies as being driven by one of five[2] implicit—if not explicit—fundamental approaches: *(1)* reduction of inequity, *(2)* utopian ideals, *(3)* professional development, *(4)* data-driven, *(5)* and regulatory. We will briefly describe each of these approaches and the corresponding set of intervention strategies, as well as the roles of empowerment and participants in each approach. We will demonstrate that "buy-in" of participants is a critical tactic in assuring empowerment outcomes. Next, we will examine each strategy with regard to its initial target of intervention—social processes, resources, and the organization of resources as well as each of their subcomponents, as shown in Table 2–1. (When pertinent to an intervention strategy, the secondary target will be explored as well).

In practice, few of these intervention strategies have a single underlying approach; the approaches often "bleed" into one another and employ multiple strategies, especially in terms of the tactics used and objectives pursued.

When settings are the focus of change, community psychologists are often drawn toward directly changing social processes (e.g., changing relationships between teachers and students, norms) or doing so indirectly by altering the organization of resources to potentiate change in these social processes. However, policymakers, public administrators, lawyers, and economists view resources (e.g., per-pupil spending) and their arrangement or organization (i.e., financial incentive structures) as more tangible targets of change that may be modifiable with regulatory strategies. For each strategy, we explore whether the social processes, resources, or the organization of resources of a setting are the initial or secondary target of intervention and the interrelationships among these primary and secondary targets. Strategies within one approach are utilized with different objectives under different approaches. What are the trade-offs between directly changing setting-level social processes and practices versus changing resources and/or the organization of resources? We explore these questions, as well as others concerning the comparative advantage and disadvantage of several different strategies of intervention.

---

2 We do not intend that this schema be comprehensive or representative of all possible approaches and strategies.

Table 2.1   Approach, Strategy, and Target(s) of Social Intervention

| Approach | Strategy | Target(s) of Intervention | | |
		Resources	Organization of Resources	Social Processes
Reduction of Inequity	Grassroots Organizing	S	I	I
	Consciousness-Raising	I		I
	Advocacy/ Litigation	I	S	S
Utopian	Creation of Alternative Setting	I	I	I
Professional Development	Education/ Training	I		
	Coaching/ Mentoring			I
Data-Driven	Feedback	S	I	I
	Participatory research	I	I	I
	Experimental social innovation		S	I
Regulatory	Policy/ Legislation	I	I	
	Administrative order	I	I	

I = initial target of intervention
S = secondary target of intervention

Because our focus is on intervention, we are not depicting the multitude of bidirectional and transactional influences among setting concepts. Instead, in Figure 2–1, we use unidirectional arrows to depict: *(1)* the *initial* focus or target of intervention (i.e., resources, organization of resources, and social processes as indicated by wide lines); and *(2)* the radiating pathways of influence that alter social processes and, in turn, stimulate change in setting outcomes (as indicated by thin lines).

As Tseng and Seidman (2007) have postulated, changing resources or the organization of resources is unlikely to change setting outcomes unless the change also affects the daily social processes (i.e., practices, routines, interactions, and norms). For this reason, social processes are portrayed as larger in Figure 2–1. However, this does not imply that the initial target or focus of intervention has to be social processes. Instead, it implies that when resources or the organization of resources is the initial target of intervention, a corollary must be a change in the daily experiences and practices of setting members or in the setting norms. Changes in resources and the organization of resources can also operate as levers, stimulating or conditioning change in social processes. By our estimation, however, without a change in these social processes, restructuring of the system is unlikely. In other words, changing resources or their organization alone is likely to result in only a fine-tuning of the system (Seidman, 1988).

We next describe the strategies of intervention that are most commonly employed to impact resources, organization of resources, and social processes. For each selected strategy of intervention, we describe and illustrate the anticipated directions of influence (*see* Table 2–1). For simplicity, we limit our examples to school- and community-based organizations that serve youth.

Reduction of Inequity Approach and Strategies of Intervention

The reduction of injustice, inequity, and/or unfairness approach is the most common social intervention approach among social change agents. Strategies that exemplify this approach include grassroots organizing, consciousness-raising, advocacy, and litigation. These strategies can be employed separately, but they are often used in combination.

For the inequity-driven approach, the central premise and corollary goal is to alter the role relationships, power differential, or resource balance between the haves and have-nots (e.g., government and the people; management and workers; principals, teachers, and students; see, for example, Alinsky, [1971]). In terms of our social settings framework, the target of change is social processes. Despite this objective, in strategies such as advocacy, the initial target of intervention may be a change in resources, not social processes.

Empowerment of the have-nots and their narratives are crucial components of most inequity-driven strategies. Empowerment is used to mean both individual psychological and collective empowerment (Zimmerman, 2000). However, in practice, each of these inequity-driven strategies differs in the salience of empowerment and the voices of the constituents, especially when advocacy strategies are employed.

Grassroots organizing. The initial targets of the grassroots organizing strategy are twofold—the alteration in the balance or distribution of resources (e.g., physical, economic) and the simultaneous change in the role relationships between those in and out of power. The tactics employed to rearrange the allocation of resources, including buy-in, are empowering both at the individual and setting levels, are attentive to the participants' concerns, and, if successful, inherently change the social processes.

Speer (2008) describes how the People Improving Communities through Organizing (PICO) National Network approaches youth organizing in a setting. PICO's theory of change is that adverse conditions in settings and communities are a result of the powerlessness of those affected by the conditions. "To change these conditions, those in society with little power must develop and exercise power to advocate on behalf of their own interests" (p. 219). Speer explicates three critical tactics—relationship development, leadership development, and action—by which the PICO approach alters settings. This must be a youth-led process, although the youth are trained by an adult PICO member.

For relationship development to be realized within a setting, youth have to be connected or reconnected through one-on-one communication. This ongoing process uncovers commonalities and helps build relationships. Sustaining these relationships is the basis for long-term power. PICO organizers work to create settings in which there are numerous distinct, specific roles with opportunities for youth to participate and learn. Moreover, leadership development requires youth to participate in and learn from their experiences in multiple roles. From the one-on-one conversations, themes emerge that become the basis for action and continued assessment. For PICO and many other organizing groups, a paid organizer is brought in at the outset. These principles, strategies, and tactics can be employed by indigenous youth and adults as well as outside agents.

In one example of youth organizing, Speer describes how youth leaders organized county-wide community action meetings and won commitments from three school district superintendents to help prioritize and implement policies to close the achievement gap. In one instance, youth leaders campaigned to alter a policy that was automatically placing students with Spanish surnames into remedial English classes with little effort to return these students to mainstream classes. The youth-led efforts resulted in an 800% increase in transfers to mainstream courses.

In assessing the effectiveness of organizing, Speer asserts that network analysis is a key method with which to examine whether the pattern of relationships or connectedness has changed. In these network analyses, we can examine changes in patterns of relationships, as well as the amount of participation among youth. A corollary would be a change in norms for youth and adults in the setting.

Consciousness-raising. Consciousness-raising also focuses on inequities, but here the tactics consist of education and increasing the participants' awareness of the inequities. In this way, the unfairness and adverse consequences become apparent, reminiscent of the work of Friere (1970) and others. This is intended to push individual and collective action in order to realign the balance of power, altering the social processes and, eventually, the allocation of resources. Although targeting social processes is important, so is an increase in the knowledge resources of the participants. Empowerment of individual participants, which leads to collective empowerment, is paramount.

Pollock (2008) uses her basic research on discussions about race to mount a consciousness-raising intervention in schools. In a previous 3-year ethnographic study in California, Pollock (2008) discovered that school personnel's refusal to explicitly discuss race, which she defines as "colormuteness," can have harmful consequences in schools. The personnel used very imprecise language such as "low achievers" and "the kids getting suspended." In part as a result, the achievement gap and the racially disproportionate numbers of suspension went unchanged. In contrast, Pollock states:

> "When people work to solve dilemmas, tensions, and inequities in their social settings, they must seek to discuss and analyze those issues *precisely and thoroughly*. Hence, I work with pre-service and in-service educators to think through how they talk (and do not talk) precisely about racial issues in their institutions. I define precise race talk as talk that *thoroughly and clearly analyzes the various actors, actions, and processes involved in the issue under discussion."*
>
> (2008, pp.103–104)

To achieve improved youth outcomes and equity in a setting—consistent with a consciousness-raising strategy—Pollock has school personnel talk skillfully and precisely about race, focusing on "student subpopulations and their needs," "the causes of racial disparities," and "the everyday educator acts that actually assist students of color and those that actually harm them." It is through precise discussion and analysis of issues such as these (what linguists call metapragmatic analysis) that consciousness is raised and tools and solutions are created and implemented.

The tactics of consciousness-raising directly target discussions among educators in a setting. Such talk has both interactional and normative dimensions, and talking is participatory. Thus, knowledge resources, social practices, and norms are the initial and primary foci of intervention. These discussions can create tools or resources with which educators can achieve the setting-level goals of equity in opportunities for learning.

Advocacy/Litigation. In comparison to grassroots organizing and consciousness-raising strategies, the advocacy/litigation approach tackles the inequities by trying to garner more resources for the relatively more disadvantaged and/or disempowered group. Resources are often the direct target of intervention when advocacy or litigation strategies are employed. (There are, however, times when advocacy is used to enforce a statute or policy that ensures equity, as in the case of affirmative action or racial or sexual harassment. Here, the initial target would be the social processes or practices. Thus, advocacy used for enforcement purposes would more likely fall under the rubric of the regulatory family of strategies discussed below.)

When advocacy is performed by an expert, there is little opportunity for the disadvantaged to engage in the process or for empowerment processes to unfold. (Litigation is always performed by an expert, and thus, empowerment can only be hoped for as a long-term consequence of successful litigation.) The voices of the disadvantaged are rarely heard, except in an anecdotal fashion. If the disadvantaged/disempowered engage in advocacy for themselves, the picture is much different.

Advocacy can be used to increase the amount of human, social, physical, or financial resources or, more specifically, the amount of experience or educational level of service deliverers, amount of services delivered, space available, or per-client expenditures in a setting. However, there is no prescription or specified mechanism through which the increased resources alter the balance of resources or power in the setting; it is assumed that it will follow naturally.

According to Edelman (1973), an advocate or small group of citizen advocates "must identify the problem and set the process for action in motion." The advocate(s) has to lead throughout the process. The problem has to be small enough to be addressable by specific remedies. Also, "the problem must be comprehensible to the public and capable of evoking the sort of strong emotion that attends the demonstration of a clear injustice."

Edelman (1973) describes the use of task forces as a type of advocacy mechanism. Once a problem has been identified, it is essential to gather data in the form of individual stories backed by statistical data. (Here the "voices" are of the victims and are used in a dramatically different way than those of participants engaged in community organizing or consciousness-raising strategies.) The constellation of the task force is critical for its final report to have credibility and influence. Membership on the task force needs to be balanced by stakeholder interests, walk of life, profession, and ideology, but ideally each member should fall within a broad-based definition of the mainstream.

Edelman (1973) uses the report of The Task Force on Children Out of School (1970, 1971) as an illustration. The report, "The Way We Go to School: The Exclusion of Children in Boston," begins with a gripping series of individual stories and images of school exclusion. It "includes a short chapter on each type of exclusion, with documentation of the meager amount of financial and human resources the Boston school system devotes to each area and enough proof of the magnitude of each problem to show that tragedy is occurring daily." Use of the media was a critical tactic to garner increased resources and delivery of services. Thus, increased human, social, and economic capital became the targets of intervention. This might lead to a reorganization of resources and/or different social practices. The task force approach of advocacy has been followed by many other successful organizations, including the Children's Defense Fund. This type of advocacy approach is partly data-driven and employs a variety of tactics, including media and victims' stories, to achieve its goals.

Litigation, another form of advocacy, should only be used as a last resort because it "is an expensive, time-consuming, adversarial, and antagonistic process" (Dale & Sanniti, 1993). Also, the interveners have much less control over potential outcomes. Litigation focuses primarily on altering resources. In this way, both advocacy and litigation focus foremost on resources (e.g., increasing educational and financial resources for inner-city schools). Whether increasing resources results in or conditions an equalization of opportunities for learning and youth outcomes is an assumption. Thus, advocacy and litigation can be viewed as more akin to policy strategies where the primary target is a change in resources. This is in contrast to grassroots organizing and consciousness-raising strategies in which the more explicit target of change is equalization in the distribution of these types of resources (i.e., a second-order change or a change in the social processes).

Utopian-Driven Approaches and Strategies of Intervention

Utopian-driven approaches are exemplified by the creation of new or alternative settings (e.g., Cherniss & Degan, 2000; Sarason, 1972). The settings that exist are viewed as ill-conceived, dysfunctional, and/or unchangeable, and consequently, the only alternative is to create an alternative setting based on a more appropriate conceptual approach with different kinds, amounts, and qualities of resources, organization of resources, and social processes.

These alternative settings should be empowering for the individual and the collective and interdependent with its participants' narratives.

Creation of new or alternative settings. For strategies that are motivated by utopian ideals, the "old" setting is seen as difficult, if not impossible, to change in the desired directions. Thus, it is believed that a new setting needs to be created or the old setting completely overhauled with a different normative culture and practices. As Weinstein (2008) stated in describing the difference between setting creation and school change, "While the creation of new school settings enables increased freedom (e.g., in teacher selection, student recruitment, and policy development), new settings come with tougher resource challenges," such as incorporation of staff and students, long-term funding, and planning. When creating an alternative setting, resources and their organization also become targets of change, but changing the normative culture and practices remains the first priority. In the youth field, we often hear about the creation of alternative schools; most recently, these have been charter schools and single-sex educational settings. In the last two decades, the movement to create schools-within-schools can also be seen as an illustration of the creation of an alternative setting (*see*, for example, Oxley, 2000).

One example of the creation of a new setting within a larger one is provided by Maton, Hrabowski, Ozdemir, and Wimms (2008). Maton and his colleagues describe the successful creation of an alternative college program designed to foster the achievement of African-American and Latino minority students in the hard sciences. Historically, these minority students have been severely underrepresented in undergraduate or graduate programs in the sciences. At the University of Maryland, Baltimore County, the Meyerhoff Scholars' Program was created. This multicomponent program consists of resources, including financial aid, summer bridge programs and tutoring, an opportunity role structure in the form of summer research internships, community residence halls, and research experience during the academic year as well as a multifaceted support system that includes study groups, personal advising and counseling, faculty and administrative support, mentors, and family involvement. This program provides supportive emotional and instructional interactions to students. Perhaps, most importantly, a positive, shared normative belief system is established through the inculcation of the program values of high academic goals with an emphasis on the attainment of PhDs and research careers. We can see the wide array of tactics that are employed to simultaneously alter resources, the organization of resources, and social processes and practices.

This process empowers the Meyerhoff students; in recent years, 50% of them have entered PhD programs in the sciences. Moreover, this program appears to have transformed the institutional culture of the university.

Professional Development-Driven Approaches and Strategies of Intervention

Training is a hallmark of professional development-driven approaches[3]. Training approaches are more skills- than empowerment-oriented. More recently, coaching/mentoring has been added to the repertoire of professional development strategies, and it is often used in tandem with training. However, these two strategies are different in their primary focus—resources (human capital in particular) are the primary focus of training, whereas coaching/mentoring approaches focus on social processes (emotional and instructional supportive relationships). Individual empowerment is believed to be achieved by the accumulation of knowledge and skills. Setting-level empowerment is not a driving concept here nor are the voices of "street-level bureaucrats" (Weatherly & Lipsky, 1977). In contrast, coaching/mentoring focuses more on the interactions between the expert and novice.

Education/Training. Educators and trainers often target improvement in the skills, knowledge, and expertise of the service deliverers (i.e., human resources). Thus, a strategy (and industry) of professional development continues to grow and flourish. Believing that teachers or youth workers will be more effective if they increase their skills and knowledge seems intuitive. Professional development workshops are the most common scenarios, but they are, at best, a prelude. Neither empowerment nor the "voices" of the participants play a significant role in this strategy. Training and education directly increase human resources and knowledge in particular, yet a number of evaluations have failed to demonstrate that they actually change practice (Bouffard & Little, 2004). Training may be necessary, but it does not appear to be a sufficient condition for changing professional practice. Consequently, we focus exclusively on the professional development strategies of coaching and mentoring, which almost always follow and complement a training component. In this way, coaching/mentoring strategies help bring skills from training to practice and thereby affect social processes, not just human resources.

Coaching/Mentoring. Coaching/mentoring focuses directly on improving the quality of practices and interactions between youth and service deliverers (e.g., teachers, youth workers). Formal training components are necessary but not sufficient to cause this type of change. Training targets improved human resources or knowledge. When training is successful, human

---

3 Education and training are often lumped together as education/training approaches. We choose not to follow that convention because the two are different conceptually and practically. Training is appropriate when there are a known set of effective skills to master. Education, on the other hand, fosters awareness and reflection.

capital or resources are increased and resources are likely to be allocated differently. Training alone, however, does not target the daily isolation and lack of practical support teachers and youth workers experience within their settings. This is where regular and frequent coaching/mentoring by more experienced peers can play a critical role in putting knowledge into practice. Coaches/mentors provide understanding and emotional support, as well as practical instructional knowledge. Coaching/mentoring strategies place a premium on understanding the narratives of the participants and, when successful, result in individual empowerment.

Illustratively, Jones, Brown, and Aber (2008) describe the 4Rs Program (Reading, Writing, Respect, and Resolution), which targets the classroom setting and, in particular, teacher pedagogical practices, teacher–child relationships, and classroom emotional and instructional climate. Teachers are afforded intensive professional development experiences in this program. As in many professional development programs, 4Rs begins with 5 days of training, which introduces teachers to the specific activities and lessons of each unit, provides practice through role playing and experiential learning, and inspires teachers to adopt the new concepts and skills in their personal and professional lives.

Most importantly, the critical coaching/mentoring components, as the authors describe, consist of ongoing classroom coaching. This intensive and extensive process uses a staff developer and teachers to model class lessons, co-plan and teach lessons, and observe and provide feedback. "In addition, staff developers convene regular conferences with teachers either in a one-on-one format or with a group of teachers from one or multiple grades" (p. 59). The strategy is to provide intensive and extensive coaching to support each teacher in altering their practices and emotional and instructional interactions with their students. Recent results from this school-level randomized cluster trial revealed that emotional and instructional support was successfully impacted (Brown, Jones, LaRusso, & Aber, 2010) as were child-level academic and socio-emotional outcomes (Jones, Brown, & Aber, in press).

Data-Driven Approaches and Strategies of Intervention

Data-driven approaches are exemplified by data feedback (e.g., Smith & Akiva, 2008), participatory research (Minkler & Wallerstein, 2008), and experimental social innovation (Fairweather, 1972) strategies. A very rational and scientific approach underlies this set of strategies. As Minkler and Wallerstein (2008) have pointed out, participatory and action research represent opposite ends of a continuum that grew out of the Lewin (1946) tradition of action research. Action research has come to represent the more conservative form, whereas participatory research approaches have a more values-based and emancipatory focus, similarly to the inequity approach strategies. Experimental social innovation (ESI) also grows out of this tradition. ESI falls near the middle of this continuum, as it focuses on more rigorous research methods driven by scientists and collaboration with participants to change role relationships between service deliverers and recipients.

Each data-driven strategy varies with regard to the role played by empowerment and the voices of participants. Feedback of data, or knowledge of results, is inherently empowering. The same can be said for experimental social innovation in which altering the role relationship between service deliverer and recipient is a key feature. In participatory strategies, empowerment is inherent in the process of partaking in the research enterprise.

Among these data-driven strategies, constituent narratives are most salient in the participatory strategy. Setting-level empowerment is most central to the experimental social innovation strategy and least central to a simple knowledge of results strategy. However, although theoretically important, neither ESI nor participatory research approaches assess setting-level outcomes. Data-driven tactics are often incorporated under the rubric of other strategies of intervention (e.g., advocacy, coaching/mentoring). Similarly, strategies like consciousness-raising are incorporated into some data-driven strategies, especially participatory research.

Data-driven strategies of intervention are characterized by their focus on targeting change in social processes. For participatory research strategies, resources and the organization of resources are of equal importance as primary targets of intervention with social processes. Feedback differs only slightly in that resources are a secondary or ancillary target. For ESI, the emphasis on social processes is followed by secondarily targeting the organization of resources.

Feedback. Creating change by feeding back information about professional practices or the nature and quality of interactions between staff and clients is not a new intervention strategy. Early in the history of experimental psychology, individuals were given feedback about how close or far they were from perfect performance; this feedback lead to rapid and dramatic improvements in that performance (e.g., Butler & Winne, 1995).

Smith and Akiva (2008) describe how they employ feedback with regard to safety, support, interaction, and engagement to improve the nature and quality of after-school settings. These constructs are depicted within a pyramid structure (p. 193) with engagement of youth at the top of the pyramid and safety at the bottom. (So, engagement is a necessary but not sufficient condition to achieve quality programming.) The authors frame this intervention process conceptually as a way to achieve accountability. Safety is determined by assessing the amount and availability of various resources (e.g., emergency supplies, adequate physical space, and healthy foods). The constructs of support, interaction, and engagement are measured largely by the organization of resources (e.g., session flow is planned, presented, and paced for youth; opportunities to participate in small groups exist) and by the social processes and practices (e.g., staff support youth with encouragement). The engagement construct also aids youth empowerment by prioritizing their voices. This is evident in the specific items used to assess the construct—for example, youth opportunities to reflect, make choices based on interests, set goals, and make plans. As one can discern from the pyramid, resources are a necessary condition for change, but the primary targets are the organization of resources and social processes.

To accomplish their accountability goals and provide feedback, the authors employ a sequence of four tactics. First, presentations are made to a setting's decision-makers and pilot data is collected to generate local learning and feedback. Second, assessment is conducted with an instrument developed to tap the constructs mentioned above (safety, support, interaction, and engagement), which are the substantive targets of change. The assessment can be performed by the participants, external assessors, or both. Self-assessment has greater potential for individual and collective empowerment than external assessment, although self-assessment alone may have less impact on changing key setting regularities. Third, automated reports are produced for each program/site. This is the key stimulus for change in a feedback strategy. Fourth, in this specific example, additional technical assistance, coaching, or training using the feedback often follows. This additional step begins to blend feedback strategies with professional development strategies. Recent results from a randomized cluster trial of after-school settings indicated that managers were successful in getting front-line staff to engage in a greater number of continuous improvement practices and those instructional practices were of higher quality than those practices in the control sites (Smith, Sugar, Pearson, Lo, & Frank, 2009).

Participatory research. According to Israel, Eng, Schulz, and Parker (2005), the core principles of community and participatory research include the active participation of community members and researchers in a co-learning process to which they contribute equally. In addition, participatory research involves systems development and capacity-building. The process is empowering to its participants and their voices are relevant. There is a simultaneous and co-equal focus on changing available resources, their organization, and social processes.

In many participatory research endeavors, the leaders often work in consultation with youth to help youth identify the most pressing issues. Youth are taught how to assess community needs. To do so, they might use surveys or interviews, record data, or employ more creative data collection methods. Youth learn how to create, use, and interpret data from these different methods. In essence, the scholar-interventionists are "giving away" the tools of the trade. After interpreting the data, youth and leaders collaborate on the development of an action plan. The young people play a very active role in every phase of the project,

Cheatham-Rojas and Shen (2008) describe how an organization—Asian Communities for Reproductive Justice (ACRJ)—engaged young Cambodian women and girls in Long Beach, California, to study and address issues of sexual health. Community-based participatory research was preceded by community organizing and popular education or consciousness-raising (Freire, 1970). Sexual harassment became the central focus. With the help of ACJR staff and their knowledge of a variety of research methods, the students created a 40-question survey. They only included questions that "would elicit information helpful to the development of their organizing campaign, would not be repetitive, and would produce new knowledge for future use" (p. 129). The youth learned about the use of standardized tests, pretesting, and how to shorten the instrument. They chose a target population, learned about sampling, and engaged in data collection. Although they did not have the inclination to engage in data analysis, they did pose the questions they wanted addressed. They then took direct action and organized the Community Forum on School Safety. They used the Forum to release their survey results and present their recommendations to ensure a safe learning environment for girls in Long Beach. Every one of their recommendations was adopted.

Experimental social innovation. According to Fairweather (1972), the goal of experimental social innovation is social change and, in particular, changes in the nature and structure of role relationships among members of a setting. This strategy of intervention is carried out according to the highest standards of science (i.e., with a randomized experimental design). The primary targets of intervention are the social processes and practices and, secondarily, the organization of those resources that may facilitate a change in social processes.

Pianta and Allen (2008) have developed a program called My Teaching Partner (MTP), which works to change teaching practices and relationships between teachers and students, specifically in terms of emotional support, instructional support, and classroom organization. MTP is evaluated in the context of randomized control experiments in both elementary and high schools. The researchers have also developed an observational device—known as the Classroom Assessment Scoring System (CLASS)—which measures 10 dimensions of teacher–student interactions and practices in the areas of emotional support, instructional support, and classroom organization.

After professional development training on these constructs, teachers are asked to videotape a classroom lesson. The video is sent to a master teacher, who analyzes it and then provides feedback to the teacher, including ways to respond to situations in a more effective manner. This cycle is repeated every 2 weeks for the entire academic year. We can see that this experimental social innovation incorporates a variety of strategies we have discussed, such as training, coaching/mentoring, and feedback. If this intervention is successful, then teachers are empowered and can then help to more effectively empower their students. Preliminary findings from a randomized cluster trial of 90 classrooms/teachers suggested that the patterns of instructional transactions and youth are positively altered (Allen & Pianta, 2009).

Regulatory-Driven Approaches and Strategies of Intervention

Finally, regulatory-driven approaches are exemplified by policy (e.g., legislation) and administrative-order strategies of intervention, which are based on authority. Issues of empowerment and the voices of the participants play, at best, a remote role in this approach. As we will see, the objectives of regulatory strategies are to change the resources or organization of resources in a setting.

As we have stated, resources can be altered in a straightforward manner by the implementation of regulatory policy. For example, a policy or administrative order may impose a credentialing requirement on youth workers with the assumption that certified workers will be more effective at improving their daily interactions with youth. Alternatively, the courts could mandate improved physical facilities or an increase in per-pupil expenditures for education. In a different vein, a city department of education might increase the number of computers in schools, implement a new curriculum, or add an hour of instruction to each school day. An increase in any of these resources will likely be beneficial, but will these policy strategies lead directly to improvements in the daily experiences (social processes) among youth and teachers or among youth and workers? Such resource changes alone are unlikely to change daily social processes. However, added instruction time or a new curriculum is more likely to precipitate positive changes than more distal resources. These strategies represent desirable and even necessary changes, but it is difficult to see them as both necessary and sufficient to achieve positive setting-level change.

Policy. Based, in part, on a long history of research on class size, Wisconsin passed legislation known as the Student Achievement Guarantee in Education (SAGE) program. The primary goal of SAGE was a reduction in class size to 1 teacher per 15 students (Graue, Hatch, Rao, & Oen, 2007). The hope was that this reduction would lead to different teacher practices and, ultimately, improved academic and socio-emotional outcomes. However, the only tool at legislators' disposal was to mandate a class-size reduction to a specified student–teacher ratio (i.e., a change in the resources). The 15:1 ratio was implemented by arranging the resources in several different ways: 15 students to 1 teacher in a single classroom, 30 students to 2 teachers in a shared space, 30 students team taught by 2 teachers, and a hybrid approach in which a part-time teacher is added for core subjects so the ratio for these students is reduced to 15:1. None of the different organizations of resources used to achieve the 15:1 student to teacher ratio focuses on changing daily social practices and processes. We look in vain for a focus on empowerment of the participants within classroom and school settings. Similarly, there is no attention paid to the voices and concerns of the participants.

Administrative orders. Administrative orders function in the same way as a policy, in that they are based on authority and target change in resources and/or the organization of resources without directly targeting change in daily social practices of processes. Again, empowerment goals play little role as do the voices of the participants.

CHANGING SOCIAL SETTINGS: WHAT STRATEGIES OF INTERVENTION SHOULD BE CHOSEN?

As we have seen, the approaches—reduction of inequity, utopian, professional development, data-driven, and regulatory—underlying the different strategies of intervention are varied. These approaches and strategies aren't perfectly aligned with each other. Misalignment occurs in at least two different ways. First, similar strategies are employed in the context of different approaches, although at times, as tactics. Second, the primary focus of setting-level intervention strategies is not consistently aligned with the specified approaches.

The Mixing of Approaches and Strategies

Intervention strategies are not pure. Mixing and matching different strategies within and across approaches is common. Even when strategies fall within the framework of a particular approach, the strategy is commonly employed as a tactic under the rubric of a different strategy/approach. For example, we often find community organizing strategies being used within the context of the creation of an alternative setting or in participatory research that are considered to be part of utopian and data-driven approaches, respectively.

Within data-driven approaches, we also saw feedback employed as an experimental social innovation strategy of intervention, whereas the coaching and mentoring illustration also took the form of an experimental social innovation.

Primary Focus of Intervention Strategies

The primary focus—resources, organization of resources, social processes/practices—of a setting-level intervention strategy is not always consistent within a specified approach. Table 2–1 reveals that the primary or exclusive target of several strategies (e.g., advocacy/litigation, education/training, and regulation [policy, administrative order]) is resources and their organization. Here, social processes/practices are neither a primary focus nor an implicit secondary focus. Thus, these strategies, at best, condition the setting or serve as levers so that change in social practices, interactions, or norms might be possible. Such strategies may, however, set in place critical conditioning factors, the effects of which are mediated by changing social practices and norms.

For the other strategies of intervention discussed—community organizing, consciousness-raising, the creation of settings, mentoring/coaching, feedback, experimental social innovation, and participatory research—social processes/practices are the primary focus of intervention. These strategies are also more likely to foster individual and collective empowerment. Using strategies of intervention to directly change social setting practices, interactions, and norms and, in particular, the daily experiences of the participants in these varying settings, provides an initial armamentarium and *place for community psychologists and others to stand*.

AUTHORS' NOTE

The authors would like to express their appreciation to Krishna Knabe for her meticulous and constructive editorial feedback on this chapter.

References

Alinsky, S. (1971). *Rules for radicals–A practical primer for realistic radicals*. New York: Random House.

Allen, J. P., Pianta, R. C. (2009). *My Teaching Partner: Classroom-level impact analyses*. The William T. Grant and Spencer Foundations' Intervention/Measurement Winter Workshop. Chicago, IL.

Altman, I., & Rogoff, B. (1987). World views in psychology: Trait, organismic, and transactional perspectives. In D. Stokols & I. Altman (Eds.), *Handbook of Environmental Psychology* (pp. 7–40). New York: Wiley.

Ball, D. L., & Forzani, F. M. (2007). What makes education research "educational?" *Educational Researcher. 36*, 529–540.

Bennett, C., Anderson, L., Cooper, S., Hassol, L., Klein, D., & Rosenblum, G. (1966). *Community psychology: A report of the Boston Conference on the Education of Psychologists for Community Mental Health.* Boston: Boston University.

Bennis, W., Benne. K., & Chin, R. (1976). *The planning of change.* New York: Holt, Rinehart, & Winston.

Bouffard, S., & Little, P. (2004). Promoting quality through professional development: A framework for evaluation. *Harvard Family Research Project, 8*, 1–12.

Bronfenbrenner, U. (1979). *The ecology of human development.* Cambridge, MA: Harvard University Press.

Bronfenbrenner, U. & Morris, P. (2006). The bioecological model of human development. In R. M Lerner (ed.), *Handbook of Child Psychology* (6th ed.) (Volume 1, pp.793–828). New York: Wiley.

Brown, J. L., Jones, S. M., LaRusso, M., & Aber, J. L. (2010). Improving classroom quality: Teacher influences and experimental impacts of the 4Rs Program. *Journal of Educational Psychology,* 102 (1), 153–167.

Buckley, W. (Ed.) (1968). *Modern systems research for the behavioral sciences: A sourcebook.* Chicago: Aldine.

Butler, D. L. & Wimme, P. H. (1995). Feedback and self-regulated learning: A theoretical synthesis. *Review of Educational Research, 65,* 245–281.

Cheatham-Rohas, A., & Shen, E, (2008). CBPR with Cambodian girls in Long Beach California: A Case study. In M. Minkler & N. Wallerstein (Eds.). *Community-based participatory research for health: From processes to outcome* (pp. 121–135). San Francisco: Jossey-Bass.

Cherniss, C., & Degan, G. (2000). The creation of alternative settings. In J. Rappaport & E. Seidman, *Handbook of community psychology* (pp. 359–378). New York: Kluwer Academic/Plenum Publishers.

Cohen, D. K., Raudenbush, S. W., & Ball, D. L. (2003). Resources, instruction, and research. *Educational Evaluation and Policy Analysis, 25,* 119–142.

Crowfoot, J., & Chesler, M. A. (1974). Contemporary perspectives on planned social change: A comparison. *Journal of Applied Behavioral Science, 10,* 278–303.

Dale, M. J., & Sanniti, C. (1993). Litigation as an instrument for change in juvenile detention: A case study. *Crime & Delinquency, 39,* 49–67.

Eccles, J., & Gootman, J. A. (2002). *Community Programs to Promote Youth Development.* Committee on Community-Level Programs for Youth.

Board on Children, Youth, and Families, Division of Behavioral and Social Sciences and Education. Washington, DC: National Academy Press.

Edelman, P. B. (1973). The Massachusetts Task Force Reports: Advocacy for Children. *Harvard Educational Review, 43*, 639–52.

Fairweather, G. W. (1972). *Social change: The challenge to survival.* Morristown, NJ: General Learning Press.

Foster-Fishman, P. G., & Nowell, B. (2007). Putting the system back into systems change: A framework for understanding and changing organizational and community systems. *American Journal of Community Psychology, 39*, 197–215.

Friere, P. (1970). *Pedagogy of the oppressed.* New York: Continuum.

Fullan, M. (2001). *The new meaning of educational change* (3rd ed.). New York, NY: Teachers College Press.

Gallimore, R., Goldenberg, C. N., & Weisner, T. S. (1993). The social construction and subjective reality of activity settings: Implications for community psychology. *American Journal of Community Psychology, 21(4)*, 501–20.

Graue, E., Hatch, K., Rao, K., & Oen, D. (2007). The wisdom of class-size reduction. *American Educational Research Journal, 44*, 670–700.

Israel, B. A., Eng, E., Schulz, A. J., & Parker, E. A. (Eds.) (2005). *Methods in community-based participatory research for health.* San Francisco: Jossey-Bass.

Jarrett, R. L., Sullivan, P., & Watkins, N. (2005). Developing youth social capital in extracurricular programs. *Journal of Research on Adolescence, 33*, 41–55.

Jones, S. M., Brown, J. L., & Aber, J. L. (2008). Classroom settings as targets of intervention and research. In M. Shinn & H. Yoshikawa (Eds.), *Toward positive youth development: Transforming schools and community programs* (pp. 58–77). New York: Oxford University Press.

Jones, S. M., Brown, J. L., & Aber, J. L. (in press). Two year impacts of a universal school-based social-emotional and literacy intervention: An experiment in translational developmental research. *Child Development.*

Kelly, J. G., Ryan, A. M., Altman, B. E., & Stelzner, S. (2000). Understanding and changing social systems: An ecological view. In J. Rappaport & E. Seidman (Eds.), *The Handbook of Community Psychology* (pp. 133–159). New York: Plenum.

Lewin, K. (1946). Action research and minority problems. *Journal of Social Issues, 2*, 34–46.

Lewin, K. (1951). *Field theory in social science.* New York: Harper & Brothers.

Maruyama, M. (1963). The second cybernetics: Deviation amplifying mutual causal processes. *American Scientist, 51*, 164–179.

Maton, K. I., Hrabowski, F. A., Özdemir, M., & Wimms, H. (2008). Enhancing representation, retention, and achievement of minority students in higher education: A social transformation theory of change. In M. Shinn & H. Yoshikawa (Eds.), *Toward positive youth development: Transforming schools and community programs* (pp. 115–132). New York: Oxford University Press.

Minkler, M., & Wallerstein, N. (2008) Introduction to community-based participatory research: New issues and emphases. In M. Minkler & N. Wallerstein (Eds.). *Community-based participatory research for health: From processes to outcome* (pp. 5–23). San Francisco: Jossey-Bass.

National Research Council & Institute of Medicine (2004). *Engaging Schools: Fostering High School Students' Motivation to Learn.* Committee on Increasing High School Students' Engagement and Motivation to Learn. Board on Children, Youth, and Families, Division of Behavioral and Social Sciences and Education. Washington, DC: National Academy Press.

O'Donnell, C., Tharp, R., & Wilson, K. (1993). Activity settings as the unit of analysis: A theoretical basis for community intervention and development. *American Journal of Community Psychology, 21(4),* 501–520.

Oxley, D. (2000). The school reform movement: Opportunities for Community Psychology (pp. 565–590). In. J. Rappaport & E. Seidman (Eds.), *Handbook of community psychology* (pp. 309–330). New York: Kluwer Academic/Plenum Publishers.

Pianta, R.C. (2006). Classroom management and relationships between children and teachers: Implications for research and practice. In C. M. Evertson & C. S. Weinstein (Eds.), *Handbook of classroom management: Research, practice, and contemporary issues.* (pp. 685–709). Mahwah, NJ: Lawrence Erlbaum Associates Publishers.

Pianta, R. C., & Allen, J. (2008). Building capacity for positive youth development in secondary school classrooms: Changing teachers' interactions with students. In M. Shinn & H. Yoshikawa (Eds.), *Toward positive youth development: Transforming schools and community programs* (pp. 21–39). New York: Oxford University Press.

Pollock, M. (2008). An intervention in progress: Pursuing precision in school race talk. In M. Shinn & H. Yoshikawa (Eds.), *Toward positive youth development: Transforming schools and community programs* (pp. 102–114). New York: Oxford University Press.

Rappaport, J. (1977). *Community Psychology: Values, Research, and Action.* New York: Holt, Rinehart, and Winston.

Rappaport, J. (1981). In praise of paradox: A social policy of empowerment over prevention. *American Journal of Community Psychology, 9,* 1–25.

Rappaport, J. (1987). Terms of empowerment/exemplars of prevention: Toward a theory of Community Psychology. *American Journal of Community Psychology, 15,* 121–144.

Rappaport, J. (1995). Empowerment meets narrative: Listening to stories and creating settings. *America Journal of Community Psychology, 23,* 795–807.

Rothman, J. (1974). Three models of community organization practice. In F. Cox, J. L. Ehrlich, J. Rothman, & J. E. Trapman (Eds.), *Strategies of community organization.* Itasca, IL: Peacock.

Sarason, S. B. (1972). *The creation of settings and the future societies.* San Francisco: Jossey-Bass.

Sarason, S. B. (1982). *The Culture of the School and the Problem of Change* (2nd ed.). Boston, MA: Allyn & Bacon.

Seidman, E. & Rappaport, J. (1986). *Redefining Social Problems.* New York: Plenum.

Seidman, E. (1988). Back to the future, community psychology: Unfolding a theory of social intervention. *American Journal of Community Psychology, 16,* 3–24.

Seidman, E. (1990). Pursuing the meaning and utility of social regularities for Community Psychology. In P. Tolan, C. Keys, F. Chertok, & L. Jason (Eds.), *Researching Community Psychology: Issues of theories and methods* (pp. 91–100). Washington, DC: American Psychological Association.

Smith, C., & Akiva, T. (2008). Quality accountability: Improving fidelity of broad developmentally focused interventions. In M. Shinn & H. Yoshikawa (Eds.), *Toward positive youth development: Transforming schools and community programs* (pp. 192–212). New York: Oxford University Press.

Smith, C., Sugar, S., Pearson, L., Lo, Y., & Frank, K. (2009). Youth Program Quality Intervention Study: Impact findings for management practice and instructional quality. The William T. Grant and Spencer Foundations' Intervention/Measurement Summer Workshop. Washington, DC.

Speer, P. (2008). Altering patterns of relationship and participation: Youth organizing as a setting-level intervention. In M. Shinn & H. Yoshikawa (Eds.), *Toward positive youth development: Transforming schools and community programs* (pp. 213–228). New York: Oxford University Press.

Task Force on Children Out of School (1970, 1971). *The way we go to school: The exclusion of children in Boston.* Boston: Beacon Press.

Tseng, V., & Seidman, E. (2007). A systems framework for understanding social settings. *American Journal of Community Psychology, 39,* 217–228.

Tyack, D., & Cuban, L. (1995). *Tinkering toward utopia: A century of public school reform.* Cambridge, MA: Harvard University Press.

Von Bertalanffy, L. (1957). General systems theory. In R. Taylor (Ed.), *Life, language, and law: Essays in honor of Arthur F. Bentley* (pp. 58–78). Oxford, England: The Antioch Press.

Weatherly, R., & Lipsky, M. (1977). Street-level bureaucrats and institutional innovation: Implementing special education reform. *Harvard Educational Review, 47,* 171–197.

Weinstein, R. S. (2002). *Reaching higher: The power of expectations in teaching.* Cambridge, MA: Harvard University Press.

Weinstein, R. S. (2008). Schools that actualize high expectations for all youth: Theory for setting change and creation. In M. Shinn & H. Yoshikawa (Eds.), *Toward positive youth development: Transforming schools and community programs* (pp. 81–101). New York: Oxford University Press.

Weisner, T. S. (2002). Ecocultural understanding of children's developmental pathways. *Human Development 45* (4), 275–281.

Zimmerman, M. A. (2000). Empowerment theory: Psychological, organizational, and community levels of analysis. In J. Rappaport & E. Seidman (Eds.), *Handbook of community psychology* (pp. 43–63). New York: Kluwer/Plenum Publishers.

3   Empowering Community Settings: Theory, Research, and Action

Kenneth I. Maton and Anne E. Brodsky

Empowerment has been conceptualized and defined in many different ways, depending in part on the population of interest, the area of focus, and the level of analysis (Rappaport, 1981; Zimmerman, 2000). For the current analysis, empowerment is viewed as a group-based, group-member driven, developmental process through which marginalized or oppressed individuals and groups gain greater control over their lives, enhanced access to valued resources, and reduced societal marginalization (Maton, 2008). Psychological, social, and civic empowerment are the three specific areas of focus examined. *Psychological empowerment* refers to group members gaining a greater sense of mastery or control over their daily personal lives. The primary emphasis is on individual change. *Social empowerment* can be viewed as gaining access to valued social roles, including high status roles, which group members have historically been denied (e.g., professional roles, leadership positions). Change in both the individual and the status of the group are encompassed. *Civic empowerment* can be defined as acquisition of basic human rights by severely oppressed groups (e.g., women in repressive third-world countries, poor people in every society). Primary emphases include individual change, the group's status in society, and larger social and cultural change. In each case, for marginalized or oppressed groups, the process of empowerment can be expected to take place over a substantial period of time, in community settings that are salient in group member's lives.

Previous research has suggested some of the organizational characteristics of empowering community settings. For example, based on a review of the literature of empowering settings in multiple community sectors, Maton (2008) delineated six organizational factors that characterize empowering settings: group-based belief system, core activities, relational environment, opportunity role structure, leadership, and setting maintenance and change. The belief systems of empowering settings inspire change among members, are strengths-based, and focus members beyond themselves. Core activities are engaging, involve active learning, and are of high quality. The relational environment provides extensive support, caring relationships, and a sense of community. The opportunity role structure is highly accessible to members and pervasive (i.e., meaningful roles are available throughout the setting) and involves both development of skills and opportunities for member voice and influence. The leadership in empowering settings is inspirational, talented, shared, committed, and empowered. Finally, setting maintenance and change features are learning-focused and characterized by both bridging mechanisms and external linkages.

Other studies have suggested additional organizational characteristics that may be important, including participation incentives, participatory decision making, and co-empowerment across subgroups (Bond & Keys, 1993; Gruber & Trickett, 1987; Prestby, Wandersman, Florin, Rich, & Chavis, 1990; Speer & Hughey, 1995). There has also been some focus on the ways that empowering community settings influence the external community and society (e.g., Maton, 2008; Janzen, Nelson, Hausfather, & Ochocka, 2007; Zimmerman, 2000; Peterson & Zimmerman, 2004). Maton (2008), for example, emphasized three pathways: increased numbers of empowered citizens, empowered member radiating influence (i.e., empowered members influencing the community through their personal activities in their neighborhood, workplace, and policy arena), and external organizational activities (e.g., public education, community services, policy advocacy)

In the current chapter, we draw upon research on three different kinds of empowering settings to delineate, in more detail, the setting-specific: *(1)* mediators through which organizational characteristics empower setting members and *(2)* pathways through which community betterment and positive social change occur—member-radiating influence and external organizational activities. Figure 3–1 depicts the primary model that has emerged from the research, and the bolded lowercase letters indicate the subset of areas of focus in the current chapter. The arrow marked by "a" in the figure refers to the mediating processes through which community settings empower their members. In turn, the arrow marked by "b" in the figure refers to the indirect influence of settings on the community and society through empowered member radiating influence. Finally, "c" refers to the

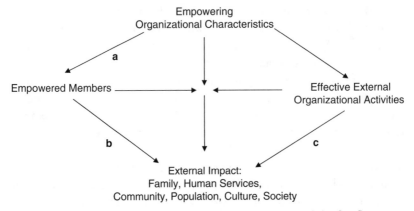

Figure 3.1   Empowering Community Settings: Model of Influence

direct influence of settings on the community and society through their external organizational activities.

The mediating processes and external pathways of influence proposed are illustrated from research involving three, diverse empowering community settings. One is Alcoholics Anonymous (AA), a self-help organization that focuses on individual psychological empowerment. The second is the Meyerhoff Scholars Program (MSP), a multifaceted support program that enhances the psychological and social empowerment of African-American college students with interests in the sciences. The third is The Revolutionary Association of the Women of Afghanistan (RAWA), a humanitarian and political organization that works toward psychological, social, and civic empowerment for Afghan girls and women in Afghanistan and Pakistan. Research to date suggests a number of commonalities across the three settings in terms of mediating processes and pathways of external influence, along with some distinct areas of difference.

THE THREE SETTINGS AND EVIDENCE OF MEMBER EMPOWERMENT

The three settings that constitute the focus of the current chapter will first be briefly described, along with evidence related to their empowering influence on members. In the case of AA, a recent book by Keith Humphreys (Humphreys, 2004) constitutes the source of much of the information; his book includes extant quantitative and qualitative research on AA. The available information on the MSP is primarily based on extensive qualitative and quantitative research conducted over the past 20 years by the first author and colleagues (e.g., Maton & Hrabowski, 2004; Maton, Sto. Domingo, Stolle-McAllister, Zimmerman, & Hrabowski, 2009). In the case of RAWA, the available information is based on extensive qualitative research conducted over the past 10 years by the second author (e.g., Brodsky, 2003).

Alcoholics Anonymous

Alcoholics Anonymous (AA) is a worldwide, 12-step, self-help group for alcoholics. AA views alcoholism as a disease with moral, physical, and spiritual components. In the view of AA, one is an alcoholic, and there is no such thing as a cured, ex-alcoholic. AA offers its members "fellowship," meaning a supportive network of recovering alcoholics, and a "program," meaning a method of ceasing alcohol consumption, improving moral character, and fostering spiritual growth. The essence of AA's program of change are the 12 steps, which include admitting an inability to control drinking, surrendering to a Higher Power, conducting a moral inventory of oneself, and helping other alcoholics (12-stepping). All 12-step meetings include a ritual at the beginning and the end and telling one's story. Based on its most recent triennial survey, AA estimates that there were more than 100,000 extant groups in 2002, with 2.2 million members worldwide, including 1.16 million in the United States (Alcoholics Anonymous, 2007; Humphreys, 2004).

Evaluation research to date has provided evidence of a positive impact on problem drinking and related indicators (e.g., depression, job performance) for AA members versus comparison samples. Humphreys (2004) provides a recent summary of experimental and quasi-experimental studies, including meta-analysis studies, of AA. He concludes that the "average effect of AA as a stand-alone intervention ... is of meaningful size" (p. 119). In addition, he notes that although some of the studies have methodological flaws, the better designed evaluations provide evidence of AA effectiveness that are equal to or stronger than the studies with weaker designs. There is evidence, then, that AA members are psychologically empowered in terms of gaining control over their drinking and their daily lives.

The Meyerhoff Scholars Program

The MSP is a multicomponent educational support program primarily focused on talented African-American college students interested in research careers in the sciences. The program is located at a predominantly European-American university at which, prior to the program's inception, African-American students in the sciences had not fared well. Primary program components include a summer bridge program prior to freshman year, comprehensive financial scholarships, study groups, peer community, program-specific academic advisors, strong campus administration involvement and support, and parent involvement. From its inception in 1988 to 1995, the program only accepted African-American students; in 1996, admissions was opened to all students committed to the advancement of underrepresented minority students in the sciences. The program has become a national model of a race-focused program enabling minority students to succeed in the sciences at a predominantly European-American campus and go on to PhD programs in the sciences (Building Engineering and Science Talent, 2004). Now in its 21st year, the program has a total current enrollment of 252 students—about three-fifths are African-American.

Prior to the advent of MSP, academically talented African-American students entering UMBC with a science focus rarely succeeded in science nor proceeded to graduate or medical school or careers in science or engineering. In contrast, more than 75% of entering African-American MSP students have entered graduate programs in the sciences, or medical school; furthermore, the students are almost five times more likely to enter into science PhD (or MD/PhD) programs than equally talented African-American students who were accepted into the program but declined the offer and attended other universities instead (Maton, Sto. Domingo, Stolle-McAllister, Zimmerman, & Hrabowski, 2009). Another indicator of the program's success is that UMBC is now one of the top three predominantly European-American universities in the nation in terms of producing African-American students who go on to receive science and engineering doctorates (the other two are University of Michigan at Ann Arbor and Duke University) (National Science Foundation 2008). Thus, the program demonstrates strong evidence of psychological empowerment leading to individual successes and social role empowerment for African-Americans, a group with very low rates of science PhD receipt (1.8% in 2006; Hoffer, Hess, Welch, & Williams, 2007).

The Revolutionary Association of the Women of Afghanistan

RAWA is an Afghan women's humanitarian and political organization founded in 1977 by a 20-year-old college student named Meena[1]. Meena, along with a small group of educated, urban women, formed RAWA to advocate for women's basic rights in a country where the familial, tribal, and

---

1 As is common among many Afghans, Meena used only one name.

societal traditions circumvented these rights, keeping 90% of women illiterate and often treating them as chattel and second class citizens. RAWA is an underground organization active in both Pakistan and Afghanistan and provides humanitarian assistance in the forms of literacy classes for women, schools for girls and boys, hospital and mobile medical teams, income-generating projects for women, and aid distributions. They are also a political organization, maintaining a political voice through their website, political magazine, international speaking tours, political protests, and conferences, all of which have advocated for women's basic rights, peace, and human rights, as well as for a secular, democratic Afghanistan. Through all of their activities, they have concentrated on bringing education, as well as a message of empowerment and resistance, to women and men and have been able to recruit an estimated 2000 female members and an estimated equal number of male supporters—both of whom carry out the work of the organization.

RAWA's ability to survive and thrive as an organization during the past 30 years of nearly constant war and oppression of women is a case in point for their ability to empower their members to participate in this difficult endeavor. Over the years, their impact has been felt by the women and children they have served, the empowerment of the women and men who volunteer with them to provide services and advocacy, and the message of women's rights and a secular-democratic Afghanistan that they have continued to voice both in Afghanistan and internationally. Thus they can be seen as an empowering community that impacts all three domains of empowerment.

Next we turn to the interesting question of how these three different organizations empower their members with regard to each setting's content focus; demographics in terms of age, gender, ethnicity, and country; and different types of empowerment. We focus on both what these settings have in common as well as the ways in which they are unique.

MEDIATORS OF MEMBER EMPOWERMENT

Table 3–1 depicts the mediators of member empowerment delineated by Maton (2008), here separated into cognitive/affective, relational, and instrumental categories. In addition, the table summarizes the unique content focus through which the mediators lead to empowerment within each setting. Given space limitations, we can only briefly depict the mediators in each category, illustrating with several quotes their unique manifestation and content focus in each of the three settings. The quotes vary in the extent to which they describe the mediator or illustrate how the mediator impacts member change.

Table 3.1   Mediators and Content Focus of Member Empowerment

	Alcoholics Anonymous	Meyerhoff Scholars Program	The Revolutionary Association of the Women of Afghanistan
Cognitive/Affective			
Mediators	Awareness	Awareness	Awareness
	Motivation	Motivation	Motivation
	Self-efficacy	Self-efficacy	Self-efficacy
Content Focus	Transformation of view of self, alcoholism	Development of identity as an outstanding science student	Consciousness-raising related to women's rights
Instrumental			
Mediators	Skills development	Skills development	Skills development
	Meaningful roles	Meaningful roles	Meaningful roles
	Engagement	Engagement	Engagement
Content focus	Abstinence coping skills	Strategic academic skills	Literacy, service, income generation, & social action skills
Relational			
Mediators	Caring	Caring	Caring
	Mutual support	Mutual support	Mutual support
	Belonging	Belonging	Belonging
Content focus	Recovery-focused	Achievement-focused	Emancipation-focused

Cognitive/Affective Mediators: Awareness, Motivation, and Self-Efficacy

Fundamental alterations in awareness, motivation, and self-efficacy mediate member empowerment within each of the three settings. Consistent with their very differing goals and contexts, however, each of the three settings can be seen as having a distinct content focus through which these mediators result in member empowerment. These are transformation in the view of self and one's alcoholism in the case of AA, identity development as a future scientist in MSP, and consciousness-raising related to basic women's rights in RAWA.

Alcoholics Anonymous. AA appears to empower members psychologically through a fundamental change in member's view of self and alcoholism. Specifically, members come to view alcoholism as a disease, accept the need to rely on a "higher power," develop self-efficacy related to drinking cessation, and to varying degrees experience emotional healing and spiritual transformation, as illustrated in the following excerpts from an AA member:

> "For weeks I sat in the back of the rooms, silent when others shared their experience, strength and hope. I listened to their stories ... I learned that alcoholism isn't a sin, it's a disease. That lifted the guilt I had felt. I learned that I didn't have to stop drinking forever, but just not to pick up that first drink one day, one hour at a time. I could manage that."
> (Alcoholics Anonymous, 2007b, p. 344)

> "Above all, I healed spiritually. The steps took me on that path. I had admitted that I was powerless over alcohol, that my life had become unmanageable ... Then, nurtured by the program, [my] inner spirit grew, deepened, until it filled the emptiness I had so long felt inside. Step to step I moved to a spiritual awakening. Step by step I cleared up the past and got on with the present."
> (Alcoholics Anonymous, 2007b, p. 346)

Meyerhoff Scholars Program. Central to the cognitive/affective process of empowerment in MSP is development of an identity as a science student and future scientist capable of outstanding academic performance. Students incorporate key program values, including achievement at the highest levels in difficult science majors, commitment to redress the shortage of African-American science PhDs, seeking help from a variety of sources to achieve As, drawing on peer support and peer study, and giving back to the community. Students are inspired and challenged to meet the high academic expectations that surround them:

> "I want to set a good example for [my two younger siblings] and also an example for Blacks in general, so that they can see that somebody can make it. There aren't a lot of [black] PhDs, which is what I want to [become]."
> (MSP student; unpublished data)

"They [the Meyerhoff Program] had high expectations for me ...
I internalized those expectations ... The most important thing it
gave me ... confidence that I could succeed in school but also that
I could be one of the best."

(MSP student; unpublished data)

"That feeling of family when everybody came together in the
(program-wide) meetings ... I learned that all of these people are
doing so well. Those things were an inspiration to me. I think that
made me do so well my freshmen year, and made me continue on
to doing well."

(MSP student; unpublished data)

Revolutionary Association of the Women of Afghanistan. Raising of
consciousness, through an educational approach that shares much with
Freire's (1972) emancipatory education, is a primary psychological mechanism through which RAWA empowers its members. The manifestations of
consciousness raising are illustrated in the following quotes—the first from a
RAWA leader, and the next three from RAWA members:

"We always thought deeper than just giving women education. We
thought the purpose was giving women a consciousness—political,
social, cultural—giving them that consciousness meant a revolu-
tion. We obviously had to start with basic education, but
couldn't stop there."

(Brodsky, 2003, p. 106)

"I learned to read and write but also attended other activities
and functions and became a RAWA member. All these years I
finally learned who I am as a woman. We ... can help our country
and our people."

(RAWA member; Brodsky, 2003, p. 136)

"The most important thing was recognizing our rights as
women and when we live in a family with men we should also
have our rights as human beings and woman. In some families the
value of women for men is like their shoes, but we also know that
women are human beings and have their rights and should live
equally..."

(RAWA member; Brodsky, 2003, p. 124)

"...at RAWA everyone has the consciousness that no one is living here for personal life; all are together for one goal. What RAWA teaches women and all people is to put others first."

(RAWA member; Brodsky, 2003, p. 263)

Instrumental Mediators: Skills Development, Meaningful Roles, and Engagement

Skills development, meaningful roles, and engagement have been identified as critical instrumental mediators in empowering community settings (Maton, 2008). Consistent with their differing goals and contexts, the content focus of these mediators varied greatly across the three settings of focus. In the case of AA, instrumental mediators focus on active coping to maintain abstinence, in MSP the focus is on strategic academic skills linked to academic success in science; and in the case of RAWA, the focus is on literacy, income-generation, service to others, and social action skills.

Alcoholics Anonymous. Research studies suggest that development of active coping skills and the opportunity to participate in meaningful, helping roles and engagement over time are important mediators of AA effectiveness (Humphreys, 2004).

"In working the Twelve Steps, my life and my old way of thinking have changed. I have no control over some of the things that happen in my life, but with the help of God I can now choose how I will respond. Today I choose to be happy, and when I'm not, I have the tools of the program to put me on back."

(AA member; Alcoholics Anonymous, 2007d, p. 381)

"Commitment and service were part of recovery. I was told that to keep it we have to give it away. At first I made the coffee and later volunteered at the intergroup office answering telephones on the evening shift. I went on 12th-step calls, spoke at meetings, [and] served as group officer. Ever so gradually I began to open. Just a crack at first, with my hand on the door ready to slam it shut in a moment of fear. But my fears subsided too. I found that I could be there, open to all kinds of people from this solid base that we shared. Then I began to go back out into the world, carrying that strength with me."

(AA member; Alcoholics Anonymous, 2007b, p. 345)

Meyerhoff Scholars Program. MSP helps students learn strategic academic and research skills to achieve both short-term (college) and longer-term (graduate school) success in science fields. These skills include getting to know professors and the best students in the class, seeking help, participation in study groups, getting tutoring to help achieve As, tutoring others, and summer research experiences in labs of eminent scientists around the country. Furthermore, the program provides multiple opportunities for engagement and meaningful helping roles. These include opportunities for community service with inner city children and representing the program to the external world.

> "I think that the things the Meyerhoff Program stresses, like working in groups and getting to know your professors and sitting in front of class—those things help you in graduate school.
>
> (MSP student, unpublished data)

> "The research experiences have been very valuable. I worked with Dr. Jones ... first ... he set a basis for everything that I was going to be using later on. Then Dr. Farkson—I presented at three difference conferences on the research that I did with him about myoglobin. Then I worked with Dr. Howard ... in neuroscience ... [Most valuable has been] the thinking process, how you go about trying to solve a problem, and all the different techniques you can use to get around problems..."
>
> (MSP student, unpublished data)

> "When you go out in public, you're not only representing yourself, but you are representing the program. So you carry yourself with a little more pride, and a little more dignity."
>
> (MSP student; Maton & Hrabowski, 2000, p. 644)

Revolutionary Association of the Women of Afghanistan. The development of basic skills, civic engagement, and the provision of meaningful social roles are important mediators of empowerment in a society experiencing ongoing decades of war and social upheaval, in which all noncombatants—particularly women—found their social roles degraded. Skills acquired include not only literacy and numeracy but also additional abilities learned through practical experiences that serve the needs of the organization as well as individuals. Thus, older adolescents have been students as well as teachers, women in literacy classes quickly have come to make up the ranks of contributing organizational members, and participants in income-generating projects simultaneously learned a skill and an interpretation of the political situation in which they were not alone. All of these have led women to active involvement as political and social change agents:

> "RAWA ... discovers the abilities and potential of members in different fields. For example, one might be working in publication, the website, literacy classes, or in other fields. RAWA tries to improve and promote those skills that they already have the natural gift or talent for."
>
> (RAWA member; Brodsky, 2003, pp. 113–114)

> "When I first came to stay in the [refugee] camp I was impressed by the interactions between women in camp because of RAWA. Before this I had a lot of time to think about how terrible the situation was for me and for my country. I had no children, no work, and all this thinking made me depressed. The things I could get involved with in the camp, literacy courses, other involvements made me feel better."
>
> (Brodsky, 2003, p. 141)

Relational Mediators: Caring, Mutual Support, and Belonging

In the relational domain, common to all settings is the importance of caring, mutual support, and belonging. Consistent with their differing goals and contexts, the content focus of these mediators varied greatly. Specifically, caring, mutual support, and belonging are recovery-focused in the case of AA, achievement-focused in MSP, and emancipation-focused in RAWA.

Alcoholics Anonymous. Research suggests that recovery-focused social support constitutes one of the key mediators of AA effectiveness (Humphreys, 2004). This support occurs in the context of caring relationships with other alcoholics and is aided by a sense of belonging to a community of recovering alcoholics. The following quotes illustrate several aspects of these mediating influences.

> "Over the course of my sobriety I have experienced many opportunities to grow. I have had struggles and achievements. Through it all I have not had to take a drink, nor have I ever been alone. Willingness and action have seen me through it all, with the guidance of a loving Higher Power and the fellowship of the program. When I am in doubt, I have faith that things will turn out as they should. When I'm afraid, I reach out to the hands of another alcoholic to steady me."
>
> (AA member; Alcoholics Anonymous, 2007c, p. 309)

"AA is my home now, and it is everywhere. I go to meetings
when I travel here or in foreign countries and the people are family
I can know because of what we share ... In my 28th year of
sobriety, I am amazed to look back and ... see how far I've come
out of the abyss."

(AA member; Alcoholics Anonymous, 2007b, p. 346).

Meyerhoff Scholars Program. Along with high levels of expectation and
challenge, MSP provides a relational environment characterized by high
levels of mutual support, caring, and belonging related to achievement
in science. Various aspects of these relational resources are revealed in the
following interview excerpts:

"Number one in my book is the support. Having other
smart, talented African Americans around you at all times
is an asset."

(MSP student; Maton & Hrabowski, 2000, p. 644)

It would have taken me a while to become social with people.
But in my first year of college [after summer bridge program],
I knew about thirty people [MSP peers], so it was easy. I had
friends. I didn't feel like an outcast."

(MSP student; Maton & Hrabowski, 2000, p. 644)

"Peers played a big role in my academic success ... I'm always
studying with them. So (for) anything I don't understand, they're
the ones who help me understand the concept."

(MSP student, unpublished data)

Revolutionary Association of the Women of Afghanistan. The emancipation-focused caring, mutual support, and belonging that RAWA provides
for members represent a key component of its ability to empower Afghan
women. Support includes material support (e.g., free communal housing
in exchange for work, aid distributions for destitute refugees, income-
generating projects) as well as emotional support. Caring and belonging are
an integral part of membership given the repressive society in which RAWA
operates.

"I've always been impressed with the behavior and kindness of
other members toward me—they've constantly asked about me and
helped me with my sickness as well as taking care of my children."

(RAWA member; Brodsky, 2003, p. 247)

"First of all women generally in Afghanistan have very close relationships with each other, mainly probably related to the kind of pain we are all suffering.... But at RAWA, from the very first days, we made creating this feeling of community very much conscious."

(RAWA member; Brodsky, 2003, p. 257)

"Mainly it is our political standpoints and goals that keep members together. We all struggle for the same cause. Unity, friendship, sisterhood, love, and camaraderie occur on top of political unity."

(RAWA member; Brodsky, 2003, p. 256)

NATURE AND LEVELS OF EXTERNAL IMPACT

There is little extant research in community psychology on the impact of empowering community settings on the surrounding community and society. In theory, empowering community settings have the potential for influencing beliefs, norms, practices, and policies at multiple levels of analysis ranging from the family, workplace, and neighborhood to the larger community and society, including population-level indicators related to the marginalized or oppressed population. The specific nature of the external impact varies tremendously across the three settings studied, consistent with their focus and context. Table 3–2 depicts possible external impacts at various levels of analysis for AA, MSP, and RAWA.

In the case of AA, one indicator of external impact is its ongoing growth, along with diffusion of the 12-step model over the years to other self-help organizations and professional treatment agencies (Kurtz, 1997a). Most notable among the latter are the "Minnesota Model" treatment programs, which, although distinct from AA, have facilitated its growth in societies such as Denmark, Iceland, Israel, and Sweden. AA has now spread from the United States to more than 50 other societies (Humphreys, 2004). In terms of population impact, evidence suggests that a reduction in liver cirrhosis has been associated with the continuing rise in AA membership (and alcoholism treatment programs) (Smart & Mann, 1993).

One important area of impact for MSP is the institutional culture and reputation of the university in which it is embedded. The culture has become much more accepting of the potential of minority students to succeed in science (and indeed in all fields). The university's reputation has increased nationwide, in part because of the fact that MSP has attracted attention as a national model for enhancing the success of underrepresented

Table 3.2   Empowering Community Settings: External Impact

Alcoholics Anonymous	Meyerhoff Scholars Program	The Revolutionary Association of the Women of Afghanistan
Microsystem		
Spouse, children	Younger siblings	Nuclear & extended family
Workplace	University	Supporters & aid recipients
Community		
Human services	Educators	Local community services
Alternate settings	Black parents	Local community norms
Society		
Diffusion of model	Social policy	Persian intellectual community
Social Norms	Funders	International community
Population prevalence (alcoholism; liver cirrhosis; health care costs)	Population representation (% black scientists)	Emancipation (% empowered women)

minority students in the sciences (e.g., Building Engineering and Science Talent, 2004). In terms of population influence, the increasing numbers of MSP graduates receiving their doctorates and entering the workforce conceivably, over time, will result in a substantive increase in the (now extremely small) number of African-American scientists, with potentially important implications for the settings in which they work.

In the case of RAWA, their name recognition and prestige in the international community, ability to meet in international contexts with high-ranking government officials, and attendance—both overtly and covertly at many of the meetings and conferences related to the formation of the new Afghan state—all point to their external impact. Less easily documented, but hypothesized by Brodsky, is that through taking relatively extreme standpoints on Afghan secular democracy, against warlords and fundamentalist jehadis, and for women's rights and role in society, RAWA has made room for more moderate political women's voices, which, by comparison, come to appear more acceptable in this traditional society. Thus the existence of radical agitation with international support makes space for other women who consciously set themselves apart from RAWA while advocating for similarly directed progress for women and the country.

PATHWAYS OF INFLUENCE LEADING TO EXTERNAL IMPACT

Two pathways of external influence appear important in the case of empowering community settings, leading to the specific impacts noted above. These are empowered member-radiating impact and external organizational activities. Each pathway is described below, with differences across settings manifest in both content and level of analysis. We also consider, at the end of this section, the important role social science can play in contributing to the external impact of empowering community settings.

Empowered-Member Radiating Influence

One pathway of external influence is empowered-member radiating impact. This refers to the extent to which empowered members, as individuals and citizens, influence the settings, communities, and larger society in which they reside. Modeling, interpersonal influence, and policy advocacy are three means through which radiating external impact can be achieved. The nature and level of such influence is directly related to the content focus of the empowering community setting, as illustrated below.

Alcoholics Anonymous. AA members have the potential to influence their families, coworkers, fellow alcoholics, and, through obtaining positions of policy relevance, human services policies related to alcoholism. The two quotes below illustrate the potential for influence on family and on other alcoholics.

> "Growing up in AA, I have been blessed with children who have never seen their mother drunk. I have a husband who loves me simply because I am, and I have gained the respect of my family.
> (AA member; Alcoholics Anonymous 2007c, p. 318)

> "My favorite AA story is about this woman who went on a 12th-step call. She picks up this drunk, you know, and she gets a cab to take him to a treatment center. So she's there in the back of the cab 12th-stepping this guy and telling him about AA. She drops him off at the detoxification center and then never sees him again. But about a week later she's waiting for a meeting to start

and the cab driver walks in and says, 'Lady, I heard every word
you said.'"

(AA member; Humphreys, 2000, p. 503)

Two specific examples illustrate the radiating influence of certain AA
members on national level policy. First, many members of the influential
National Council on Alcoholism, including its founder Marty Mann, have
been AA members (cf. Humphreys, 2004). Second, influential AA member
Democratic Senator Harold Hughes was the force behind the Comprehensive
Alcohol Abuse and Alcoholism Prevention Act of 1970 that established the
National Institute on Alcohol Abuse and Alcoholism (NIAAA). In each case,
mobilization of resources to treat and prevent alcoholism can be attributed,
at least in some part, to the radiating influence of empowered AA members.

Meyerhoff Scholars Program. Two primary domains of influence of
empowered MSP scholars are the university in which the program is embedded and potential policymakers and funders. The three quotes below reflect
the influence on the university from the perspective of faculty members.

"In the past (prior to the Meyerhoff Program), a student in your
class who was Black was likely not to do well. The Meyerhoff
program changed that almost immediately. As soon as Meyerhoff
students started earning As ... becoming very insistent on going
into research programs and being successful, all of a sudden you
couldn't make that assumption. Looking for success rather than
failure [in your black students]. That's a big change. That's a big
institutional change. That happened in my department and it
happened throughout the institution."

(Maton & Hrabowski, 2000, p. 647)

"In the research lab ... they [Meyerhoffs] are role models for
[other minority students.]"

(Maton & Hrabowski, 2000, p. 647)

"The minority students who don't get into the program still
want to come to our campus because they want to be around that
type of person. They just want to be surrounded by minorities that
care about education and are driven and trying to be the best
people they can be."

(Maton & Hrabowski, 2000, p. 647)

Evidence also exists for Meyerhoff student influence beyond the local
setting, as influential role models for younger siblings, as ambassadors for the

program effectively influencing foundations and national policy group representatives, and on their graduate student peers and faculty. Time will tell if they exert a substantive influence, as they enter into roles in the workforce, including those in education and science policy.

Revolutionary Association of the Women of Afghanistan. RAWA influences the families of members, supporters, and aid recipients, local communities in which they operate, and the Persian intellectual and the wider international community who view their political writings and website and interact with their foreign affairs committee members. Nuclear and extended family members are the first to be affected by an individual's association with RAWA:

> "My affiliation with RAWA changed the mentality of my family. In the beginning my brother and sister wondered if I was mad to live in a refugee camp with an uncomfortable life. But they visited and saw the freedom, education, and what I had learned. They changed and now my brother distributes Payam-e Zan (RAWA's political magazine) and is very supportive. My sister reads it even though her husband was initially very restrictive and critical .... But after several visits he ... changed."
>
> (RAWA member; Brodsky, 2003, p. 146)

This advocacy can extend to neighbors:

> "I always try to help others in our neighborhood. For example, the daughter of our neighbor was in the name of her cousins from childhood [i.e., their marriage was prearranged], but she wasn't happy ... she [came] close to having killed herself. After that we talked to her uncle and family members ... And we talked and talked and talked and finally they were convinced and the girl became free of that pressure [to marry the boy]."
>
> (RAWA member; Brodsky, 2003, p. 125)

Women and men who observe RAWA women leading activities that women are not thought generally capable of are also impacted by their contact with RAWA:

> "I first learned about RAWA through friends. I told them that they were being deceived, and couldn't trust it, women couldn't possibly be doing the things they said. They invited me to attend a demonstration and there I saw other members. It was then that I thought that my place should be with RAWA."
>
> (RAWA member, Brodsky, 2003, p. 110)

At the policy level, the potential for influence of empowered RAWA members exists through involvements in varied policy relevant groups, including government councils and agencies in Afghanistan. Policy influence also occurs through RAWA members' open and direct advocacy with foreign governmental officials, including the United Nations, with direct impact on the post-Taliban government. Much of the work in Afghanistan, however, has necessarily been performed over the years in secretive ways because of the dangers perceived by RAWA members were their affiliations to become known.

External Organizational Activities

A second pathway is the influence of the external organizational activities that the empowering setting performs. Activities include recruitment, public education, dissemination/diffusion of information and programming, community actions (e.g., social action), community services, resource mobilization, and policy advocacy (Janzen, Nelson, Hausfather, & Ochocka, 2007; Maton, 2008; Peterson & Zimmerman, 2004). Some activities are focused at the microsystem and community levels and others at the societal level. The three settings studied varied in the content focus of their external activities and, as illustrated in Table 3–3, to some extent in the types of activities and the level of focus of external influence.

Alcoholics Anonymous. The primary external activities of AA are member recruitment/outreach, public and professional education, and dissemination. The 12th step of the AA program involves reaching out to other alcoholics. AA also has an active information dissemination program, including hard copies and online copies of the AA Blue Book and a speaker's series. As an integral part of its program, AA reaches out to alcoholics through the participation of members in "12th-stepping."

The long-term, sustained growth of AA in the United States and around the world likely results in part from its own information dissemination and outreach activities and in part from positive portrayals in the media. Evaluation research indicating positive outcomes may also contribute to its external influence, in part as it legitimizes AA as a viable resource in the face of ongoing professional discrediting of AA's 12-step approach, including its lack of professional involvement (Humphreys, 2004). In terms of policy, as indicated in Table 3–3, AA does not participate as an organization in explicit national resource mobilization, political and policy advocacy, or challenge of cultural norms. Thus, in this domain, empowered AA members and available research serve as the "voice" of AA rather than the organization *per se*.

Table 3.3   External Organizational Activities and Levels of Influence

	Alcoholics Anonymous	Meyerhoff Scholars Program	The Revolutionary Association of the Women of Afghanistan
Community			
Member recruitment	XX	XX	XX
Public education	XX	XX	XX
Dissemination/ diffusion	XX	XX	XX
Seeking external funding		XX	XX
Community services			XX
Community actions			XX
Society			
National Resource Mobilization			XX
Political and policy advocacy			XX
Challenge cultural norms			XX

Meyerhoff Scholars Program. Major external organizational activities include student recruitment, public education, dissemination of information about the program, and seeking of external funding (for student scholarships, staff support, and support for long-term evaluation). Each of the above activities is uniquely facilitated by the fact that the African-American program founder is also president of the predominantly European-American university in which MSP is situated.

Student recruitment is facilitated by dissemination of information to leading high schools in Maryland, as well by its increasing state and national reputation. Procurement of funding from foundations and the federal government has been aided by the positive results from the ongoing program evaluation, started in 1990 as a result of the initiative of the program founder. Public and professional education is greatly facilitated by two published books describing the strengths-based parenting practices that led to the MSP student's pre-college success, along with the outcome and process outcomes resulting from the program's evaluation (Hrabowski, Maton, & Greif, 1998; Hrabowski, Maton, Greene, & Greif, 2002). More than 32,000 copies have been sold, and first-author Dr. Hrabowski, MSP program creator and university president, has had the opportunity to discuss and sell (signed copies of) the book to large audiences of educators (national and statewide meetings of superintendents and teachers) and African-American parents (PTA; concerned parent groups).

The program itself does not take part in national resource mobilization, political and policy advocacy, or challenge of cultural norms. It does have an indirect influence in some of these areas, however, as Dr. Hrabowski serves, or has served, on many influential national committees and boards that mobilize and earmark funding and develop policy related to the success of minorities in the sciences. In these roles, he acts as an advocate for his program, as well as the larger social problem on which the program focuses. These include influential committees and boards within the American Association for the Advancement of Science (AAAS), National Academy of Sciences (NAS), National Institutes of Health, and the National Science Foundation.

Revolutionary Association of the Women of Afghanistan. RAWA's external organizational activities, as a social change-focused setting, explicitly includes a focus on both the community and societal levels. Specific activities include educational and humanitarian service provision, advocacy in the local community, member recruitment, dissemination of information, national resource mobilization, political and policy advocacy, and challenging cultural norms. Educational and humanitarian services are provided by RAWA members; thus, empowered RAWA members are important for effective external activities. Local advocacy is done by addressing problems in people's lives in the local community, as illustrated in the following example:

> A man was beating up his wife and his mother-in-law ... RAWA members went to talk to him several times as did the camp council (of men).... Other men who were beating their wives heard that RAWA goes to other houses and about the council warning ... it changes their behavior directly. Men also see how much changing their behavior helps relationships in the family and affects the kids, and this convinces them to change their mentality.
> (RAWA member; Brodsky, 2003, p. 130)

RAWA has sought to impact public policy at the local, national, and international levels. Under Jehadi and Taliban, their public policy work took the form of impacting the running of local refugee camps headed by sympathetic resistance leaders, or through attempting to convince local religious councils that girls should be allowed and encouraged to attend their school. At the international level, RAWA works with contacts in the European Union Parliament, certain sympathetic local towns and villages in Europe who made it policy to support RAWA programs monetarily and through advocacy, through war crime tribunal judges in Europe, and through lobbying the United States and the United Nations. Currently, at the national level, RAWA has been successful in seeing several former and current members of the organization as well as various supporters take an active part in advocating policy for the new Afghanistan. This comes through RAWA's connections to international policy shapers, as well as their placement as trusted, giving members of their local communities who have been thus recommended or voted onto national level groups, even if not under the name of RAWA *per se*.

SOCIAL SCIENCE INFLUENCE

Social science has a potentially important role to play contributing to the external influence of empowering community settings through enhancing legitimacy and helping to mobilize resources. As noted above, in the case of AA and MSP, evaluation research by social scientists has helped to establish the viability and legitimacy of each of the programs. In the case of AA, as noted earlier, this is important given the tendency of professional guilds to discredit the 12-step approach, in part because of the lack of professional involvement. In the case of the MSP, social science evaluation evidence indicating positive results has directly contributed to the program being proclaimed a national model; few other programs that have focused on the advancement of minorities in the sciences have any systematic evidential support.

Social science research also contributes to changing public and professional attitudes and stereotypes concerning empowering settings and their members. In the case of the two books about the MSP students and their families, the publications help alter perceptions so that the public and educators view minority students as academic stars, raise expectations of the students' potential, and recast African-American families as similar to European-American families in their hopes, dreams, and practices related to educating their children. In the case of RAWA, research documents organizational activities and processes, allows the public to gain a more realistic appraisal of the daily life experienced by Afghan women and their resistance in the face of long-standing repression, and more generally provides an analysis of RAWA as a model of resilience of possible utility to other movements and organizations.

Finally, social scientists can also more directly support the external activities of empowering community settings. In the case of RAWA, the second author played an active role, along with other U.S. supporters, in facilitating media-based, public educational and resource mobilization activities of RAWA representatives in the United States. Specifically, from 2000 through 2003, Brodsky worked with other supporters to facilitate meetings between RAWA representatives and U.S. governmental officials and private agencies with an interest in the issues facing Afghan women, arrange press interviews and coverage of events, plan and organize fundraisers, and further educate and interest U.S. audiences through public speaking to raise awareness of issues for Afghan women and organizations that could be supported on their behalf, such as RAWA. The writing of a book, *With All Our Strength*, which documents the organization and the history of Afghan women's community resilience, also serves to benefit Afghan women by reaching a wider audience and providing money-generating possibilities through book sales.

IMPLICATIONS AND FUTURE DIRECTIONS

This chapter is a modest attempt to build on Rappaport's (1977, 1981, 1987) vision of a community psychology in which empowerment is the guiding motif to life. Clearly, much work remains to be done in conceptualizing and defining the construct of empowering community settings and identifying the key organizational characteristics, mediating processes, and pathways of external influence on the community and larger society.

The strength of the current research—its inductive, multiple-case study methodology—also represents the source of its weaknesses. First, only three settings were included, selected in part based on available research. The generalizability of findings to other settings is not known. Second, the absence of comparison, nonempowering settings precludes any definitive demonstration that the processes and pathways delineated are unique to empowering settings.

One important line of future scholarship is determining the extent to which the proposed mediating processes and pathways of external influence are present in other types of empowering settings. A review of extant research in settings such as youth development programs, religious settings, and social action programs has helped to delineate some commonalities in mediating factors and activities related to external influence (Maton, 2008). Future empirical research that directly examines mediating processes and external pathways of influence will be critical in answering questions of commonality versus specificity across types of settings.

Another important area of research is to examine the arrows in Figure 3–1 that were not focused on in the current research. One important focus is the linkage between empowering organizational characteristics and effective organizational activities (arrow in top-right hand portion of the figure). For example, to what extent do the organizational characteristics that lead to member empowerment also lead to effective organizational activities, and to what extent are other factors involved? A second important focus is the reciprocal linkage between member empowerment and effective organizational activities (arrows in middle-left and middle-right portions of the figure). For example, does the extent to which empowered members are central to the conduct of effective organizational activities differ by type of setting? A third important question is whether there are other mechanisms through which organizational characteristics lead to external impact in addition to the empowerment of members and effective external organizational activities.

Relatedly, further research is needed to clarify and refine the key concepts examined. For example, the extent to which each of the proposed mediators is distinct and separate from each other is unclear (e.g., caring relationships versus provision of support). Similarly, the two pathways of external influence—empowered member-radiating influence and external organizational activities—will not always be distinct. For example, it may not always be clear when members (or leaders) of empowering settings are acting as individuals on their own (empowered member-radiating influence) and when they are acting on behalf of their setting (external organizational activities). Research is needed to examine the nature and import of these, and related, pathways of influence.

Advances in understanding empowering community settings will depend in part on advances in our definition and conceptualization of empowerment more generally. For example, it may reasonably be argued that the too-common practice in our field of defining and examining empowerment solely as an individual level process or outcome diverts attention from social group-level, setting-level, and community-level empowerment. Although each has a role to play in social change, the latter likely holds maximal potential to truly make a difference in the lives of disempowered lower income populations, for whom transformative social change—not individual change—appears most critical in contemporary society (Maton, 2000). Thus, future work in this area will especially benefit from a focus on empowerment that involves changing social norms, practices, and policies affecting the lives of our most oppressed citizens.

Varied types of research methods will be called for in future work. Of special importance is the use of narrative methods to give voice to those silenced by society and to understand the setting and dominant cultural narratives necessary to bring about change and transformation. To date, narrative methods research remains relatively scarce in social science research on community-based settings. In the current context, narrative methods have provided critical insights into both distinct and common pathways and processes of influence in each setting. Also important is mixed-method models and, in the case of external pathways of influence, historical and sociological methods that may very well require interdisciplinary collaborations across levels of analysis.

The current chapter has focused on the potential of social science to enhance the impact of extant empowering settings. Equally important is theory development, research, and action that help to transform currently unempowering or disempowering settings into empowering ones (Maton, 2008). Consistent with Julian Rappaport's vision and contributions to the field, such work will require multilevel conceptualizations of empowerment, ecological theory development, narrative methods, interdisciplinary collaboration, and collaborative partnerships with citizens, community groups, and policymakers. Such work is most likely to bear fruit if it is grounded in the fundamental aspects of Julian's contributions to our field: taking the empowerment ideal seriously, amplifying the voices of those who are oppressed and silenced, taking context seriously, and raising important questions about individual and social change. Indeed, being true to oneself and to the larger questions that one is passionate about—these are some of the most enduring, and important, aspects of Julian's gifts to our field.

AUTHOR'S NOTE

Special thanks to Keith Humphreys for his contributions to the overall manuscript, and his expertise concerning Alcoholics Anonymous in particular. Revised version of paper presented at Festschrift for Julian Rappaport, University of Illinois Champaign-Urbana, June 9, 2005.

REFERENCES

Alcoholics Anonymous (2007a). *A.A. at a glance.* Retrieved October 16, 2007 from www.alcoholics-anonymous.org/en_information_aa.cfm?PageID=10.
Alcoholics Anonymous (2007b). *The Big Book Online,* 4th Edition. Chapter 8: Because I'm an alcoholic. Retrieved June 14, 2007 from www.aa.org/bigbookonline/en_theystoppedintime8.pdf.
Alcoholics Anonymous (2007c). *The Big Book Online.* 4th Edition. Chapter 5: My chance to live. Retrieved June 14, 2007 from www.aa.org/bigbookonline/en_theystoppedintime5.pdf.

Alcoholics Anonymous (2007d). *The Big Book Online*. 4th Edition. Chapter 8: Winner Take all. Retrieved June 14, 2007 from www.aa.org/bigbookonline/en_theystoppedintime12.pdf.

Building Engineering and Science Talent (2004, February). *A Bridge for All: Gateways of Higher Education into America's scientific and technological workforce*. Retrieved May 8, 2008, from http://www.bestworkforce-March.org/PDFdocs/BEST_High_Ed_Rep_48pg_02_25.pdf

Bond, M. A., & Keys, C. B. (1993). Empowerment, diversity and collaboration: Promoting synergy on community boards. *American Journal of Community* Psychology, *21*, 37–58.

Brodsky, A. E. (2003). *With all our strength: The Revolutionary Association of the Women of Afghanistan*. New York: Routledge.

Freire, P. (1972). *Pedagogy of the oppressed*. New York: Continuum.

Gruber, J., & Trickett, E. J. (1987). Can we empower others? The paradox of empowerment in the governing of an alternative public school. *American Journal* of Community Psychology, *15*, 353–371.

Hoffer, T. B., Hess, M., Welch, Jr. C., & Williams, K. (2007). *Doctorate Recipients from United States Universities: Summary Report 2006*. Chicago: National Opinion Research Center. Retrieved May 13, 2008 from http://www.norc.org/SED.htm

Hrabowski, F. A. III., Maton, K. I., Greene, M. L., & Greif, G. L. (2002). *Overcoming the odds: Raising academically successful African-American young women*. New York: Oxford University Press.

Hrabowski, F. A. III., Maton, K. I., & Greif, G. L. (1998). *Beating the odds: Raising academically successful African-American males*. New York: Oxford University Press.

Humphreys, K. (2004). *Circles of Recovery: Self-help organizations for addictions*. Cambridge, England: Cambridge University Press.

Humphreys, K. (2000). Community narratives and personal stories in Alcoholics Anonymous, *Journal of Community Psychology*, 495–506.

Janzen, R., Nelson, G., Hausfather, N., & Ochocka, J. (2007). Capturing system level activities and impacts of mental health consumer-run organizations. *American Journal of Community Psychology*, *39*, 287–300.

Maton, K. I. (2000). Making a difference: The social ecology of social transformation. *American Journal of Community Psychology*, *28*, 25–57.

Maton, K. I. (2008). Empowering community settings: Agents of individual development, community betterment, and positive social change. *American Journal of Community Psychology*, *41*, 4–21.

Maton, K. I., Zimmerman, J. L., & Hrabowski, F. A. III. (2008, May). *Analyzing the impact of the Meyerhoff Scholars Program*. Paper presented at the Understanding Interventions National Workshop, Atlanta, GA.

Maton, K. I., & Hrabowski, F. A. III. (2004). Increasing the number of African American Ph.D.s in the sciences and engineering: A strengths-based approach. *American Psychologist, 59*, 629–654.

Maton, K. I., Sto. Domingo, M. R., Stolle-McAllister, K., Zimmerman, J. L., & Hrabowski, F. A. III (2009). Enhancing the number of African Americans who pursue STEM Ph.D.s: Meyerhoff Scholarship Program outcomes, processes, and individual predictors. *Journal of Women and Minorities in Science and Engineering, 15*, 15–37.

National Science Foundation (2008). Unpublished Data. Generated from WEBCASPAR Integrated Science and Engineering Resources Data System (NSF Survey of Earned Doctorates Data Base). Retrieved on May 15, 2009 from https://webcaspar.nsf.gov.

Peterson, N. A., & Speer, P. W. (2000). Linked organizational characteristics to psychological empowerment: Contextual issues in empowerment theory. *Administration in Social Work, 24*, 39–58.

Peterson, A., & Zimmerman, M. (2004). Beyond the individual: Toward a nomological network of organizational empowerment. *American Journal of Community Psychology, 34*, 129–146.

Prestby, J., Wandersman, A., Florin, P., Rich, R., & Chavis, D. (1990). Benefits, costs, incentive management and participation in voluntary organizations: A means to understanding and promoting empowerment. *American Journal of Community Psychology, 18*, 117–150.

Rappaport, J. (1977). *Community psychology: Values, research and action.* New York: Holt, Rinehart, & Winston.

Rappaport, J. (1981). In praise of paradox: A social policy of empowerment over prevention. *American Journal of Community Psychology, 9*, 1–25.

Rappaport, J. (1987). Terms of empowerment/exemplars of prevention: Toward a theory for community psychology. *American Journal of Community Psychology, 15*, 121–148.

Smart, R. G., & Mann, R. E (1993). Recent liver cirrhosis declines: Estimates of the impact of alcohol abuse treatment and Alcoholics Anonymous. *Addictions, 88*, 193–198.

Speer, P., & Hughey, J. (1995). Community organizing: An ecological route to empowerment and power. *American Journal of Community Psychology, 23*, 729–748.

Zimmerman, M. A. (2000). Empowerment theory: Psychological, organizational and community levels of analysis. In J. Rappaport & E. Seidman (Eds.), *Handbook of Community Psychology* (pp. 43–63). New York: Plenum.

4 Pursuing Paradox: The Role of Adults in Creating Empowering Settings for Youth

Reed W. Larson and Rachel M. Angus

"... the medicine for mediocrity is the pursuit of paradox."

(Rappaport, 1981, p. 8)

Adolescence is a period when young people have the potential to develop powerful new skills for action: skills to plan a community event, create a multilevel work of art or business plan, or formulate strategy for a lobbying campaign. During this period, new cognitive capacities come online that permit youth to acquire higher-order executive abilities: skills for means–ends thinking and for organizing actions over time to achieve a goal (Gestsdóttir & Lerner, 2008; Keating, 2004). As part of this, adolescents become more able to understand dynamic real-world human systems and thus to be more effective in thinking through how to influence people and institutions (Heath, 1999; Larson & Angus, 2011). These new high-order cognitive potentials, however, are just that: *potentials*. Their realization depends on adolescents having the requisite experiences (Kuhn, 2009).

Many adults and professionals working with youth want to help them develop these action skills–to learn leadership, develop agency, or become "empowered." But they often encounter problems and paradoxes when they try to do so. Teachers who want to empower students run up against institutional structures that require faculty to play superordinate roles over students as authority figures, disciplinarians, and evaluators (Pace & Hemmings, 2007). It is hard to provide students genuine opportunities to develop actions skills within a tightly controlled institutional environment in which authority and accountability are vested in a hierarchy of adults.

Youth programs—including community-based programs and extracurricular activities—appear to be more suitable than school classrooms for adolescents to develop these action skills. Youth participate voluntarily. The mission of many programs includes providing opportunities for youth leadership and empowerment. Programs for high-school-aged youth often engage them in decision-making roles in large individual or group projects that demand actions skills, such as creating a website, planning an event, or impacting their community (Eccles & Gootman, 2002; Ginwright, Noguera, & Cammarota, 2006; Larson, Hansen, & Moneta, 2006). Nonetheless, there are many instances in which the adults have embraced the goal of youth empowerment, only to have things go awry. A common scenario is for adults to make a commitment to youth's control of a project, but then turn on youth when problems emerge, reasserting their authority and leaving youth angry and humiliated (Camino, 2005; Hogan, 2002; Ozer et al., 2008). Now, savvy youth professionals are generally able to avoid this scenario, but they still struggle with contradictions in how to reconcile youth freedom with setting limits, when to challenge versus support youth, and how to use their own agency to support young people's development of agency (Halpern, 2009; Kirshner, 2006).

This chapter builds on Julian Rappaport's (1981) description of the paradoxes professionals face in attempts to help others. He argues that their efforts to serve a client population—in our case, to develop action skills among youth program members—easily drift to one-sided solutions. Rappaport observes that professionals easily let their authoritative knowledge of clients' needs trump clients' own knowledge and abilities, resulting in clients' disempowerment. To support people's empowerment, Rappaport urges us to understand rather than avoid contradictions: "to play within the dialectic and to pursue paradox" (p. 16).

To pursue the paradoxes of empowering youth, we will begin with accounts from participants in different programs regarding how they developed action skills. As developmental psychologists we are interested in the *processes*—particularly the conscious processes—of development. In this chapter, we focus on the processes occurring in some (but not all) programs through which youth develop a specific set of action skills that we think is central to individual empowerment. *Strategic thinking,* as we will explain, entails higher-order skills for agency in complex real-world contexts.[1]

After describing strategic thinking and how youth develop it, we will turn to the focal question of how adults support the developmental process. How do they thread the paradoxes? Although this process is not something institutions or adults do *to* youth, we examine how advisors facilitate youth having experiences that help them learn strategic skills. Our investigation employs grounded theory analyses of data from a large longitudinal study. We compared leaders' interactions with youth in programs that did and did not facilitate strategic thinking, giving special attention to the unfolding of these interactions in one program.

STRATEGIC THINKING AND HOW IT DEVELOPS: YOUTH'S ACCOUNTS

Skills for Action in Real-World Contexts

Young people are rarely taught in school how the real world works or how to accomplish goals in it. In social studies classes, for example, students in most nations are taught how government is supposed to work, not how it actually works; and they receive no training in how to influence governmental bodies (Torney-Purta, Lehmann, Oswald, & Schultz, 2001). School instruction typically presents the world as more logical and principled than it really is. Returning to our theme, young people are rarely told that the real world contains paradoxes and Catch-22s. Of course, as they move into adolescence, they begin to realize that the world isn't quite as orderly and easy to understand as they are being taught. But this discovery often only begets cynicism and avoidance of adulthood, not skills for navigating this more complex reality.

Our perspective for understanding what is missing from youth's learning combines elements of chaos theory and classic American pragmatism, integrated within Bronfenbrenner's (1979) ecological theory. The first posits a universe that includes substantial disorder: metaphorically, there are lots of butterflies flapping their wings that shape events in seemingly random ways. The pragmatists described "a universe shot through with contingency" (Menand, 2001, p. 360). But in our view, much of the disorder and contingency in the human world is not so much illogical as ecological; it has a rationality to

---

1 In choosing to focus on youth's development of skills, we, of necessity, give less attention to accompanying changes in motivation, efficacy beliefs, and critical consciousness that are included in discussions of youth empowerment (e.g., Ginwright et al., 2006; Jupp, 2007).

it that stems from the complexity of human social systems (Gigerenzer, 2008; Larson, 2010). To function in this world, young people need to learn how human environments are shaped by nested layers of personality processes and micro-, meso-, and macrosystems (Bronfenbrenner, 1979). Each of these systems partly functions according to its own history, constellation of goals, and power dynamics; they are living systems animated by active and reactive human intentions (Lerner, 2002). Further, because these systems contain multiple actors and intersecting influences, contradictions and conflicts occur; things are not always what they seem on the surface. There may be unstated rules, hidden power dynamics, and leverage points for getting things done that are not immediately apparent. To become actors in the real world and make their way as adults, youth need to learn to think and act in strategic ways that anticipate the dynamics of human systems and how these systems interact with each other.

Our interest in strategic thinking was inspired by the work of linguist Shirley Heath, who found that young people in high-quality arts, technology, and other project-oriented youth programs appeared to learn new language forms that provide tools for dealing with these real-world dynamics. Heath observed that new entrants to these programs began using language adapted to doing work and achieving goals in real-world settings. They learned:

- Language forms for anticipating, planning, and acting in human settings (hypotheticals, modals, and scenario building; Heath, 1998, 1999)
- Language constructions for identifying real-world contingencies (e.g., if–then)
- Genres of communication employed by members of different professions whom the youth were attempting to influence (reporters, police, administrators, etc.)

Heath observed these changes in youth's verbal behavior. We wanted to understand the corresponding changes in youth's conscious thinking (Larson, 2000). What insights, concepts, heuristics, understandings, tools, and other skills for action were youth acquiring?

We first heard youth describe learning strategic thinking in a case study of Youth Action, a program in which African-American and Latina/o high school students were lobbying the Chicago City Schools to address capricious use of suspensions (Larson & Hansen, 2005). Youth in this program became motivated to correct these injustices (Pearce & Larson, 2006), and they reported learning strategic skills that helped them be effective in doing so. In biweekly interviews over 4 months, they reported learning to understand and predict how different groups of people think: not just school officials but also teachers (whom they were trying to recruit as allies) and fellow students (whom they were trying to recruit for their rallies). The youth also described how understanding these groups' ways of thinking allowed them to plan effective strategies to influence them. For example, Miguel described learning that school board members valued data, and thus to influence them, one needed to "always have information that you can count on. State the facts and always state where you got the facts."

What caught our attention was that these skills entailed the development of adolescents' capabilities for advanced, higher-order reasoning, which we mentioned earlier. These youth were learning to think about how complex systems function and how to use this knowledge to achieve goals within them. They were developing their cognitive potentials to think about the dynamics—not just of logical systems but of irregular, "messy" real-world systems, like the rationality of different groups of people, the functioning of institutions, and how systems change (Habermas & Bluck, 2000; Labouvie-Vief, 1990; Selman, 1980, 2003). A key adolescent capability that adolescents can develop is hypothetical thinking—abilities to generate reasoned deductions about future or counterfactual possiblities. Members of Youth Action were developing this capability and using it to think through plans (e.g., in formulating their presentation to the school board) and to choose actions that they deduced would be most effective. They were developing higher-order executive skills for acting with deliberate foresight, in ways adapted to specific ecological contexts.

Since our study of Youth Action, we collected similar data on 10 more programs, and analyses of these data have allowed us to better define strategic thinking and understand how it develops. Seven of the 11 programs (counting Youth Action) were in Chicago, with members who were primarily Latino/a and African-American. The other programs were in rural areas or small cities and were predominantly European-American. All were leadership, arts, or media arts programs and each was studied over a 2- to 9-month period in which youth worked on projects. The final sample of 108 youth (8–12 per program; 712 total interviews) included about equal numbers of high-school-aged youth of both genders. The findings we report first were based on analyses using the person (not the program) as the unit of study.

This larger sample helped us conceptualize strategic thinking as it was learned by youth across diverse programs (*see* Larson & Angus, 2011). Forty of the 108 youth reported learning elements of strategic thinking. Our analysis led to this definition: *Use of advanced executive skills to anticipate possible scenarios in complex dynamic systems (particularly human systems) and to formulate flexible courses of action that take these different possible scenarios into account.* In the leadership programs, the "dynamic systems" were the officials in the community they were trying to influence or children they were trying to teach. Youth learned how to anticipate how these different groups would react to different actions or activities, then to plan their course of action accordingly. In the arts programs, they were the processes involved in creating a work of art within the context of real-world constraints. Across programs, the data suggested that youth progressed from formulating actions based on rote steps to use of flexible strategies: from following fixed rules to becoming able to make up their own guidelines for regulating their actions based on reasoned forethought.

An important finding was that many youth described transferring these new strategic skills to other domains of their lives, such as schoolwork, solving personal problems, and pursuing goals for their future. Although some of the skills they reported involved context-specific knowledge (e.g., how school board members think), the basic executive skills for strategic action seemed to generalize across contexts, at least for some youth. Of course, this finding needs to be validated with longitudinal research.

The Developmental Process

Scholars who study the development of adolescents' advanced reasoning skills stress that these skills do not materialize as an automatic product of brain maturation. They depend on a youth having *experiences* through which they actively develop these skills (Kuhn, 2009). Our analyses were aimed at identifying what the requisite experiences were for strategic thinking, based on accounts from the 40 youth who reported learning this skill set (*see* Larson & Angus, 2011). These analyses identified three key components of episodes through which youth reported learning strategic skills.

Youth as producers of their own development. First, we discovered that youth almost always described themselves as the agents of these episodes and of their learning process. They experienced control over their projects (as individuals and sometimes as part of a group). We know from educational research that experiencing control is associated with more effective learning (Eccles & Gootman, 2002; Zimmerman & Campillo, 2003), and indeed, when we asked youth *how* they had gained a strategic insight or skill, they often said, "I realized that ..." or "I figured out that ..." They had created their own strategic knowledge. They also described learning through active experimenting, "tinkering," and "trial and error." Youth experienced themselves as the producers of their own development of strategic skills.

Learning from engagement with challenges. The second component in youth's accounts of their learning process was their mental *engagement in the challenges* they faced within the episode. These challenges were *tactical challenges*: they involved problems, demands, and obstacles related to achieving their goals in their projects. Youth described learning strategic thinking as a necessary response to these challenges: they use terms like "we had to," "you gotta," or "I needed to." They reported learning because they had to analyze a situation, solve a problem, or figure out a way around something that stood in their way. Youth said their learning was driven by mental activity aimed at addressing the tactical demands of their projects. In Halpern's (2009) words, youth learned from "wrestling with" the challenges.[2]

Maria, a 16-year-old, provides a useful example of this process. Throughout the period of our study, she and other youth in El Concilio planned activities for young people in their Chicago precinct—activities aimed at keeping them off the streets and out of gangs. Over the course of the interviews, Maria described encountering numerous tactical challenges, such as:

- Figuring out how to distribute toys to children in the neighborhood
- Choosing dates for events: "Adults didn't like dates we had chosen."
- Asking stores to donate money and restaurants to donate food
- Coordinating use of resources with other programs: "Buses are in use by dance program"

It was not surprising, then, that what Maria reported learning over 4 months was: "How to solve problems: 'We can't do this. We have this, this and this. So we have to find other ways to solve the problem.'" Notice that she is describing solving multidimensional real-world (or ecological) problems in which "this, this, and this" need to be taken into account. When asked *how* she learned these skills, Maria said, "Like in everything we do, you can have an obstacle that you need to find a way around [to] make the event come true." For her, obstacles became challenges and they initiated new episodes of learning.

The analyses indicated that youth learned strategic thinking, in part, from individual and group brainstorming, creative worry, and, in some cases, laying awake at night thinking through different possibilities. The tactical challenges appeared to push youth into the realm of future-oriented thinking about contingencies, options, and the likely effectiveness of different courses of action. In other words, the necessity of the situations (the "you need to," "we had to,") appeared to initiate a creative process of developing new insights and strategies (Nurmi, 2004). Necessity is not only the "mother of

2 This relationship between "engagement with challenges" and learning strategic thinking was confirmed with a statistical test. We counted how often each youth reported experiencing tactical challenges across all of his or her interviews and how often they reported learning strategic thinking. We then computed a partial correlation between these two scores (with statistical controls for program and a youth's number of interviews). As predicted from the qualitative findings, these two were significantly correlated, rpartial = 0.22, $p < 0.05$.

invention," it can be the stimulus for youth's active developmental processes.

Learning from results. The third key component in the learning episodes was feedback youth received from outcomes of their work. When they were successful in a step of a project, or the project as a whole, they concluded that their strategy was effective.[3] Youth also described learning strategic thinking from things that went wrong. Jack, an actor in a theater production reported: "Something would get mixed up, and you had to recover from it. It definitely teaches you how to plan ahead and how to time things." Sara, from El Concilio, described learning from both the mistakes and successes in a sleepover they had planned. In many cases, youth reported learning from comparing the results of multiple events or projects in the program.

Often, youth described their learning process by relating a narrative of their work. These included descriptions of short learning cycles and the longer cycle of their entire project. Youth were the protagonists in these narratives (either as individuals or a group), and the narratives postulated causal links between the tactical challenges they had wrestled with, how they addressed them, and the outcomes that followed. Studies of expertise have found that even accomplished professionals (e.g., teachers, engineers, military commanders) often draw on narratives of prior experiences to make plan courses of action (Ross, Shafer, & Klein, 2006). These narratives are useful, we believe, because they encode complex thinking about why certain actions were effective in one type of situation but not in others.

In sum, the youth described learning strategic thinking through an active process of struggling with tactical challenges and deriving conclusions (or formulating narratives) from the outcomes of their responses to these challenges. We are now ready to turn to our focal question.

THE ROLE OF PROGRAM ADVISORS IN YOUTH'S DEVELOPMENT

Youth's Accounts of Adults' Contribution

If youth are the protagonists in these narratives and the agents of their own development, what is the role of advisors? Their position has been portrayed

---

3 This relationship between experiencing successes and learning was confirmed with a statistical test. We evaluated this finding by counting how often each youth reported experiencing successes in their projects during their biweekly interviews. These counts were significantly correlated with higher rates of learning strategic thinking, $r_{partial} = 0.31$, $p < 0.01$. However, experiencing negative outcomes from their work was not significantly correlated with strategic thinking.

as that of mediator, broker, or bridge between the worlds of youth and adults (Rhodes, 2004). Youth's relationship with advisors (as compared to with teachers in school) is more likely to be based on trust and mutual respect than on unilateral authority (Deutsch & Jones, 2008). But this bridging and this mutuality often rest on unstated assumptions. When push comes to shove, are you a friend or authority figure (Jeffs & Bank, 1999)? Straddling two worlds creates contradictions.

Not surprising, when we asked youth what contribution their advisors made to their strategic learning, their responses reflected these contradictions (Larson & Angus, 2011). The first theme that emerged from these analyses was that advisors aided them by *getting out of their way*. They helped them learn by allowing them freedom. When asked how leaders helped, one young man said, "They really just laid back, and let us take everything in control." However the second major theme, often expressed by the same youth, was that advisors helped them by *providing assistance when and if they needed it*. Advisors suggested useful ideas, kept them from making bad decisions, provided back-up support, and helped them if they got stuck. But how do advisors decide when to provide freedom versus assistance?

This is where we need to turn from examining the youth's to the advisors' accounts. The advisors are making decisions about when to provide support and when to step back. So we want to learn about the decision-making situations they face, how they respond to them, and how these situations ultimately relate to youth's learning experiences. How do they juggle competing imperatives to provide freedom and assistance?

Methods for Analyses of the Advisor Interviews

This section provides methodological information on our interviews with the advisors and our analyses of them. Our objective was to understand how advisors addressed the contradictions in their role and what they did to facilitate youth's experience of strategic learning episodes (e.g., engagement with tactical challenges, learning from outcomes)? Figuring out the connections between advisors' actions and youth's developmental experiences is, of course, a difficult task, and our attempt to understand it should be seen as only a beginning.

The approach we took to these questions involved two interrelated analyses. The first entailed comparing programs in which youth had high versus low rates of learning strategic thinking. Five of the 11 programs had high rates (40%–62% of program youth), and we shall call these the "strategic learning programs." In the other six, these rates were low (0%–25% of youth). The strategic learning programs included both urban settings (including Youth

Action) and rural settings[4]. The strategic learning programs included more leadership (including youth activism) programs and fewer arts programs, but there were exceptions going both ways. It is possible that this difference contributed to the findings, but our case-by-case comparison suggested that the results were more attributable to advisors' philosophies and actions than to the type of program. Other researchers have described arts programs in which youth learned higher-order strategic skills (Halpern, 2009; Halverson, 2009; Heath, 1999).

The principal data for these program comparisons came from longitudinal interviews with the one or two primary advisors from each of the 11 programs ($n = 17$ advisors). All were paid professionals, with the exception of one. Their tenure in the program averaged 7 years (range: 2–30), and this did not differ between the strategic learning programs and the others. Advisors were interviewed over the same schedule as the youth ($n = 125$). To provide an additional viewpoint, we conducted site observations in each program over the same periods (a total of 159).

The aim of these comparative analyses was to identify differences between high and low strategic learning programs that might account for greater strategic learning in the high ones. To conduct these comparisons, we employed a discovery approach (Miles & Huberman, 1994). The first stage generated preliminary hypotheses about the features of advisors' philosophy and behavior that differentiated the high programs. To do this, we read all the advisor and observational transcripts and looked for differences between programs in advisors' statements and actions that might provide theoretical explanations for differences in youth's rates of strategic learning.[5] Based on this initial reading, we identified six features that we hypothesized to differentiate the strategic learning programs and developed preliminary operational definitions to use for coding each. In several iterative cycles, we read back through all the data, coded passages, and revised operational definitions. We then compared the high and low programs on the frequency and intensity of passages for each of the six features. This process led to two features being eliminated because they did not differentiate programs (the time-length of projects, community relevance) and two being combined because of considerable overlap (activity structure and youth control were combined

4 The strategic learning programs included three urban and two rural programs (vs. four and two, respectively, in the other group); and they included four leadership and one arts program (vs. two and four, respectively). They did not differ in leader characteristics. It should be noted that youth in most of the programs that had low rates of strategic thinking reported development in other areas (e.g., developing responsibility, emotional resiliency), and these might also be seen as components of empowerment. All names used from programs, advisors, and leaders are pseudonyms.

5 In the six programs that had two primary leaders, the two provided quite similar statements on the dimensions that we coded.

into commitment to youth control). These analyses yielded three features that differentiated advisors' philosophy (*commitment to youth control, philosophy of experiential learning*) and actions (*leading from behind*) in the high versus low programs.

The second set of analyses was aimed at understanding advisors' roles in specific episodes of strategic learning. These analyses focused primarily on the five strategic learning programs and on episodes in which both advisors and youth provided at least some data pertinent to the three components of strategic learning episodes discussed previously. We employed an interpretive approach to reconstruct the sequence of youth's and advisors' experiences. These interpretive analyses were used to help understand and illustrate the three distinctive features of the high programs and how they were related to youth's active process of learning in context.

We give particular attention to one program in which the principal advisor, Lisa, was attempting to foster a more empowering setting for youth. The Federation was a 4-H leadership program in which members helped run events for young children in the local rural community. In prior years, these events had been planned by Lisa's colleague, Janet, a paraprofessional. But Lisa, who had a masters degree, had ultimate responsibility for the program as part of her job, and she wanted to change the social contract with the youth so that *they* organized the events. She wanted youth to take roles as leaders in the community and learn the strategic skills that would come from being in charge of the planning. Over the 9-month period that we studied the Federation, Lisa worked to change the setting, and, indeed, this program ended up as one of the five high-strategic learning programs. The experience of Lisa and the youth over this period provide a valuable example for understanding adults' roles.

Unlike youth in many studies of empowerment, members of the Federation were not from a marginalized ethnic group or social class. But as "adolescents" they were marginalized in their community. Young people's role in society is limited; they are viewed as naïve, irresponsible, and troublesome by the majority of adults (Gilliam & Bales, 2001). The Federation was located in an isolated, European-American (97.4%), and comparatively poor county (median household income = $31,000). Lisa described the youth as:

> … a very interesting, mixed bag of kids. We've got kids that come from all economic cross sections in the county, we've got kids from different high schools, different interest levels, and different levels of willingness to participate.

Lisa admitted that her goals for these youth were "pretty lofty," but she had also spent a few months in the prior spring trying to prepare the youth for the change.

ADVISORS' PRINCIPLES, PHILOSOPHIES, AND STARTING POINTS

Sarason (1972) describes how a setting exits in the minds of its creators before it is formed. Similarly, front-line practitioners bring guiding ideas, values, and principles to their work that shape the setting. Two of the features that differentiated the advisors of the strategic learning programs from the others were of this nature. They were foundational principles or philosophies that advisors articulated to us in their initial interviews and to youth at the start of program, then demonstrated in their actions. The first feature was a *strong commitment to youth control.*

Commitment to Youth Control

Lisa launched her effort to change the Federation by putting it right on the table, by telling youth that were now in charge. The program had an annual summer retreat at a 4-H camp in which advisors and youth planned activities for the following year. After doing an icebreaker, Lisa gave a short speech in which she told the 15 youth that she was "passing the torch" to them. It will be "your planning process," she said, adding that they collectively had more experience than she and Janet. Furthermore, because the youth were closer in age to the children they served, they had the knowledge "to take ownership of the vision." She and Janet would be there to provide support, but they needed to take the responsibility.

Lisa's language typified how advisors in the five strategic learning programs expressed their commitment to youth control. They repeatedly told youth "it is your program." The advisors did not take themselves out of the picture. In fact, they kept a foot in the door; they were still the "adult" who was ultimately responsible for the program. But they stressed the principle that youth should take "ownership" over decisions. For the Federation's rural White youth, there was no talk of oppression, or throwing off chains. Lisa did not use the word "power." Her philosophy was more John Dewey than Paulo Freire.

Although similar, there were also variations in how the advisors of these five programs articulated youth control. At El Concilio, where the mostly Latina/o youth also planned activities for children (as well as for youth their age), the advisor, Lucho, was more emphatic than Lisa. He often communicated that youth were in charge by leaving the room, telling them he would check back later to see what they had planned. At Youth Action, the advisor, Jason, used some Freire-like, empowerment language. He emphasized that the youth were "not only the leaders of tomorrow, but leaders today," and he described his role as working "side-by-side" with youth in working to address issues they chose.

In the two other strategic learning programs, the advisors were committed to youth ownership—but within a structured framework the adults had created. Harambee was an activism program in a low-income African-American urban neighborhood. For their summer session, the advisor (Mike) felt he needed to create structure in advance, because they would be meeting daily, 5 hours per day for only 6 weeks, and he wanted to get the 32 youth off and running on the first day. The advisors chose a theme for the summer (discrimination in transit service for their neighborhood) and preplanned the activities. But youth exercised control over major decisions *within* these activities. For a team working on a video, Mike described how: "Kids are shooting the footage, deciding what to edit, deciding what's important." Similarly, two adults leading a theater production of *Les Miserables* set the schedule and ran most of the rehearsals because they learned that their management skills were essential to coordinating the large cast of 107 members. But they encouraged youth to take ownership and control over development of their roles, and across the 3 months of rehearsals, they progressively allowed youth's control to increase. As described by Kirshner (2008), the adults "faded" as the youth developed the needed skills.

Across these five programs, then, the nature of youth control was adapted according to the number of youth, their developmental levels, and other contextual factors. But the commonality was a stated philosophy that youth had control over at least some of the higher-order decisions directing their work. A youth at El Concilio explained, "Lucho wouldn't tell us, 'You have to do this!' We wouldn't put as much effort in, because it wasn't our idea, it wasn't what we wanted." Youth saw their control over decisions as important to their engagement.

In contrast, advisors in four of the other six programs (those in which few or no youth learned strategic thinking) did *not* emphasize youth control.[6] These adults emphasized that they were in charge. On the first day at Media Masters, a media arts program, the advisors provided no introduction or opportunities for input from youth. One of them stood in front of the group and started taking them through a number of difficult procedures in a software program. The most adult-controlled program was an evangelical dance group, Faith in Motion, in which the advisor taught dance moves and controlled rehearsals from the front of the room. Advisors of these four programs

---

6 One of the other two programs was a consciousness-raising program for young women, and the advisors, like Lisa, told youth that they were in charge of their agenda. But despite the advisors' hopes and encouragement, the youth decided they did *not* want to do a leadership activity in the community; they wanted to discuss personal issues that affected them. So there were few tactical challenges for youth to learn from. The sixth program was a leadership program in which youth were allowed quite a lot of control over planning activities, and we are not clear why youth did not report developing strategic skills (Larson, Hansen, & Walker, 2005).

appeared to be less concerned with allowing youth choice than with structuring activities so they would learn technical skills. As a result, these youth did not have a role in higher-order decisions and thus had fewer opportunities to learn strategic thinking.

A Philosophy of Experiential Learning

The second feature that differentiated the advisors of the five strategic learning programs was that they had a well-developed philosophy of experiential learning. Without prompting, they described placing high value on youth having *direct* and *active* real-world experiences. Jason, at Youth Action, told us:

> A lot of things with [community] organizing you can't teach, you have to experience it. I think the most important piece is providing opportunities for them to actually use their talents in real-life settings.

Lisa said she started out as a school teacher, but her interest shifted to after-school programs, partly because: "I'm a firm believer in the experiential learning process." In her opening speech, Lisa encouraged youth to take risks with new ideas. She told them they would learn even if an activity was not a big success. Lucho at El Concilio took this further, saying they would learn "even if we have the worst event ever." Parallel to our findings from youth's accounts of how they learned strategic thinking (Larson & Angus, 2011), advisors believed that mistakes provided useful corrective feedback and that successes provided validation of their actions.

But advisors' philosophy of experiential learning sometimes included playing a stronger role than youth described. Jason at Youth Action believed in "pushing [youth] out of their safety zone, so it's like a new situation for them, and they can test out their skills." He coaxed youth to take roles directing workshop sessions, reading at a poetry jam, and presenting to the school board. Jason explained that this "pushing" would help youth learn, "Oh, that wasn't so hard," or see, "This is what I have a problem with."

Most of these advisors believed youth benefited not just from the outcomes but from adult guidance in interpreting the events that shaped them. (No youth mentioned this contribution.) Lisa felt she had to help youth process the success or failure of what they had done: "Did it work? Did it not work? What should we do differently?" She encouraged youth to analyze what happened and why it happened. This adult role may be important because the underlying causal factors shaping real-life events can be masked or confounded with other factors (Byrnes, 2005); so youth may see the underlying machinery at work. In some cases, advisors helped youth recognize success in what they saw as failure. The advisors helped youth shape the narrative of what had taken place (*see also* Priest & Gas, 1997).

In contrast, advisors of the six other programs made far fewer statements about experiential learning. Their philosophy centered on providing predictable, structured activities that would help youth learn skills and that avoided real-world risks. Rather than wanting youth to figure out the strategies and steps to reach a goal, they created structures and directly instructed youth on how to proceed. In short, these advisors largely superseded the possibility of a discovery process in which youth could uncover, engage with, and learn from tactical challenges.

Beyond Philosophy

This philosophy of youth control and experiential learning, however, was not enough. For one thing, advisors' commitment to youth control meant little unless it was accepted by the youth. At the Federation, Lisa made a unilateral declaration about passing the torch. Then, after provided a brief training, she turned the planning for the year over to the youth.

The youth didn't balk. They generated a list of activities they wanted to plan (a bike safety training; a campout; a state fair trip) and volunteered for committees to work on each. Lisa was especially happy when Tricia (the new President) and Adam (the Vice President) took charge of planning the next meeting's agenda:

> They asked if I had anything the group needed to discuss. I reviewed a few items with them and asked that the group give each some attention. With that, the two of them dismissed me—asked me to leave. I was so incredibly pleased that they felt comfortable enough to kick me out, and confident in themselves to do the job.

Lisa's opening move was successful. As the year began, however, difficulties started to emerge.

WHEN GOOD IDEAS HIT THE FAN

Sarason (1972) observed that, time and again, when new settings are created, optimistic expectations are replaced by pessimism as reality takes over.

There is often a large gap, Sarason suggests, between people's vision for the setting and what can actually be achieved in the complex ecology of real life. Schwandt (2003) expresses a similar idea in writing that the expectations of practitioners are inevitably compromised when they have to be "carried out on a rough ground of paradox and contingency, ambiguity and fragmentation" (p. 361).

Adults working with youth can make a commitment to youth control and experiential learning, but sustaining these principles on the "rough ground" of daily practice is a different matter. It is then that contradictions rear their head. Just as youth in our study faced challenges in their projects, advisors faced challenges (or meta-challenges) in creating and sustaining circumstances for youth to learn strategic skills from these projects. The diverse challenges Lisa faced and the mixed success of her responses are instructive.

The Rough Ground of Practice

When Lisa began checking in with youth a few weeks after the summer retreat, some were making excellent progress with planning the events they had chosen. Rhonda, for example, was thoroughly absorbed in the tactical challenges of planning a party for 5- to 12-year-old children. She reported trying to figure out "stuff for little kids to big kids; a 7-year-old isn't going to be interested in the same thing as an 11- or 12-year-old, but [we are] trying to connect them all." Not surprisingly, Rhonda later reported learning strategic skills from her experiences.

Other youth, however, were already stuck or spinning their wheels. Lisa realized that although her training had helped youth think about the outcomes of their planning, it did not include the *processes* of planning, including how to start: "A lot of them very naively approached the first activities, 'Oh, we'll just do this.'" Some youth didn't seem to get the bigger picture. Zeldin and Camino (1999) have found that program advisors often overestimate young people's abilities, letting them take on complex planning tasks that would be difficult even for adults. As a result, youth can get off on the wrong foot or get overwhelmed.

Lisa felt she needed to act but wanted to do it in ways that kept ownership with the youth. For a committee that had made little progress planning a carwash, she described trying to stimulate their higher-order thinking processes. Rather than telling them what to do, she primed them with guiding questions, "What has to come first, and what has to come second?" Use of questions can direct youth's thinking to problems they need to address, while keeping accountability for solving them with the youth (Kirshner, 2008). As Lisa explained, "I wanted them to feel like it's their responsibility."

A more difficult challenge was the President's shyness. Tricia had trouble commanding attention. At one Federation meeting, our observer noted that while Tricia was trying to set a date, many youth started talking to each other. Despite Lisa's commitment to youth control, she decided she needed to step in and help Tricia get the date. In the next interview, Lisa explained:

> This is where I'm going to get a little bit bossy—I won't allow Tricia and Adam to not perform their [jobs]. That's where coaching, supporting, facilitating and sometimes prodding is going to come into play on my part: to be pretty aggressive to make sure they take responsibility and initiative to lead their group. ... That's probably the harshest thing you'll hear me say (chuckle). I won't allow them to slough on this one, because it's so important for the group that they do the job.

This scenario was repeated at the next meeting. The group discussion was going nowhere, so Lisa interjected, "Why don't you move this forward, Tricia?" Tricia sought volunteers and set up a committee to plan the event. But then Tricia turned to Lisa for instructions on what to do next. Lisa's help only seemed to increase Tricia's dependency on adult guidance.

In our interviews, however, Tricia said she was unhappy with the disorder in the group, and over time, she started to plan in advance how to be effective in choosing dates and keeping the group on task. She also asked Lisa to give the group lessons on parliamentary procedure. As a result, by the end of the year, Tricia was better able to run the meetings by herself.

Lisa faced another challenge when she realized the officers had not been coordinating the work by different committees (something the advisors had done in years past). Two groups were both planning overnight campouts. One was for older youth the following summer; that was not a concern. But Becky's committee, assigned to 5- to 7-year-olds, was also planning a campout for the spring. Lisa spoke up, indicating that parents would not accept an overnight for young children, but Becky's solution was to shift it to an older age group.

Lisa formulated her situation in this paradoxical way, "How can I redirect them without making them think I'm redirecting them?" She went on, "I guess that's manipulative, but at the same time I don't want to squelch their enthusiasm; I don't want them to see me as the person who's always saying 'No.'" Lisa had ultimate responsibility for the group's activities but struggled with how to nix the overnight in a respectful way that did not undermine youth control.

Things came to a head when Becky made a motion to switch the target group for her campout from 5- to 7-year-olds to older elementary children.

Lisa responded by posing a host of logistical questions: Even with older children, parents would have a list of concerns. These questions led the group to vote down Becky's campout. Lisa followed up by encouraging Becky's committee to be more critical in evaluating their ideas but then concluded with a cheery, "Thank you, good thinking."

Afterward, most youth said Lisa had done the right thing. They recognized that this was an occasion where they had needed advisor input to keep them from a bad decision. Adam, who was on Becky's committee, conceded, "We were kind of drifting off." But Becky felt bruised. She did not accept that her plan was unviable and saw Lisa's quashing it as arbitrary exercise of adult authority: "Sometimes we come up with things and the advisors want something different. Like ours is a good idea but they want something [else]." For the next 2 months, Becky reported feeling disgruntled and disengaged.

Lisa, however, took on the goal of repairing Becky's sense of ownership. She met with Becky, trying to get her interested in doing a daycamp for 5- to 7-year-olds. Over several meetings, Lisa's patient encouragement had an effect. Becky conceded, "You just have to kind of compromise," and gradually she became engaged and excited by the challenges of figuring out how to help young children put up tents and build a campfire. As the camp approached, she was able to say: "It's my ideas; Lisa's helping me make it more attractive to little kids." The camp went well, and afterward Becky said, "I really had a lot of fun helping out all the kids." Lisa's extended campaign to restore Becky's ownership and engagement had succeeded.

The Art of Judicious Support

Reflecting at the end of the year on her attempt to change the program, Lisa said, "I've not made as much progress as I would like. I've had to do too much intervening." Although she had made a commitment to youth control, Lisa found herself responding to one challenging situation after another, exerting adult influence in subtle and sometimes less subtle ways. Youth did not know how to start, so she primed them with guiding questions. Tricia lost control of meetings; Lisa felt she had to step in. Becky started out with a full head of steam; Lisa reined her in, then pumped her back up when she was deflated.

This is the rough ground of practice. "It's always a tightrope you walk," Lisa said. She was repeatedly challenged by the pulls between helping youth and giving them freedom. She did resist many youth's bids for help, saying: "You guys need to make the decision. You run it the way that you want it to be run." And when Lisa did intervene, she tried to minimize her footprint. Although it felt "manipulative," she tried to redirect youth, rather than being seen as controlling. "Every time I have an interaction with them, I have to really be conscious of what I'm saying and how I'm saying it. I don't want to come across as the authority." When she intervened, however, Lisa felt she compromised her goal of youth control.

But although Lisa felt she intervened too often, the youth seemed unaware. Tricia, told us: "We pretty much planned a lot of the activities. [The advisors] were kind of there if we needed help with anything, but they kind of let us run the show." We, as researchers, saw that Lisa and Janet provided assistance at many key moments, but the youth took credit for the many activities they had worked on. Similar to the results of the person-level analysis mentioned earlier in the chapter, the Federation youth reported that the advisors had helped them by allowing them freedom combined with the right amount of help when needed. From youth's point of view, Lisa had lived up to her side of the new social contract. With the exception of Becky's period of disgruntlement, Lisa's actions were not perceived as diminishing youth's control. Indeed, from our viewpoint, her judicious interventions appeared to keep youth on track. They helped *sustain* conditions for youth to feel control. It is possible that *experiencing* control is more important to youth's engagement than degree of *actual* control (Zimmerman & Campillo, 2003).

The youth justified the advisors' role developmentally in terms of adults' greater knowledge and experience. When asked about the adults' help, they explained: "They know what we're capable of doing;" "They're making sure we were staying on task;" "They know what workshops have failed in the past and what we can pull off." The youth trusted the advisors and viewed them not as a threat to their ownership but as benevolent overseers looking out for them, helping them keep their work at a level manageable for them. The advisors helped keep their work in what Lev Vygotsky (1978) described as *the zone of proximal development.* This is work at a level of difficulty that is challenging to youth but within their capacity when they have assistance from peers or mentors.

But one might ask: Were the advisors complicit in sustaining youth's dependency? Were they undermining youth's empowerment? What we observed was that youth were engaging in the processes for learning strategic thinking. Because they felt ownership, youth reported many occasions of mental engagement in the higher-order tactical challenges of planning events. These challenges included how to run a meeting, how to plan activities for children of different ages, and thinking systematically about how different plans would unfold. Indeed, many of these youth reported learning strategic thinking. This included Becky, who described learning to think through an activity from the children's point of view (e.g., setting up tents), imagining problems that might come up, and how they could steer around them.

The youth were also learning from the outcomes of their planning. They learned from mistakes, for instance, to expect the unexpected: "always have extra" and "plan for more people."

The most important finding may be that youth needed less adult help as the year went on. They reported feeling more competent and, as one said, the advisors "were more likely to accept our plans." Although Lisa experienced many "stops and starts," the youth and adults had succeeded in changing the setting to one in which youth were exercising considerable control.

LEADING FROM BEHIND

Results of Program Comparisons

When we compared programs, we found that advisors of the five strategic learning programs worked as hard as those in the other six programs. Although they were committed to youth control, they were very engaged in supporting youth's work. But like Lisa, they often did so in subtle, indirect ways. This included devoting much mental energy to watching, listening, and trying to figure out whether, when, and how their intervention was needed.

The third feature we found that distinguished these five programs (in addition to advisors' commitment to youth control and philosophy of experiential learning) was that the advisors *led from behind*. This is the art of supporting youth's leadership while providing light touch guidance and assistance as needed.[7] Consistent with their philosophy of experiential learning, these advisors found ways to respect youth's dominion over higher-order decision making, while assisting or redirecting as needed. They were not charismatic leaders; most were self-effacing and didn't draw attention to themselves.

Leading from behind was not easy, as we saw with Lisa. These advisors dealt with the "rough ground" of ambiguous and unexpected challenges. Each situation was different and required tailored decisions. They struggled with how to navigate situations in which youth dropped the ball, lost motivation, were in over their heads, or set out on plans that were not likely to succeed. At first blush, "leading from behind" sounds contradictory. Indeed, these advisors were "pursuing paradox." They had to weigh competing

---

7 Grossman, Campbell, and Raley (2007, p. 40) use the term *leading from behind* in describing advisors' interactions with younger children in which there was a higher level of adult control. For our high school-aged youth, the advisors' actions might as accurately be described as "supporting from behind." The concept of "autonomy support" (Ryan & Deci, 2000) might also be used.

imperatives and figure out when to intervene and how to do so in ways that were effective but minimally intrusive.

To deal with different situations, they employed the approaches Lisa used that balanced these competing concerns, from guiding questions to priming and redirection. Youth at Harambee, for example, were trying to interview people on the street for their video on local transit service, but frequent refusals made the youth frustrated. So after every street session, advisors debriefed youth, giving them praise and redirecting their attention from their frustration to thinking about techniques for getting good statements from people who did show interest.

A common objective of these advisors was to take a problem that was overwhelming and help break it down to be manageable for youth. When members of Youth Action were going to run a large meeting, Jason helped write out the agenda on butcher block paper, drawing open boxes identifying decisions the group had to make (e.g., Do we hold a rally or not? If so, what date?). When youth at El Concilio were building a haunted house, Lucho did the work of getting the materials, then let youth take it from there. Adolescents can have difficulty with problems requiring that many dimensions be considered at once (Byrnes, Miller, & Reynolds, 1999). By breaking problems down, advisors kept youth in their zones of proximal development and thus helped them learn. In comparing youth activism programs, Kirshner (2008) concluded that youth learned *fewer* organizing skills in a program where adults provide less structure and guidance. Young people may learn more when they grapple with strategic decisions within their capability.

Although these advisors mostly led from behind, we observed occasions in all five programs when they were more assertive, as Lisa was in prodding Tricia and redirecting Becky. Even Jason at Youth Action, who put the most emphasis on youth control, vetoed ideas; he also described sometimes "hounding" youth, including calling them at home, to get them to do things they had committed to do. But as with Lisa, these more assertive interventions made the advisors uncomfortable, and they followed up with efforts to restore any negative effects on youth's sense of control. At *Les Miserables*, the director engaged in a similar campaign as Lisa's to repair a breach in the actors' sense of ownership after it had been violated by a dialect coach (Walker & Larson, 2006). Pursuing paradox required not avoiding, but addressing, contradictions.

What is important developmentally is that these advisors sustained conditions for youth to experience episodes of strategic learning. By leading from behind they reinforced youth's ownership, helping them engage with deepening levels of challenges. Youth in these five programs (compared to the six others) reported dealing with more tactical challenges in their work: how to plan an interesting discussion, how to get store owners to donate food, planning a session on safe sex, and how to get a play to gel. Youth were engaged with higher-order strategic decisions. They had to learn to anticipate, brainstorm, and think about real-world contingencies.

In contrast, advisors in the programs reporting low levels of strategic thinking often short-circuited opportunities where youth could have taken responsibility for tactical decisions. This was apparent at The Studio, when the advisor, Neisha, described guiding youth's development of artwork for the cover of a CD they were producing:

> Not that I'm an artist, but I tend to know what looks good. The students were coming up with something that I really liked, and from there I just kind of coached them, and said, "Okay, you know, that looks good right there. Try making that line bolder, or try changing that color. Try duplicating that on the other side."

She was "leading from the front." Youth were told by an authority what would look better, eliminating the struggle with challenges that leads to learning through experience.

Youth in the five strategic learning programs also reported more learning from outcomes than did youth in the other programs. Because of their advisors' prompting, questioning, and redirecting, their work was often successful. It is an axiom of community organizing that one tries to provide novices with "easy wins" in their action campaigns (Kirshner, 2008). That is probably true in other types of youth projects as well. Successes not only confirm the strategies used, they build self-efficacy. Although youth in these programs had received quite a bit of assistance from their leaders, it was low-visibility assistance that allowed youth to *perceive* ownership of the work and its outcomes. They came away with the experience of being the protagonists in narratives of challenge and decision making that usually (but not always) led to success.

But if the goal is to create perceptions—to provide youth these narratives—the question becomes, How far should adults go in orchestrating optimal learning episodes?

Engineering Experiences for Youth's Learning

Lucho, the advisor of El Concilio, used what he described as "national security, CIA tactics" to shape some learning experiences in his program. For example, Sara was in charge of getting help from a local business for a party they were planning. But Lucho, who knew the people at the business, didn't think they would respond to a request from a teenager, so:

> I called ahead and said, "This is what we're doing, can you help us out?' And when he said "Yes," I said, "You know, one of my young people is going to give you a call and set up a meeting." That's when I pulled myself out of it. So when Sara called, it was already to a point where they knew she was coming, but they acted as if it was the first time she was calling.

Lucho in effect staged an experience in which Sara negotiated what he had already negotiated. In the interview, he was proud and adamant about the value of these "backdoor" actions. He said that telling Sara about his prior call would have been wrong:

> In her eyes, and in my eyes as a youth development person, I would have been like, "I just cut her development out." And she probably would have been thinking, "What, he doesn't trust me, he thinks I'm going to fuck it up." And I didn't want her to feel that.

Lucho provided Sara with an illusion that she was the agent in these negotiations, so she could experience an episode in which she engaged with the challenges and received affirmative feedback from the results of her efforts. "We need to bring youth along," Lucho explained. In this and other situations, he created ready-made epiphanies for the youth.

Lucho was quite deliberate in presenting his "CIA tactics" to us (and to you!) as a challenge to our thinking. Is this a confidence trick or legitimate experiential learning? Our feeling is that Lucho's tactics created new contradictions. Although Lisa admitted to manipulating situations, she was leading from behind, not "from off stage," so youth saw what she was doing. We are concerned that Lucho's approach creates a breach of trust and that it may create experiences that are inauthentic to the real world. Lucho, however, might respond that breaches of trust are quite authentic to the rough and tumble Chicago world that he knows.

CONCLUSION: PURSUING PARADOX AND CULTIVATING EMPOWERING SETTINGS FOR YOUTH

What is the role of adults in facilitating youth's empowerment? How do we create settings that allow youth to develop strategic skills and other elements of empowerment? We have a human tendency to look for simple and singular answers to these kinds of questions. Youth policymakers are currently concerned with identifying stable features of youth settings that can be used for establishing quality standards and improving programs. Quantitative researchers have a parallel concern with determining setting variables that predict positive youth outcomes (Larson, Eccles, & Gootman, 2004). We believe these efforts are valuable, but they get us only so far. They provide limited assistance in understanding *how* practitioners create and sustain positive developmental settings, on the ground, in response to the complex ecology of daily practice: How to cultivate conditions for positive developmental experiences, especially ones in which youth are the agents (Larson, Rickman, Gibbons, & Walker, 2009)

Part of the challenge they face, as Rappaport (1981) argues, is that "human social systems ... are paradoxical in nature" (p. 2). One-sided solutions for influencing or changing a setting rarely work. Indeed, a term that comes up again and again in writings on effective practice is *balancing*. Across applied fields from education to engineering to business, it is often recognized that practitioners' expertise lies in their abilities to balance, integrate, or adjudicate conflicting situational demands (Sternberg, 1998). It follows that to create settings in which youth empower themselves, it is necessary to embrace the contradictions inherent in that concept. What we found here is that practitioners who were effective in supporting youth's development of strategic thinking do this: they balance. Both from the youth's and the advisors' accounts, we found that youth's strategic learning appeared to depend on advisors maintaining a dynamic equilibrium between supporting youth's agency and intervening to keep their work on track. Effective advisors found ways to simultaneously respect youth's rights, ownership, and voice, while using their professional knowledge to provide measured assistance as needed.

Another part of the challenge is that human development (including empowerment) is a process that occurs over time. Although stable features of the setting—positive relationships, trust, and a commitment to youth control—appeared to be necessary to this process, youth reported learning strategic thinking through their participation in episodes. They learned through immersing themselves in the tactical challenges of trying to reach a demanding goal and then obtained feedback from their efforts. The role advisors played in supporting this learning, therefore, included not just maintaining stable conditions but facilitating youth's experience of these cycles. They stood back when they could, supporting youth's freedom, experimentation, and engagement with challenges. But they intervened when they judged it necessary, to help shape an authentic experience—and narrative memory—in which youth were the protagonists and the outcome was successful, or at least laden with useful information.

We must stress that even the most skilled leaders had both hits and misses in cultivating these learning episodes (Larson & Walker, 2010). As with Lisa, sometimes they were able to intervene in effective ways, and sometimes they were not. Some situations they faced lent themselves to easy solutions, and some were harder. Just as the youth were learning basic strategic skills, the advisors were engaged in their own process of learning "meta" strategic skills—skills for facilitating youth's experiencing these episodes.

In concluding, we should emphasize that this research employed discovery methods and is limited in scope. Empowerment involves more than learning skills, it involves development of motivation and sense of self- or group-efficacy to use those skills. We believe youth in our study gained these through the same types of cycles of learning, but more research is needed. Further research is also needed to build on existing knowledge on processes related to development of political consciousness and issues unique to marginalized groups of youth (e.g., Ginwright & Cammarota, 2002). Further knowledge about creating empowering settings for youth should also build on Seidman and Tseng's (this volume) valuable work, consider the role of program culture (Maton & Salem, 1995), and examine youth's co-construction of collective setting narratives (Rappaport, 1995).

Authors' Note

We would like to thank Lisa, the other leaders, the youth who shared their experiences with us. We also thank the William T. Grant Foundation for its support of this research and Kathrin Walker, David Hansen, Colleen Gibbons, Aimee Rickman, Patrick Sullivan, Nickki Dawes Pearce, Aisha Griffith, Philip Hoffman, and Katherine Sweeney for valuable contributions to this work.

REFERENCES

Bronfenbrenner, U. (1979). *The Ecology of Human Development*. Cambridge, Mass: Harvard University Press.

Byrnes, J. P. (2005). The development of self-regulated decision making. In J. E. Jacobs & P. A. Klaczynski (Eds.), *The development of judgment and decision making in children and adolescents* (pp. 5–38). Mahwah, NJ: Erlbaum.

Byrnes, J. P., Miller, D. C., & Reynolds, M. (1999). Learning to make good decisions: A self-regulation perspective. *Child Development, 70*, 1121–1140.

Camino, L. (2005). Pitfalls and promising practices of youth-adult partnerships: An evaluator's reflections. *Journal of Community Psychology, 33,* 75–85.

Deutsch, N. L., & Jones, J. N. (2008). "Show me an ounce of respect": Respect and authority in adult-youth relationships in after-school programs. *Journal of Adolescent Research, 23,* 667–688.

Eccles, J., & Gootman, J. A. (Eds.). (2002). *Community programs to promote youth development. Committee on community-level programs for youth.* Washington, DC: National Academy Press.

Gigerenzer, G. (2008). Why heuristics work. *Perspectives on Psychological Science, 3,* 20–29.

Gestsdóttir, S., & Lerner, R. (2008). Positive development in adolescence: The development and role of intentional self-regulation. *Human Development, 51,* 202–224.

Gilliam, F. D., & Bales, S. (2001). Strategic frame analysis: Reframing America's youth. *Social Policy Report, XV(3),* Ann Arbor, MI: Society for Research in Child Development.

Ginwright, S., & Cammarota, J. (2002). New terrain in youth development: The promise of a social justice approach. *Social Justice, 29,* 82–95.

Ginwright, S., Noguera P., & Cammarota, J. (2006). *Beyond resistance: youth activism and community change.* New York: Routledge.

Grossman, J., Campbell, M., & Raley, B. (2007). *Quality time after school: What instructors can do to enhance learning.* Philadelphia, PA: Public/Private Ventures.

Halpern, R. (2009). The means to grow up: Reinventing apprenticeship as a developmental support in adolescence. Chicago, IL: Routledge.

Halverson, E. R. (2009). Artistic production processes as venues for positive youth development. *Revista Interuniversitaria de Formacion del Profesorado, 66(23,3).*

Habermas, T. & Bluck, S. (2000). Getting a life: The emergence of the life story in adolescence. *Psychological Bulletin, 126,* 748–769.

Heath, S. B. (1998). Working through language. In S. M. Hoyle & C. T. Adger (Eds.), *Kids talk: Strategic language use in later childhood* (pp. 217–240). New York, NY: Oxford University Press.

Heath, S. B. (1999). Dimensions of language development: Lessons from older children. In A.S. Masten (Ed.), *Cultural processes in child development: The Minnesota symposium on child psychology, Vol 29,* (pp. 59–75). Mahwah, NJ: Erlbaum.

Hogan, K. (2002). Pitfalls of community-based learning. *Teachers College Record, 104,* 586–624.

Jeffs, T., & Banks, S. (1999). Youth workers as controllers. In S. Banks (Ed.), *Ethical issues in youth work* (pp. 93–109). London, UK: Rutledge.

Jupp, E. (2007). Participation, local knowledge and empowerment: research-ing public space with young people. *Environment & Planning, 39,* 2822–2844.

Keating, D. (2004). Cognitive and brain development. In R. M. Lerner & L Steinberg (Eds.), *Handbook of adolescent psychology* (pp. 45–84). New York: Wiley.

Kirshner, B. (2006). Apprenticeship learning in youth activism. In S. Ginwright, P. Noguera, & J. Cammarota. *Beyond resistance: Youth activism and com-munity change.* (pp. 37–57). New York: Routledge.

Kirshner, B. (2008). Guided participation in three youth activism organiza-tions: Facilitation, apprenticeship, and joint work. *Journal of the Learning Sciences, 17,* 60–101.

Kuhn, D. (2009). Adolescent thinking. In R. Lerner & L. Steinberg (Eds.). *Handbook of Adolescent Psychology,* Vol 2. Third Edition. New York: Wiley.

LaBouvief-Viet, G. (1990). Modes of knowledge and the organization of de-velopment. In M.L. Commons, C. Armon, L. Kohlberg, F. A. Richards, T. A. Grotzer, & J. D. Sinnott (Eds.), *Adult Development, 2* (pp. 43–62). New York: Praeger.

Larson, R. (2000). Toward a psychology of positive youth development. *American Psychologist, 55,* 170–183.

Larson, R. W. (2010), Positive development in a disorderly world. *Journal of Research on Adolescence, 20,* In press

Larson, R. & Angus, R. (2011) Adolescents' development of skills for agency in youth programs: Learning to think strategically. *Child Development, 82*

Larson, R., Eccles, J., & Gootman, J. (2004). Features of Positive Developmental Settings. *The Prevention Researcher, 11* (2), 8–13.

Larson, R. & Hansen, D. (2005). The development of strategic thinking: Learning to impact human systems in a youth activism program. *Human Development, 48,* 327–349.

Larson, R., Hansen, D., & Walker, K. (2005). Everybody's gotta give: Adolescents' development of initiative and teamwork within a youth program. In. Mahoney, J., Larson, R., & Eccles, J. (Eds.). *Organized activi-ties as contexts of development: Extracurricular activities, after-school and community programs* (pp. 159–184). Hillsdale, NJ: Lawrence Erlbaum Associates.

Larson, R., Hansen, D., & Moneta, G. (2006). Differing profiles of develop-mental experiences across types of organized youth activities. *Developmental Psychology, 42,* 849–863.

Larson, R. W., Rickman, A. N., Gibbons, C. M. & Walker, K. C. (2009). Practitioner expertise: Creating quality within the daily tumble of events in youth settings. *New Directions in Youth Development.* No. 121 (pp. 71–88). San Francisco: Jossey-Bass.

Larson, R. W. & Walker, K. C. (2010). Dilemmas of practice: Challenges to program quality encountered by youth program leaders. *American Journal of Community Psychology, 45,* In press.

Lerner, R. (2002). *Concepts and theories of human development* (3rd Ed). Mahwah, NJ: Erlbaum.

Maton, K. & Salem, D. (1995). Organizational characteristics of empowering community settings: A multiple case study approach. *American Journal of Community Psychology, 23,* 631–656.

Menand, L. (2001) *The Metaphysical Club: A Story of Ideas in America,* New York: Farrar, Straus & Giroux.

Miles, M., & Huberman, A. M. (1994). *Qualitative Data Analysis.* Thousand Oaks, CA: Sage.

Nurmi, (2004). Socialization and self-development. In R. Lerner & L. Steinberg (Eds.). *Handbook of Adolescent Psychology,* Second Edition. New York: Wiley.

Ozer, E. J., Cantor, J. P., Cruz, G. W., Fox, B., Hubbard, E., & Moret, L. (2008). The diffusion of youth-led participatory research in urban schools: The role of the prevention support system in implementation and sustainability. *American Journal of Community Psychology, 41,* 278–289.

Pace, J. L., & Hemmings, A. (2007). Understanding authority in classrooms: A review of theory, ideology, and research. *Review of Educational Research, 77,* 4–27.

Pearce, N. & Larson, R. (2006). The process of motivational change in a civic activism organization. *Applied Developmental Science, 10,* 121–131.

Priest, S. & Gass, M. A. (1997). *Effective leadership in adventure programming.* Champaign, IL: Human Kinetics.

Rappaport, J. (1981). In praise of paradox: A social policy of empowerment over prevention. *American Journal of Community Psychology, 9,* 1–25.

Rappaport, J. (1995). Empowerment meets narrative: Listening to stories and creating settings. *American Journal of Community Psychology, 23,* 795–807.

Rhodes, J. E. (2004). The critical ingredient: Caring youth-staff relationships in after-school settings. *New Directions in Youth Development: After-school worlds,* Spring 2004, pp. 145–161.

Ross, K., Shafer, J. L. & Klein, G. (2006). Professional judgments and "naturalistic decision making." In K. A. Ericsson, N. Charness, P. J. Feltovich, & R. R. Hoffman (Eds.), *Cambridge handbook of expertise and expert performance: Its development, organization and content* (pp. 403–419), Cambridge, UK: Cambridge University Press.

Ryan, R. M. & Deci, E. L. (2000). Self-determination theory and the facilitation of intrinsic motivation, social development and well-being. *American Psychologist, 55,* 68–78.

Sarason, S. B. (1972). *The creation of settings and the future of society.* San Francisco, CA: Jossey-Bass.

Schwandt, T. A. (2003). Back to the rough ground: Beyond theory to practice in evaluation. *Evaluation, 9,* 353–364.

Selman, R. L. (1980). *The growth of interpersonal understanding.* New York: Academic Press.

Selman, R. L. (2003). *The promotion of social awareness: Powerful lessons from the partnership of developmental theory and classroom practice.* New York: Russell Sage Foundation.

Sternberg, R. J. (1998). A balance theory of wisdom. *Review of General Psychology, 2,* 347–365.

Torney-Purta, J., Lehmann, R., Oswald, H. & Schultz, W. (2001). *Citizenship and education in Twenty-eight countries: Civic knowledge at age fourteen.* Amsterdam: International Association for the Evaluation of Educational Achievement.

Walker, K. C., & Larson, R. W. (2006). Balancing the professional and the personal. In D.A. Blyth, & J.A. Walker (Eds.), *New Directions for Youth Development: Exceptional Learning Experiences for the Middle Years: Where High Quality Programs Meet Basic Youth Needs. No. 112* (pp. 109–118). San Francisco, CA: Jossey-Bass.

Vygotsky, L. S. (1978). *Mind and society.* Cambridge, UK: Harvard University Press.

Zeldin, S., & Camino, L. (1999). Youth leadership: Linking research and program theory to exemplary practice. *Research and Practice, 15,* 10–15.

Zimmerman, B. J., & Campillo, M. (2003). Motivating self-regulated problem solvers. In J. Davidson & R Sternberg (Eds.) *The psychology of problem solving* (pp. 233–262). New York: Cambridge University Press.

5   Settings and Empowerment

Edison J. Trickett

The concept of settings as a focus of assessment and intervention has a long history in community psychology. The field has long drawn on the behavior setting perspective of Barker (1968), the social ecology of Moos (1979), the intricacies of creating settings outlined by Sarason (1972), and the ecological metaphor of Kelly (Kelly, 1966; Trickett, Kelly, & Todd, 1972). Definitions of settings across these perspectives varied both in explicitness and content. For example, Barker (1969) defined settings as having a time/place locus, specific goal, and a pattern of activities, such as baseball parks, bars, and bodegas. Sarason (1972), on the other hand, defined settings broadly to include any instance in which "two or more people come together in new and sustained relationships to attain stated objectives." Here, settings involved goal-focused social relationships and interactions that often transcended, although included, settings defined by specific places with a time/space locus.

The concept of settings as resources for potential empowerment brings a specific imagery to social settings, their processes, goals, and effects, which narrows and focuses the broader social setting concept. A drugstore, for example, may be a behavior setting (Barker, 1969); have a social climate (Moos, 1973) that influences the experiences of patrons, including their desire to return on a future occasion; and can be viewed as a community resource (Kelly, 1971) where one-of-a-kind products are available or where locals gather to swap stories and continue the ongoing sense of community among them. It can be a setting where the pharmacist can serve as a weak tie for specific patrons who develop a conversational relationship over time. However, it would be unlikely (although not impossible) to frame a discussion of the drugstore as social setting in empowerment terms, as it does not usually constitute an explicit or implicit setting goal. In contrast to the pharmacy, the three chapters preceding these comments draw attention to settings plausibly related to empowerment goals and characterized by processes viewed as leading to such goals.

In reflecting on these chapters, both the meaning of settings and, particularly, the meaning of empowering settings, are important to articulate. The varied conceptions of settings in the three preceding chapters fall relatively well into the contrasting images of settings as locations (Barker, 1969; Moos, 1973) and settings as networks of relationships surrounding the achievement of a goal or set of goals (Sarason, 1972). Maton and Brodsky include in their definition of settings self-help groups, programs embedded in the larger college context, and movements energized by injustice with respect to the treatment and social status of women. Larson and Angus focus on youth development programs designed to facilitate the development of strategic thinking in youth, whereas Seidman and Tseng "refer to Julian's small groups and organizations as social settings, a term that encompasses classrooms, schools, community-based and human service organizations, workplaces, families, and peer groups" (current volume, p. 12). Although this definition focuses on specific behavior settings (e.g., classrooms) or aggregates of behavior settings (e.g., schools), it also encompasses settings such as peer groups defined not by place but by relationships.

Definitional aspects of settings are important not only for clarity of meaning but because contrasting definitions of settings carry contrasting implications for setting assessment and setting change. Efforts to describe classroom processes, for example, reflect a setting with a bounded context, designed to achieve educational goals, and with a defined role-related power hierarchy between teachers and students. A setting such as RAWA, however, as described by Maton and Brodsky, is not so bounded in where its activities occur or where setting members interact. Further, it seems to provide a range of possible roles in the setting for members and perhaps reflects a more nuanced expression of power dynamics among setting members. The voluntary nature of informal peer groups as settings provides a further challenge to assessing setting processes. Here, individuals form voluntary associations where processes are not shaped by formal roles such as teacher or youth leader and are more likely to revolve around informal relationships involving valued individual skills, resources, or qualities of peer-group members. Thus, the multiple definitions of settings in the chapters suggests the importance of assessing settings not only in terms of the process emphasis found in each of the chapters but in terms of their diverse goals, the degree to which participation is voluntary, the range of roles available to setting members, and the ways in which power is defined and negotiated.

Although the concept of setting is broadly defined in these chapters, the central notion of empowerment may cover even more definitional territory. Since Rappaport's (1981) persuasive discussion of empowerment as a contrasting image to that of prevention, the empowerment concept has evolved to include both processes and outcomes applicable to a range of ecological levels of analysis from the individual to the community (Zimmerman, 1995). Rappaport's (1981) early discussion of the empowerment concept emphasized the collaborative—rather than expert—role of the community researcher/interventionist, the importance of local influence in program development, the emphasis on environmental—rather than individual—change, and as viewing settings as objects of—rather than sites for—intervention efforts. Although subsequent reflection resulted in a less dichotomized construction of the concept (Rappaport, 1987), empowerment still stands as a rallying cry for the field.

The meaning of empowerment in the three chapters, however, seems to erase any potential boundary between the earlier distinction between empowerment and prevention, while simultaneously enriching the possibilities for its further development. For example, Maton and Brodsky, in reviewing three diverse settings, suggest that empowerment includes self-control (AA), academic achievement in science and career opportunity development (Meyerhoff), and involvement in civic political activities (RAWA) intended to achieve social change. The implication is that the definition of empowerment emerges, in part, from the goal or goals of the setting involved. These goals may be primarily individual (e.g., AA) or can, within the same setting, cut across varied kinds of empowering processes and outcomes (RAWA). Larson and Angus "focus on the skills dimension of empowerment"—specifically, the acquiring of strategic thinking among youth. Here, empowerment is defined in terms of a specific kind of competence promotion, although not one demonstrably tied to social actions related to any sociopolitical goals. Thus it seems that competence promotion across a variety of social skills, such as conflict management, cultural competence, and cooperative learning in the classroom, might be similarly viewed through an empowerment framework. Seidman and Tseng provide a very useful and informative list of social change strategies that vary in terms of how central the empowerment concept is to their processes or goals. In contrast to Larson and Angus, they suggest a distinction between skills approaches, such as professional development or coaching/mentoring, and empowerment approaches, such as the creation of new settings. Their assessment suggests that setting-level interventions can be compared and contrasted in terms of the nature and extent of the empowerment assumptions that underlie their goals and their processes.

Seidman and Tseng also suggest that some settings, such as alternative settings, are, in principle, "inherently empowering." Such settings "should be empowering for both the individual and the collective and interdependent with the narratives of its members" (current volume, p. 24). This perspective suggests that setting assessment might focus on the relationship between ideology and practice, in this instance how setting creators translate their ideology into the social processes within the setting. Here, the road to hell may indeed be paved with good intentions. For example, the alternative school I followed for more than a decade (Trickett, 1991) was a setting self-consciously structured to empower students, teachers, and parents (there were no formal administrators). However, the school founders quickly learned that Sarason (1972) was right when he cautioned that those who create new settings will inevitably not foresee all the implications of what they were getting into. This same issue is documented by Larson and Angus in some of their rich accounts where things did not go as planned. Thus, ideology does not always readily get translated into social processes in settings as intended. Although settings may differ in the degree to which they operate from an empowerment ideology, they are "inherently empowering" only in principle.

Seidman and Tseng suggest another seemingly self-evident empowerment principle in their discussion of a feedback model of setting change, where data on relevant setting characteristics are gathered from setting members and the results feed back to them for discussion and subsequent action directed toward setting change. "Obviously, self-assessment has greater potential for individual and collective empowerment than external assessment alone." However, I would argue caution in practice, as the same strategy for increasing empowerment simultaneously increases the potential for subsequent conflict and potential alienation among setting members if the post-assessment conversation does not go well. As Moos (1979) noted years ago in discussing the same survey feedback model Seidman and Tseng outline, the social climates of some settings are more conducive to processing feedback constructively than others.

Thus the empowerment concept ranges far and wide as applied to settings, and the preceding chapters provide a rich array of possibilities for how it may be implicated in the assessment of social settings. Although these multiple meanings of the empowerment concept may stray some from its origins as Rappaport envisioned, in no way do they lessen the importance of the varieties of goals these chapters describe. Both the goals and projects emphasizing them are exemplars of engaged and committed efforts to improve the life chances of individuals through developing settings designed to promote opportunities, instill competencies, and provide opportunities to address social issues. Rather, the intent here is simply to bring attention to the importance of placing current usage of the empowerment concept in the context of Rappaport's initial conceptualization and to retain, as always, the dialectic so central to his initial paper on this topic.

SETTING GOALS, NORMS, AND PROCESSES AS INTERDEPENDENT FEATURES

One striking aspect of the chapters is the diversity in setting goals or missions and the relationship of those goals and missions to relevant within-setting processes. From an ecological perspective, an emphasis on process—particularly when attempting to achieve some generalized notion of what constitute "good" processes—is inextricably linked to the goals of the setting itself and the norms of the setting regarding the kinds of behavior that are adaptive in the context of setting goals. With respect to the goals aspect, Larson and Angus provide a vivid example of how the goal of inculcating strategic thinking in youth is manifested in setting processes organized around that outcome. This represents a clearly conceptualized and articulated theory-based process linking activities to outcomes.

But goals are reflected not only in setting processes but also in setting norms. Indeed, it is plausible that acceptance of setting norms mediate the relationship between setting processes and outcomes. That is, intended setting effects are probably related to the acceptance of setting norms by members as preconditions for access to empowering setting processes. For example, acquiescing to a higher power would seem to be setting a norm relevant to successful participation in AA, adherence to a work ethic. A future in science seems central to the successful Meyerhoff participants, whereas RAWA involves a shared sociopolitical perspective in the service of which supportive processes were developed. Thus, in addition to portraying the processes relevant to achieving some kind of empowered outcomes in these settings, some acknowledgment of the niche requirements for benefiting from the processes is relevant as well. How such settings deal with diversity around the meaning and expression of norms is thus an interesting question relating to conditions under which empowerment processes can be expected to achieve results.

IMPORTANCE OF MULTIPLE METHODS AND VOICES

The important role and meaning of narrative processes in assessing settings with empowerment goals (Mankowski & Rappaport, 1995, Rappaport, 2000) is also reflected in the three chapters. Narratives can be broadly defined here as explicit efforts to elicit the stories of how stakeholders construct their understanding of the setting, its goals, its virtues, and its foibles. For example, Seidman and Tseng suggest that "the coaching/mentoring strategies place a premium on understanding the narratives of the participants and when successful result in individual empowerment" (p. 26). Here, narratives of program recipients are a source of data relevant to program development. Larson and Angus remind us that the narratives of the powerful—in their case, youth program leaders—are also important sources of understanding how to create empowering settings. Their inclusion of rich description of the contradictions, choices, and ideologies of youth program leaders as they juggled issues of power, power sharing, and its consequences indeed led them to conclude that the paradox of "leading from behind" was a recurrent program process whose resolution was critical in affecting setting outcomes.

Narratives can also be a vehicle for articulating setting mission and providing a sense of collective identity. Maton and Brodsky provide numerous quotes suggesting the power of personal, cultural, and setting (RAWA) narratives in defining identity and motivation for social action on the part of RAWA members. Seidman and Tseng, in discussing the potential empowering role of feedback in creating setting change, open up the possibility of viewing feedback discussion as a process in which setting members integrate quantitative or qualitative research findings about the setting into an evolving and co-constructed setting narrative. Each of these perspectives on narrative adds to a richer understanding of the multiple ways settings can use narrative for the empowerment of members.

RIPPLE EFFECTS AND THE "EMPOWERING-EMPOWERED" DISTINCTION

The chapters reflect the traditional distinction made between empowering and empowered settings, with the former focusing on processes internal to the setting and the latter on setting influence on the broader environment (Zimmerman, 2000). For example, Larson and Angus divide the youth programs they worked with into "empowering" and "not empowering" with respect to achieving the goal of strategic thinking programs, whereas Seidman and Tseng label "empowerment of the setting" as a framework for describing and altering within setting processes. Maton and Brodsky, however, cover programs designed to affect both empowering goals (self-help groups and college programs) and empowered (RAWA) goals of social influence as well as individual goals.

However, the chapters also suggest that the "empowered–empowering" distinction is not neat and tidy by bringing to the fore the issue of ripple effects. Indeed, this issue of the ripple effects of settings is one of the most important contributions of the three chapters to thinking about setting assessment and intervention. The issue is framed within the "empowering–empowered" distinction by Maton and Brodsky. They suggest, "One pathway of external influence is empowered member radiating impact (Kelly, 1971). This refers to the extent to which empowered members, as individuals and citizens, influence the settings, communities and larger society in which they reside" (pp. 53). Here, ripples include individual behaviors emerging from participation in the setting but not immediately related to it. "A second pathway is the influence of the external organizational activities that the empowering setting performs. Activities include recruitment, public education, dissemination/diffusion of information and programming, community actions (e.g., social action), community services, resource mobilization, and policy advocacy" (pp. 56). Here, empowering settings may be assessed in terms of the community ripple effects of the activities of members of those settings activated by setting participation but over and beyond setting-initiated activities.

The central point here is that settings have ripple effects regardless of their manifest empowering or empowered intent. The same possibility of assessing external activities and effects initiated by setting participation discussed by Maton and Brodsky could be applied more generally. One could, for example, assess the impact of participation in AA beyond the manifest issue of alcohol consumption, the post-program activities of youth who have learned strategic thinking, or the lifestyle ripples of those involved in grass roots organizing. Conceptualizing and assessing settings in terms of their intended and unintended ripple effects would provide important data on how and in what capacity settings affect both positive and not-so-positive effects in individuals. For example, the development of strategic thinking at point A can, in principle, be a vehicle for increasing later prosocial civic activism and the development of issue-related social networks at point B. However, as Larson and Angus themselves note, the same skills that can be used for good may also be used in "Machiavellian ways." Although they mention the importance of pre-empting this possibility, we do not have ripple effect data on their success at so doing. Alternatively, does participation in collective civic actions designed to correct a local injustice activate later like-minded efforts, or does it increase cynicism if the efforts fizzle? Such questions place the empowerment aspect of setting impact in context and over time.

Yet there are other ways in which settings can promote community-level radiating effects. For example, RAWA may serve as a motivating example to some and as an energizing abomination to others. Both may result in activities designed to affect local community processes. The success of the alternative school I studied (Trickett, 1991) spawned other types of alternative schools in the same community. Thus, many settings serve as exemplars of ideas, causes, and commitments. In opening up the ripple effects issue, these chapters broaden our ability to theorize and document the individual and collective ripple effects of social settings both on their participants and their communities.

It is important for future work on the impact of settings on behavior to theorize and document the inevitable ripples that occur at both the individual and setting level. At the individual level, do Meyerhoff scholars not only enter scientific careers but devote energy to community or civic involvement as their careers are established? How does the existence of that program alter college climate? How do settings themselves view their role as creating extra-setting impact? For example, different settings described by Maton and Brodsky have different perspective on involvement in policy; AA seems to shun direct involvement in national policy issues, whereas RAWA makes them central. Why doesn't the Meyerhoff program involve itself with national advocacy or challenging of cultural norms around ethnic minorities and science careers? How do these stances get reflected in setting socialization processes, and what do they imply for how setting members view empowerment? So the relationship of setting ideology and goals to ripples is highlighted by the chapters.

Finally, the ripple concept can apply to the multiple effects settings have on participants, not only those targeted by setting creators or evaluators. For example, Larson and Angus report, "It should be noted that youth in many of the programs that had low rates of strategic thinking (the 'non-empowered' group in their work) reported development in other areas (e.g., developing responsibility, emotional resiliency, skills for mobilizing effort)." Here, a setting (program) designed to achieve specific outcomes in its participants (high levels of strategic thinking) failed in achieving this goal but achieved goals in other areas of youth development that one might argue are equally as important in terms of their value in negotiating future life experiences or indeed defining empowerment. It is very important that these authors were close enough to their data and understood its importance to share this information rather than leaving their description within a "successful–unsuccessful" frame. The relevance of this for setting assessment and intervention is in the appreciation that although settings have intended goals that may be achieved through the self-conscious application of specific setting processes, it is unlikely that the manifest goal(s) of such program are the only effects worth going after.

ROLE OF SOCIAL SCIENCE IN SETTING ASSESSMENT AND INTERVENTION

One question raised by the chapters involves the role of social science in empowering organizations. In general, the role of social science as portrayed in the three chapters seems quite traditional in terms of its studying rather than influencing the settings it studies. How the studied organizations conceived of their relationship with the social scientists and how the social scientists conceived of their role is a matter of considerable interest as well, particularly in the spirit of Rappaport's vision of a community psychology "in which empowerment is the guiding motif to life." (Maton & Brodsky, p. 60). How does the research itself fit that motif?

Within Sarason's (1972) definition of setting, the relationship of researcher to setting is itself a setting of importance to understand and indeed assess. For some projects described in the chapters, such as Meyerhoff and the youth development projects, social science seems to serve a scientific function in documenting its processes and outcomes and a public awareness function related to disseminating its successes. The empowerment question is: Does the researcher's relationship to the setting serve an empowering function, is it conceptualized as documenting empowering functions of the setting, or both? Although the specifics of this issue are not clearly addressed in the chapters, the broader issue of how researchers assessing social settings deal with the issue of empowerment as part of the research relationship represents an agenda of consequence for empowerment theory and practice.

THEORETICAL CONTRIBUTIONS OF RICH DESCRIPTION

Although there is richness to all the descriptions of each of the social settings described in these chapters, the Larson and Angus chapter, in particular, provides extensive detail about the "on-the-ground" experiences of adults and adolescents in settings explicitly designed to facilitate strategic thinking. The emphasis on qualitative understanding of processes followed over time is exemplary as an effort to dig deeply into the working of settings in the service of specifiable goals. The emphasis on both adolescent and program leader narrative fulfills the promise of Rappaport's narrative interest in eliciting the world view of others from the inside out.

Such descriptions highlight experiential setting dilemmas and paradoxes that often escape the quantitative eye. For example, Larson and Angus found that in these youth development settings, the empowerment philosophy of program leaders emerged as an important aspect of the setting. The program philosophy of youth being in charge related to strategic thinking goals and, for leaders, involved the delicate balancing act resulting in what they called "leading from behind." As they put it, "Perhaps the most difficult question for many adults is addressing the contradiction between engineering developmental experiences for youth versus trusting their judgment and respecting their abilities (Camino, 2005)." This did not mean a relinquishing of power—they always had the power to decide how to use their power. Rather, the situation facing leaders reinforces the paradox Judy Gruber and I (Gruber & Trickett, 1987) described in our paper "Can we empower others? The paradox of empowerment in the governing of an alternative public school."

Larson and Angus also remind us that creating and maintaining conditions for youth development … depends on how leaders respond to unfolding events in the life of the program. Thus, although an articulate philosophy of experiential learning can help program leaders frame events and assess success in the moment, no description of how settings ultimately affect outcomes can omit ongoing process assessment as part of the scheme. Thus, rich description of setting processes provide critical insights into setting dynamics that reflect setting-specific goals and tensions and complement the kinds of setting frameworks outlined by Seidman and Tseng.

INTERVENTION IMPLICATIONS

There are multiple implications for intervention related to setting-level creation and change in the chapters as well. The critical component of this process is provided by Seidman and Tseng in their reminder that unless setting processes change as a result of intervention setting outcomes will not. However, the chapters suggest that setting processes may change as a function of direct intervention at the setting level or indirectly through working at higher ecological levels. Larson and Angus and Seidman and Tseng describe projects that worked directly with specific social settings to alter social processes in school and youth development settings. However, Seidman and Tseng also show how a school system policy-driven reduction in class size directly affected social processes in the classroom that subsequently resulted in changed educational outcomes. In a similar manner, national policies such as "No Child Left Behind" may directly influence such classroom processes as "teaching to the test," which may, in turn, affect both intended and unintended learning outcomes. Thus, there are both direct and indirect paths to altering setting processes.

The three chapters also clarify the importance of adopting a perspective that conceptualizes settings not only as nested within higher-order influences but also with respect to developmental differences in setting participants.

For example, Seidman and Tseng emphasize classrooms as the most important settings in schools and hence the most important to target for intervention. However, the importance of classrooms in general is perhaps more true for children in elementary schools than adolescents in high schools, where developmental changes, the rise of peer-group influence, the influence of schoolwide factors such as sense of connection to school, and community-level factors such as gang activity may moderate somewhat the centrality of classrooms in adolescent development. This is not to downplay the general importance of classrooms across the developmental spectrum but, rather, to suggest that the salience and role of classrooms may interact with other aspects of the ecology of children and youth in different ways in differing developmental stages.

In addition, although elaborated description of settings and their processes is one necessary component of assessing where and what to target in terms of setting-level change, it is insufficient as a guide for accomplishing such change. Intervention can benefit both from theories of the problem and theories of the solution. As Larson and Angus state:

> "Youth policymakers are currently concerned with identifying
> stable features of youth settings that can be used for establishing
> quality standards and improving programs. Quantitative
> researchers have a parallel concern with determining setting
> variables that predict positive youth outcomes (Larson,
> Eccles, & Gootman, 2004). We believe these efforts are
> valuable, but they get us only so far. They provide limited
> assistance in understanding how practitioners create and
> sustain positive developmental settings, on the ground,
> in response to the complex ecology of daily practice…"
>
> (current volume, p. 88)

The integration of efforts to identify key setting processes and the realization that such processes are dynamic, changeable, flexible, intuitive, and changing suggest that efforts at setting change need to resist the potential formulaic image of overly manualized evidence-based practices. In the spirit of Rappaport's appreciation of empowerment as grounded in local ecology and energized by local control, such knowledge may serve as a possibility to be shared locally but not as a blueprint for meaningful setting change. Larson and Angus' thoughts here serves as a useful conclusion. Researchers can contribute by helping define the array of situations that practitioners face, providing illuminative case studies, and helping formulate situational guidelines for different types of balancing situations.

CONCLUSION

The three preceding chapters serve an illuminating function by elaborating on how empowerment can guide both setting assessment and setting-level change. In so doing, they highlight how community psychology can walk the walk of empowerment as a guiding value of the field. They also suggest, however, the complexity of both setting assessment and change. Definitional issues remain both about settings and empowerment. Settings are complex and dynamic; they include goals, norms, processes, and ideologies; they are entities unto themselves as well as being nested in larger ecologies that affect the processes in them; and they can create ripple effects at the individual, organizational, and community level that are not well-understood. To understand their processes requires both qualitative and quantitative methods employed over time, across types of settings, and across developmental differences in those for whom they are intended. Altering them in ways that promote the goals for which they are intended requires theories of intervention that appreciate the narratives of those in them as well as the accumulated knowledge of settings developed by outsider researchers. The three preceding chapters take us a long way toward the goal of conceptualizing, creating, and changing social settings.

REFERENCES

Barker, R. (1968). *Ecological psychology: Concepts and methods for studying the environment of human behavior*. Stanford, CA: Stanford University Press.

Camino, L. (2005). Pitfalls and promising practices of youth-adult partnerships: An evaluator's reflections. *Journal of Community Psychology, 33*, 75–85.

Gruber, J. & Trickett, E. (1987). Can we empower others? The paradox of empowerment in the governing of an alternative school. *American Journal of Community Psychology, 15*, 353–371.

Kelly, J. G. (1966). Ecological constraints on mental health services. *American Psychologist. 21*, 535–539.

Kelly, J. G. (1971). Qualities for the community psychologist. *American Psychologist, 26*, 897–903.

Larson, R. W., Rickman, A. N., Gibbons, C. M. & Walker, K. C. (2009). Practitioner expertise: Creating quality within the daily tumble of events in youth settings. *New Directions in Youth Development, 121*, 71–88.

Mankowski, E., & Rappaport, J. (1995). Stories, identity and the psychological sense of community. In R. S. Wyer, Jr. (Ed.), *Advances in social cognition* Vol. 8, (pp. 211–226). Hillsdale, NJ: Lawrence Erlbaum Associates.

Moos, R. (1973). Conceptualizations of human environments. *American Psychologist, 28,* 652–665.

Moos, R. (1979). Social climate measurement and feedback. In R. Munoz, L. Snowden, & J. Kelly (Eds.), *Social and psychological research in community settings.* San Francisco: Jossey-Bass.

Rappaport, J. (1981). In praise of paradox: A social policy of empowerment over prevention. *American Journal of Community Psychology, 9,* 1–25.

Rappaport, J. (1987). Terms of empowerment/exemplars of prevention: Toward a theory for community psychology. *American Journal of Community Psychology, 15,* 121–144.

Rappaport, J. (2000). Community narratives: Tales of terror and joy. *American Journal of Community Psychology, 28*(1), 1–24.

Sarason, S. B. (1972). *The creation of settings and the future societies.* San Francisco: Jossey-Bass.

Trickett, E. J. (1991). *Living an idea: Empowerment and the Evolution of an Alternative High School.* Brookline, MA: Brookline Books.

Trickett, E. J., Kelly, J. G., & Todd, D. M. (1972). The social environment of the high school: Guidelines for individual change and organizational development. In S. Golann & C. Eisendorfer (Eds.), *Handbook of Community Mental Health,* (pp. 331–406). New York: Appleton-Century Crofts.

Zimmerman, M. (1995). Psychological empowerment: Issues and illustrations. *American Journal of Community Psychology, 23,* 581–600.

Zimmerman, M. A. (2000). Empowerment theory: Psychological, organizational and community levels of analysis. In J. Rappaport & E. Seidman (Eds.), *Handbook of Community Psychology* (pp. 43–63). New York: Plenum.

6 Voices from the Ground Up: The Use of Narrative in Understanding Recovery from Serious Mental Illness

Deborah Salem

Julian Rappaport (2000) argues that our role as social scientists is to use our tools to assist others in their efforts to "turn tales of terror to tales of joy" (p. 7). He suggests that the application of a narrative approach to research is consistent with this goal, because it spans levels of analysis and has the capacity to promote both personal and social change. Narrative research allows us to explore individuals' own stories about their lives and contributes to description and analysis of the settings and cultural narratives that assist individuals in making meaning of their experiences. In this chapter, I will draw on work from a long-term collaboration with Schizophrenics Anonymous (SA), a mutual-help organization for individuals experiencing a schizophrenia-related illness, as an example of how a narrative approach can help us to understand and facilitate the experience of recovery from serious mental illness.

Being diagnosed with a serious mental illness, such as schizophrenia, is a devastating experience. For individuals it not only means experiencing severe, confusing, and frightening symptoms; they have also been told that they are members of one of the most highly stigmatized groups in our culture. The experience has been described as the loss of one's pre-illness sense of self (Spaniol, Gagne, & Koehler, 1997) and, as Rappaport (2000) points out, can surely be characterized as a "tale of terror." As with any life-altering experience, individuals need to develop new understandings of the life changes they are experiencing, integrate those understandings into their views of themselves, and find ways to live with and/or overcome the challenges this presents.

Those living with a mental illness—particularly schizophrenia—have found limited opportunities to makes sense of the experience in a manner that holds out hope for a positive future. There are three primary reasons for this, two of which have been widely discussed in the literature. First, at a cultural level, we hold highly stigmatized views of individuals with serious mental illness (Fraser, 1994; Perlick et al., 2001). Some have even argued that the social and economic consequences of these views for individuals with a mental illness, and the accompanying feelings of decreased self-worth, are as difficult to recover from as the illness itself (Deegan, 1997; Harding, Zubin, & Strauss, 1987; Weaver Randall, 2000). Second, mental health professionals and settings have embraced pessimistic, outcome-oriented definitions of recovery, focused on return to normal functioning (Deegan, 1996; Harding & Zahniser, 1994). This has grown to be more than symptom cessation and staying out of the hospital to a focus on community adjustment, social relationships, and/or quality of life (e.g., Lieberman & Kopelowicz, 2005; Torgalsboen & Rund, 2002;). However, the standards that we set for individuals in these domains, and which they consequently set for themselves, may not represent feasible or personally desired goals after the onset of a serious mental illness.

A less widely recognized contribution to the tales of terror so many people experience is the fact that the stigma surrounding mental illness has made access to the experiences of others who are dealing with a serious mental illness very difficult. Consumers are often hesitant to share their stories candidly with each other. As expressed by an SA member, "I never talked about it [schizophrenia] before I started SA. I never talked to anybody about delusions or ... except for maybe my doctor, you know, or the nurses in the hospital."

As a result of this cultural stigma, professional pessimism, and lack of access to others' experiences of recovery, the meaning-making resources (Kloos, 1999) available to those with serious mental illness provide individuals with little hope for a fulfilling life. Over the past few decades, however, a variety of influences have begun to challenge the prevailing views of recovery from serious mental illness. Longitudinal studies have found that many people do recover, even according to traditional outcomes (DeSisto, Harding, McCormick, Ashikaga, & Brooks, 1995; Harding, Brooks, Ashikaga, Strauss, & Breier, 1987) either with or without the assistance of professional mental health services (Corrigan & Ralph, 2005).

Even more importantly, with the growth of the consumer movement in mental health, we have begun to hear more about the experience of recovery from those living with serious mental illness (e.g., Chamberlin, 1990; Deegan, 1988; 1996). These stories are based on what Borkman (1976, 1999) has called experiential knowledge, or the knowledge that comes from lived experience. Mental health consumers have made their stories of recovery available through the popular press, media, Internet, and research literature. In addition, we have seen the development of consumer-run settings, such as mutual-help groups, that are based on this lived experience of having a mental illness. These settings provide consumers with more positive meaning-making resources which reflect a radically different understanding of what it means to recover from an illness such as schizophrenia (Kloos, 1999; Weaver Randall & Salem, 2005).

The psychosocial rehabilitation literature has also helped to articulate a new view of recovery based on the personal experiences of consumers (e.g., Chamberlin, 1990; Deegan, 1988) and the work of scholars who have sought to amplify this experience (e.g., Anthony, 1993; Andresen, Oades, & Caputi, 2003; Davidson, Sells, Sangster, & O'Connell, 2005; Young & Ensing, 1999). These perspectives have begun to challenge the outcome-oriented definitions of recovery that have shaped our cultural understanding of mental illness (Deegan, 1988). They reflect the belief that recovery is the act of engaging in a process of growth with no predetermined endpoint (Anthony, 1993).

There is a growing body of literature that explores recovery from the consumer perspective and seeks to identify common stages, processes, and facilitators of recovery (e.g., Andersen, Oades, & Caputi, 2003; Baxter & Diehl, 1998); Davidson & Strauss, 1992; Pettie & Triolo, 1999; Spaniol, L. S., Wewiorski, N. J., Gagne, C., & Anthony, W. A., 2002; Young & Ensing, 1999). Although still in its infancy, some common themes have begun to emerge. They include, but are not limited to, the view that: *(1)* recovery is both a process and an outcome (Andreen, Oades, & Caputi, 2003; Anthony, 1993; Corrigan & Ralph, 2005); *(2)* recovery involves self-redefinition (Andreen, Oades, & Caputi, 2003; Davidson et al., 2005); *(3)* hope is an essential element of recovery (Andreen, Oades, & Caputi, 2003; Corrigan & Ralph, 2005; Deegan, 1988); and *(4)* recovery is an individualized and personalized experience (Anthony, 1993). As described by Anthony (1993), recovery is a personal process of changing "attitudes, values, feelings, goals, skills and/or roles" to develop "new meanings and purpose in one's life as one grows beyond the catastrophic effects of mental illness" (p. 19).

Although there is a growing awareness that recovery is a complex and individualized process, there has been limited empirical investigation of what recovery means for different individuals or what it means in different contexts.

This results in part from the complexity involved in studying a process that is individualized and has no specified endpoint. As Lieberman and Kopelowicz (2005) note, it is very difficult to distinguish between the process and outcome of recovery and is equally difficult to separate objective recovery outcomes from the subjective experience that accompanies them. Viewing recovery as an individualized process is not consistent with the theories (Corrigan & Ralph, 2005) or the methods (Loveland, Weaver Randall, & Corrigan, 2005) we have traditionally used to evaluate mental health services or mental health outcomes.

Our understanding of recovery has also been limited by the fact that most of the literature to date has focused at the individual level. There has been almost no attention in the literature to setting norms or organizational beliefs about recovery or to how consumers' involvement in specific settings, or types of settings, influences their experience of recovery. Kloos' (1999) work comparing the beliefs and structures of a consumer-run and a professionally run residential treatment center is a notable exception. In his study, he clearly articulates the differences between the meaning-making resources available in these settings and explores how they influence the self-definitions of their participants.

Loveland et al. (2005) challenge us to use research methods that are consistent with our conceptualizations of recovery. A narrative approach is both conceptually and methodologically consistent with emerging views of recovery from serious mental illness. The narrative framework proposed by Rappaport (1993) can help us to understand how settings assist individuals with identity transformation by providing contexts in which they develop new personal stories about their lives, in part through the adoption of shared community narratives. Rappaport argues that a narrative approach not only allows us to hear the voices of those whose experience we are attempting to represent, it also provides a framework that spans levels of analysis and allows us to explore the reciprocal influences between individuals, settings, and cultural norms (Rappaport, 1995, 1998, 2000). It can help us to both illuminate the process of recovery and to explore the setting and cultural factors that influence that process.

Rappaport (1993) distinguishes between narratives at three levels of analysis. Personal stories refer to an individual's cognitive representations of events that are unique to that individual's life history. Community narratives are communal stories that are common among a group of people or a setting. Dominant cultural narratives refer to overlearned stories that are communicated to everyone through mass media and other large social institutions. Rappaport suggests that individuals transform their identities through the development of personal stories. These stories are influenced by the community narratives of the settings in which people seek to make meaning of their experiences and the dominant cultural narratives to which they are exposed. He proposes a narrative approach as a model for understanding how contexts, such as mutual-help groups, can be understood as normative narrative communities that help individuals make sense of their lives and develop more positive personal stories.

THE APPLICATION OF A NARRATIVE APPROACH TO UNDERSTANDING RECOVERY

The narrative approach holds great promise for advancing our understanding of recovery and the contexts and experiences that facilitate and impede it. It is both conceptually and methodologically consistent with emerging consumer views of recovery. First, at the individual level, personal stories allow us hear the unique ways that individuals experience recovery, while at the same time allowing for the identification of common elements of recovery across people and settings. They provide mechanisms for accessing and giving voice to the experience, without the need to make arbitrary and perhaps false distinctions between the processes and outcomes of recovery. As Rappaport (1998) points out, people do not experience their lives as a list of outcomes and facilitating factors. They experience their lives as stories of where they have been, where they are, and where they believe they are going. A narrative approach allows us to hear how individuals are engaged in recovery without the imposition of externally determined endpoints or benchmarks. As such, it is well- suited to capturing the process of identity transformation. It also allows us to understand the role of factors such as hope and spirituality, which may play an important role in recovery but are not typically viewed as central constructs in the mental health literature.

In addition to allowing us to understand recovery in a manner that is more consistent with consumers' lived experience, narrative research provides a means for exploring the reciprocal influences across levels of analysis that shape, challenge, and change this experience. Through the exploration of community and cultural narratives, and the processes and structures that support them, we can better understand just how individuals develop, and maintain over time, their personal stories of recovery. A narrative approach directs our attention beyond the individual level to the setting and cultural narratives and structures that influence whether a diagnosis of mental illness will lead beyond tales of despair and hopelessness or to stories of growth and recovery.

Although a focus on the personal stories of individuals is consistent with the growing use of qualitative methods in psychological research (Davidson et al., 2005; Loveland et al., 2005), attention to the community narratives of settings in which people develop these stories has not been a focus of mental health research. A narrative perspective encourages us to explore the meaning-making resources available to individuals. It directs our attention to the variety of settings and contexts in which individuals make sense of their lives. In our work with SA, we have had the opportunity to learn how one setting has developed a community narrative around what it means to recover from schizophrenia and how it has supported its members in adopting that story as their own.

THE POWER OF NARRATIVE IN SCHIZOPHRENICS ANONYMOUS

SA is a mutual-help organization for persons with a schizophrenia-related illness. It was founded in 1985 in the Detroit area by a woman diagnosed with schizophrenia. Since then it has grown to more than 140 groups throughout the United States. SA's format and ideology were modeled in part after Alcoholics Anonymous (AA), in that there are weekly meetings for members, steps for recovery, a program philosophy, and mutual support between meetings. SA leaders are, in most cases, members of SA who have schizophrenia. Participants in SA groups are invited on the website to "share their experiences, feelings, and hopes in a confidential and non-judgmental environment" (Schizophrenics Anonymous, 2005).

Over the course of a 25-year research collaboration, we studied how SA helps its members and how it has developed and grown as an organization. Throughout our long affiliation with SA, we have been struck by the power of institutional and setting beliefs to impact both SA's growth and development and members' experiences within the organization.

Our initial evaluation explored SA's efforts to start SA groups in residential group homes (Salem, Gant, & Campbell, 1998). Our most powerful finding was that although SA was able to start model groups, engage group home members in participation, and engage group home directors and staff in facilitating this involvement, group home residents' ongoing involvement in SA was ultimately impeded by the beliefs of well-meaning group home directors. Their decisions as gatekeepers, regarding who should lead and attend SA groups, reflected traditional beliefs about the limited capabilities of those with serious mental illness. Similarly, in a study of SA's growth and development in Michigan, we found that following the development of a formal partnership with a professionally run advocacy organization, SA's own structure and organizational network became more like that of the advocacy organization. SA became more hierarchically structured, less consumer-run, and more involved with the traditional mental health system (Salem, Reischl, & Weaver Randall, 2008). Finally, in an evaluation of SA's efforts to start SA groups in prison/forensic settings, we found that conflict between the institutional beliefs of a prison and a mutual-help organization made it very difficult to start SA groups within prison settings that were truly consumer-led. The prisons required that all groups have a prison staff member (i.e., a group facilitator) present during the meetings. These staff members were able to articulate the importance of consumer leadership in mutual-help groups and did not identify themselves as the formal SA group leaders. When asked about their behaviors during group meetings, however, they described actually playing strong and primary leadership roles in the groups (Salem & Hughes, 2003). These findings drew our attention to the ability of beliefs at both the institutional and the setting level to influence the behaviors and beliefs of individuals within those settings. They also drew our attention to the fact that SA held very different beliefs from the settings it interacted with in its efforts to reach out to more individuals with schizophrenia. Although we were not initially conceptualizing these beliefs within a narrative framework, we were well-aware of their power.

RECOVERY IN SCHIZOPHRENICS ANONYMOUS

In our qualitative study of members' personal experiences in SA, our initial goal was to explore the helping mechanisms participants experienced. Although we did learn about how SA helped its members, we could not help but be struck by the fact that this emerged as an integrated part of their stories of recovery and that these stories were quite different from traditional thinking about mental health outcomes (Weaver Randall, 2000). The application of a narrative approach allowed us to parsimoniously integrate our research questions and findings into one multilevel conceptualization of how SA has developed and how it helps its members.

Data Collection and Analysis

The work described here is based on two sources of data: *(1)* interviews with SA leaders and members and *(2)* content analysis of SA's organizational literature and materials. In-depth, open-ended interviews were conducted with 46 SA leaders and members sampled from community-based SA groups to represent different lengths and levels of involvement in SA[1]. They were

1 Twelve of the 14 (86%) currently active, community-based SA groups in the lower peninsula of Michigan participated in the study. Eighty-nine percent (17/19) of the organizational and group leaders participated. Ninety-five percent of the SA members who were present at the SA meeting where participants were recruited

conducted in settings of the participants' choice, which included individuals' homes, restaurants, mental health agencies, or other community settings. The interviews varied in length, ranging between 45 minutes and 6 hours (conducted in multiple sessions). Interviews were conducted to allow individuals to tell their story within a semi-structured format, consisting of four sections: *(1)* participants' stories of involvement in SA; *(2)* participants' stories of their mental illness; *(3)* questions concerning interpersonal relationships and social support; and *(4)* demographic information and mental health service utilization.

Inductive thematic content analysis was used as the primary analysis tool to explore and understand the data. The first-order analysis involved the following steps: *(1)* reduction of the empirical materials; *(2)* cross-case analysis; and *(3)* within-case analysis (Miles & Huberman, 1994). Second-order analysis involved a more iterative process working between the cross- and within-case analysis to identify second-order themes (e.g., the four phases of recovery described below). Criteria of trustworthiness (including credibility, transferability, dependability, and confirmability) were met through insider member checks with SA participants, outsider checks with knowledgeable peers, and the authors' prolonged experiences with the setting (Lincoln & Guba, 1989). Thematic content analysis of SA literature and materials was conducted in a similar manner (*see* Hughes, 2004 and Weaver Randall, 2000, for more detail).

Personal Stories of Recovery in Schizophrenics Anonymous

Early in our collaboration with SA we were interested in learning how members felt their involvement in SA helped them to cope with having schizophrenia. In our interviews with SA members, we asked them to tell us the stories of their mental illness and of their experience in SA (Salem, Reischl, & Weaver, 2000; Weaver Randall & Salem, 2005). Our goal at the time was to identify processes and structures in SA that were helpful to its members, without imposing our own ideas on what those qualities were. Katie Weaver

volunteered to participate. For groups with more than three members present, three members were randomly selected to represent three "length of participation" groups (i.e., less than 6 months, 6 months to 2 years, and more than 2 years). For groups with three members or less present, all members were invited. This allowed for the selection of up to three members from each SA group, while maintaining the credibility of the sample and ensuring that each "length of participation" category was adequately represented in the final sample. A total of 30 members were invited to be interviewed, one of whom was hospitalized during the study, yielding a final sample of 46 SA participants (Hughes, 2004; Weaver Randall, 2000).

Randall, the graduate student who conducted many of the interviews, astutely realized that we were hearing stories of recovery and that these stories were quite different from traditional definitions of recovery. In her master's thesis she asked the question: What does recovery mean to members of SA? She found that although many members of SA described the attainment of personal goals and improved outlook and quality of life, their stories revealed an ongoing, multiphase process of recovery. These phases included: *(1)* mourning and grief (phase 1), *(2)* awareness and recognition (phase 2), *(3)* redefinition and transformation (phase 3), and *(4)* enhanced well-being and quality of life (phase 4) (Weaver Randall, 2000). Members described an ongoing process of redefinition of themselves and of their world views, as well as the ability to reach personally desired goals and achieve greater life satisfaction. Engagement in the process of recovery was widely reported, with 72%, 83%, and 69% of members describing engagement in phases 2, 3, and 4, respectively.

Within-case analysis of members' personal stories revealed that many SA members perceived themselves to be moving along an ongoing road to recovery with no identifiable endpoint. Although all members who described reaching a state of enhanced well-being (phase 4) did describe being in the other three phases at some point, reaching phase 4 did not mark the end of the recovery process. Participants described moving back and forth between the phases as they faced new challenges or grew in new ways (Weaver Randall, 2000; Weaver Randall & Salem, 2005). Their stories reflected an acceptance and optimism quite at odds with our dominant cultural narrative about recovery from schizophrenia, as illustrated in the following summary of one member's personal story.

Lisa describes how it took her more than 7 years to realize and accept that she had a mental illness. After she would experience successes in school or work, she would "still test the waters and go for a second opinion," because she did not believe that someone diagnosed with schizophrenia could achieve the things she was able to (phase 1). Next she describes how being in therapy and trying to find out as much information as possible about schizophrenia (phase 3) eventually brought her to SA. She describes her participation in SA as helpful, because it helped her to realistically assess her situation and understand how schizophrenia had impacted her life (phase 2). It also helped her to reassess her goal of being a CEO of a big company and settling for nothing less (phase 3). Later in her story she describes her recovery as really progressing when she was able to maintain a full-time job and eventually buy a car with the money she saved (phase 4)At the time of the interview Lisa was doing very well by her own evaluation and had achieved many of her goals, including being content at her job, getting married, and owning a home (phase 4). In the last year, however, she and her husband have been thinking about having children and this had made her recognize and acknowledge that it may not be possible for her to have a healthy baby (phase 2). She had also experienced recent discrimination at work, when coworkers told her that she was the only person who was not supposed to have a key to the office (phase 2). In spite of these experiences, Lisa describes herself as "coming around to another phase again" in her recovery. This comment was made in reference to her desire to become involved doing some volunteer work with a mental health advocacy organization, which she saw as providing a renewed sense of meaning and purpose in her life [phase 4]. (Weaver Randall & Salem, 2005, p. 199)

Convergence Between Schizophrenics Anonymous' Community Narrative and Members' Personal Stories of Recovery.

After hearing such process-oriented personal stories of recovery in SA, we were interested in examining the extent to which members' personal stories of recovery actually reflected explicit components of SA's community narrative. Using written materials, videos, and the SA website, we identified some of the key elements of SA's community narrative about recovery. We then analyzed members' personal stories to see if these elements were reflected in their stories.[2]

As described in Weaver Randal and Salem (2005), we focused on six key recovery messages in SA's community narrative: *(1)* schizophrenia is a life long, no-fault biological illness; *(2)* recovery is possible and all people can engage in recovery, regardless of symptom severity or other circumstances; *(3)* recovery consists of changing one's attitudes, beliefs, and approach to life; *(4)* people have inner strength and resources that can be used in their recovery and the recovery of others; *(5)* recovery can only be achieved with the help of others; and *(6)* recovery is an ongoing process with ups and downs.

Not surprisingly we found all of these elements clearly reflected in members' personal stories (*see* Weaver Randall & Salem, 2005)[3]. For example, the

---

2 In this paper we focus primarily on how SA's community narrative influences members' personal stories. It is important to remember, however, that there is a reciprocal influence between members' stories and the community narrative. The community narrative was initially developed from the founder's personal story (Hughes, 2004). Over time members' stories and experiential knowledge continue to shape SA's community narrative.

3 The following example is from Weaver Randall & Salem (2005). For examples of convergence with all six recovery messages and further discussion of these links, please *see* Weaver Randall & Salem (2005).

belief that *schizophrenia is a life-long, no-fault biological illness* is communicated in the following excerpt from SA's community narrative.

> A number of theories regarding the cause are now focused on biochemical and physical abnormalities in the brain. Chemical messengers carry signals from one nerve branch to another. Researchers believe that an imbalance in these chemicals contributes to schizophrenia-related symptoms.
>
> (Schizophrenics Anonymous, 2003)

It is also reflected in a members' personal stories:

> But I said no, it's a chemical imbalance in the brain ... Somebody might say, well, it's all my mother's fault. What I would say to them is, "I thought it was, too. I blamed my mother for years. But my mother did the best she could and I realize that this is a no-fault illness." ... A lot of them thought it was a weakness of character, like I did.
>
> (Weaver Randall & Salem, 2005, p. 187)

Setting Characteristics that Facilitate Adoption of Schizophrenics Anonymous' Recovery Narrative

After finding a convergence between SA's community narrative and members' personal stories, we explored the factors that assist SA members in adopting personal stories that are so strikingly different from the dominant cultural narratives about schizophrenia. SA members have not stopped living in a world that, for the most part, holds very different beliefs about their lives and futures. Based on our observations of SA and on members' descriptions of their experience, and influenced by past work on empowering settings (Maton & Salem, 1995; Zimmerman, 2000), we identified four characteristics of SA that support its members' adoption of SA's community narrative about the process of recovery. These characteristics are briefly described below (*see* Weaver Randall & Salem, 2005, for more detailed discussion).

First, SA provides members with ample opportunity to *share personal stories*. They are encouraged to tell and retell their stories, both formally and informally. This provides a mechanism for both making sense of one's own experience (Arntson & Droge, 1987) and for sharing experiential knowledge with others (Borkman, 1976). As one member describes, "That for me is the biggest part of it. It draws me to it because I can share my own story with them and they understand" (Weaver Randall & Salem, 2005, p. 192).

Second, SA provides *role models* who have shared similar life experiences and are engaged in coping with their illness. Perceptions of shared experience with those who are engaged in the process of recovery may increase the influence of these role models (Katz, 1993), facilitate the learning of new skills and coping strategies, and increase a sense of hope for improvement (Bandura, 1986). Speaking about the founder of SA, one member said:

> I knew in the very beginning that she was very caring and she
> was running it herself and she was describing her experience
> which, you know, was somewhat similar to me. I wasn't holding a
> full-time job at the time and I haven't since. But she was holding
> a full-time job. She had been through the hospital thing. She was
> taking her meds. She was seeing a psychiatrist. The whole, you
> know, a big portion of the experience that people that have this
> illness, in a big way she had experienced and she was making it.
> (Weaver Randall & Salem, 2005, p. 193)

Third, SA has a *pervasive and highly accessible role structure* (Maton & Salem, 1995), which provides members with access to a variety of highly valued formal and informal role opportunities that may not be available in other aspects of their lives (Levine, 1988). The role opportunities reflect the value placed on experiential knowledge (Borkman, 1990) and allow participants to experience the benefits of helping others (Riessman, 1965). SA doesn't just tell people they are valued, it depends on them to function. As expressed by one member:

> SA really kinda saved my life in a sense, because I didn't have any
> direction and so very early on, I was beginning to think of ways
> where I could make a contribution. The first way I could make a
> contribution was very small, which was making coffee and cleaning
> up the tables afterwards. Something simple. We need people to put
> literature out. You know. There's just a million little small things a
> person can do to build up a sense, you know, with the other people
> that they can follow through.
> (Weaver Randall & Salem, 2005, p. 195)

Finally, SA provides a *supportive context* in which people can grapple with difficult life changes with the assistance and support of others. Recovery has been described in the consumer literature as something that you do with other people (Deegan, 1988, 1993). The presence of those with shared experiences may make it easier to share stories that are considered deviant by those who have not experienced them (Katz, 1993), as indicated in the following interview excerpt:

> What has been the most helpful to me? The people clapped, rewarded me, what I said. What other members had to say … helped me get stronger, function through other things, to move on … I kept my job for almost two years now and [the group leader] says all right. You're working. We're so proud of you. A big clap that's encouraging, that makes me wanta go further. You get positive feedback from others and yourself.
>
> (Weaver Randall & Salem, 2005, p. 197)

In such a context, it is not surprising that SA members are able to adopt key elements of SA's community narrative and make it their own. SA provides its members with a new way of thinking about recovery. SA's more optimistic, process-oriented view of recovery is well-supported by SA's organizational structure and is highly accessible to members.

Not all elements of a setting's community narrative will necessarily be equally accessible to setting participants or equally supported by its structures and processes, however. In contrast to SA's narrative about the overall process of recovery, its community narrative regarding the role of professionals and traditional mental health services in recovery, although highly accessible, was less widely adopted by its members.

Schizophrenics Anonymous' Community Narrative Regarding the Role of Professionals in Recovery

SA is a somewhat unique mutual-help organization when it comes to its view of traditional services. Unlike many consumer-run organizations, it has a very positive community narrative regarding the role of professional services in recovery from schizophrenia. Analysis of the founder's personal story suggests that this aspect of SA's community narrative comes directly from her own experience that medication was crucial to her recovery and her own extraordinary relationship with her psychiatrist (Hughes, 2004).

In a similar analysis to the one described above (Weaver Randall & Salem, 2005), Hughes examined the relationship between SA's community narrative concerning the role of professionals in recovery from schizophrenia and members' perspectives on the roles of mutual-help and traditional services in their own lives (Hughes, 2004). In her analysis of SA's written materials and videos, she found that SA's community narrative clearly supported the use of professional services, encouraging members to view SA and professional services as complementary forms of support. This view was expressed in the SA literature and other materials in four different ways, including: *(1)* explicit support for the use of professional services (e.g., describing SA as a supplement to traditional services, encouraging members to utilize traditional services); *(2)* implicit statements of support for the use of professional services (e.g., describing SA as a *piece of the puzzle*, normalizing member's use of traditional services); *(3)* literature and information updates aimed at educating members about medication and traditional services; and *(4)* personal stories of recovery that include the use of traditional services (Hughes, 2004). SA's community narrative is replete with support for the use of medication and other professional services and clearly communicates that ideally members should be involved in both SA and professional services:

> The group also emphasizes the importance of adhering to the advice of mental health professionals, especially psychiatrists, case managers and therapists ... Many members of the group have benefited from these therapeutic methods ... SA is intended to be a supplement to professional help.
>
> (SA, 1999, p. 3)

Members' Personal Stories Regarding the Role of Professionals in Recovery

To explore members' adoption of this narrative, Hughes (2004) examined members' personal stories regarding their views of and use of SA and traditional services. She found that although most members were using some type of traditional service, their stories focused primarily on the differences they perceived between SA and these traditional sources of support, rather than on how they can work together.

Three distinctly different story patterns emerged regarding members' views of SA and traditional services: *(1)* stories that contained no reference to the role of SA and traditional services in their lives or the differences between them; *(2)* stories that described differences between SA and traditional services with regard to knowledge base, structure, and process; and *(3)* stories that identified differences between SA and professional services and went on to articulate the belief that both were important in their personal recoveries.

Given the press in SA's community narrative for members to view SA and traditional services as complementary components of recovery, we were surprised to find that less than one-fourth of the members articulated the belief that both sources of support were key to their own recovery. Because this aspect of the narrative involves members' experiences in both SA and other mental health settings, we examined whether the nature of their stories was related to their level of involvement in either SA or the traditional mental health system. We found that members whose stories contained no opinions regarding SA and professional services tended to have less experience in SA, most having been members for less than 6 months. They were, however, deeply embedded in the traditional service system, with many living in supported housing. These members may not have been sufficiently exposed to SA to really experience how it differed from the other settings they were engaged in or to have adopted its community narrative.

At the other end of the spectrum, SA participants who articulated the need for both mutual-help and traditional services in their recovery were, not surprisingly, the most integrated into SA. With one exception, they had been members for more than 2 years and were currently group leaders. As one participant stated:

> But the keys I found out worked was seeing my therapist, seeing my doctor to get my medication and coming to these meetings … If you listen to your therapist, listen to your doctor and come to group, this meeting, with all three of them combined, it really, I have forgot my past. I'm more focused on my present and future now. This gives me hope.
>
> (Hughes, 2004, p. 82)

Those who recognized differences between SA and professional services but did not articulate the need for both showed a great variety of experience with regard to both their use of mental health services and their involvement in SA. Regardless of level of involvement and experience with the two types of settings, they recognized that they were receiving different benefits from them. They did not, however, appear to internalize SA's belief that both were essential to recovery.

Many of those whose stories were limited to a focus on the difference between SA and traditional services had been in SA for a long time; this suggests that exposure alone is not enough to facilitate the adoption of a community narrative. SA may have a more limited capacity to support this aspect of its narrative, as it involves members' experiences in both their own organization and in other service settings. SA can certainly provide members with support in their efforts to effectively access and utilize traditional services by keeping them updated regarding information about medication and treatment options and providing advice about how to interact with professionals. Ultimately, however, the extent to which members view traditional services as a necessary, helpful, and complementary aspect of their recovery is probably more influenced by the experiences they have had in those settings. Although SA's founder experienced traditional services as beneficial and ultimately supportive and complementary to her experience in SA, this experience is unfortunately not universal.

The Transformation of Personal Stories Through the Adoption of Community Narratives

The use of a narrative approach to understand recovery in SA gave voice to members' personal stories of recovery. We heard tales of personal journeys from anger and despair—through awareness, recognition, redefinition and transformation—to enhanced well-being and quality of life. Movement along the path of recovery was marked by many ups and downs; individuals visited and revisited the different phases of the process and experienced different phases simultaneously with regard to different aspects of their lives. The stories we heard were about a journey more than they were about an end-point. Although members described engagement in different phases of the process, the four- phase process fit all of the recovery stories.

Our findings regarding the process of recovery are quite consistent with those emerging from both the consumer and the psychosocial rehabilitation literature. Across consumers' stories of their own recovery experiences and a developing body of qualitative research, a new more optimistic view of recovery is emerging, which focuses on identity transformation (Anthony, 1993). It is emerging, however, amidst a relative absence of attention to or understanding of the contexts that facilitate positive identity transformation.

Although both consumers and researchers have identified factors or experiences that facilitate recovery (e.g., Anthony, 1993, 2000; Deegan, 1988; Sullivan, 1994), there has been little attention paid to the settings in which these experiences take place. Just as people do not experience their lives as a list of outcomes, they do not experience the meaning-making resources available to them as a list of facilitating factors. The beliefs, supports, and opportunities that promote recovery exist within the particular settings and contexts in which individuals live their lives.

Our findings suggest that individuals' stories of recovery are influenced by the availability of positive community narratives within the settings where they seek to find meaning in their experiences. The adoption of a narrative is facilitated by the presence of structures and processes that are consistent with its underlying message. This is particularly likely to be true when the community narrative of the setting is at odds with the dominant cultural narrative or with the community narratives of other important meaning-making contexts in individuals' lives. If most of the meaning-making resources in an individual's life are communicating a pessimistic message about recovery, it will take more than a hopeful story to counter that message. Settings that provide structural opportunities and support for living that hopeful story are more likely to act as an effective antidote.

Implications for Promoting Recovery

As social scientists, we can assist individuals who are living with a mental illness in developing more hopeful personal stories by focusing our attention on the contexts in which they are created. To date, efforts to facilitate recovery at a setting level have tended to focus on identifying elements of recovery that emerge from consumers' stories as guiding principles and new outcomes for the transformation of traditional service systems and settings (e.g., Anthony, 2000; Jacobsen & Curtis, 2000). We know from past experience, however, that the adoption of innovation in complex, institutionalized systems is slow and difficult (Quirk, Strosahl, Fitzpatrick, Casey, Hennessey, & Simon, 1995). Efforts to change the attitudes and behaviors of service providers, the types of knowledge valued in professional settings, and the power differential between consumers and professionals are likely to result in slow progress at best.

We must therefore be cautious in simply trying to apply new conceptualizations of recovery in contexts that are not consistent with them. The importance of hope in recovery is an excellent example of this. As Deegan (1988) points out, as much as we would like to, professionals can not manufacture hope and deliver it to people. True hope, in the face of the devastation that accompanies mental illness, comes from access to the lived experience of others who have engaged in recovery and found hope. Although we can add "increased hopefulness" to our list of positive outcomes, the experiences that engender hope (e.g., the support of others who have shared the experience, access to role models who are positively engaged in recovery, opportunities to engage in socially valued roles) are not experiences that are likely to be available in traditional mental health settings as they are currently structured.

The application of new recovery outcomes to systems and settings that are not structured to support them may actually act to undermine the very goal they are attempting to achieve. We run the risk of simply identifying another set of externally determined and potentially unattainable goals for those seeking to make meaning of the experience of living with a serious mental illness. The development of "self-acceptance," "hope," or "new life goals" are no more attainable than the return to independent work or living in the absence of structures and processes that support this identity transformation.

The goals of promoting both personal and social change with regard to our understanding of recovery from serious mental illness can perhaps be best served by turning our attention to articulating the community narratives of the settings where people search for meaning about mental illness. By doing so, we can uncover both settings that embrace tales of terror and those that embrace tales of optimism. By revealing the beliefs that underlie different contexts and the accompanying processes and structures that give life and power to these narratives, we bring to light their capacities to facilitate and impede recovery. This will allow consumers to better choose between the alternatives that are available to them and to recognize and negotiate between conflicting community and cultural narratives. It will also facilitate the possibility of real change in settings that seek to become more recovery-oriented.

Uncovering negative community and cultural narratives about recovery is one means of liberating people from them (Rappaport, 2000). The clear articulation of the community narratives of traditional mental health settings, such as the work done by Kloos (1999), brings to light the ways in which these settings may actually impede recovery. This understanding opens the possibility for change in the structures and narratives of these settings that are fundamentally incompatible with consumer-defined recovery processes and outcomes.

The articulation of setting narratives that already support the creation and adoption of hopeful stories of recovery is also essential for promoting recovery. In many cases, these are consumer-run settings (e.g., mutual-help organizations) where individuals engage in recovery without the assistance, presence, or interference of professionals. The alternative community narratives available in such settings are based on experiential knowledge (Borkman, 1976) and can act as antidotes to the stigma that dominates our cultural view of mental illness. The articulation of these narratives can help to strengthen existing recovery-oriented settings. Settings with clearly articulated beliefs and ideologies are less likely to be intentionally or unintentionally influenced by external forces (Oliver, 1991; Salem, Foster-Fishman, & Goodkind, 2002).

As consumer-run organizations interact more and more with the traditional service system, the potential for the dominant cultural and professional narratives to influence the community narratives and organizational structures of these alternative settings is great. Institutional (Scott, 1995) and resource dependency (Pfeffer & Salanick, 1978) theories suggest environmental beliefs and resources can have a powerful influence on the ideologies and structures of settings. We have already seen how interaction with more traditional settings has influenced SA's organizational development and expansion (Salem, Gant, & Campbell, 1998; Salem & Hughes, 2003; Salem, Reischl, & Weaver Randall, 2008). Better understanding of the meaning-making resources of mutual-help settings, as well as the structures and processes that support them, may help to protect alternative settings from the unintended influence of the dominant cultural and professional narratives that have been tales of terror for many people experiencing a serious mental illness.

Increased understanding of the narratives, structures, and processes that promote positive experiences of recovery, as well as the need for convergence between them, can also assist in the creation of new types of alternative settings. Although participating in SA is clearly a positive experience for those who choose to join, SA, like any mutual-help or consumer-based setting, is not for everyone. The goal is not necessarily to create more settings like SA but to create settings that facilitate the sharing of experiential knowledge and have the capacity to create community narratives and structures that embrace participants' goals and experiences. It is important that alternative settings do not simply provide predetermined and static narratives to their members but that they create contexts that nurture the ongoing development of these narratives.

Identification of recovery-promoting community narratives can also provide a blueprint for change in more traditional mental health settings. Analysis of the ways in which these narratives are compatible and incompatible with existing setting beliefs, practices, and structures can facilitate the adoption of innovation within traditional settings.

Finally, giving voice to the personal stories and community narratives of consumer-run settings makes these narratives more available to consumers, families, professionals, and the public. This is essential for transforming our dominant cultural narratives and introducing to the cultural dialogue new ideas about the positive meanings that can emerge from a diagnosis of serious mental illness and about the kinds of settings that facilitate a positive meaning-making process.

Contributions and Limitations of Narrative Research

The work described in this chapter focused primarily on two levels of analysis—SA's community narrative and members' personal stories—and on the top-down influence of the community narrative on member's stories. Narrative research also allows us to examine reciprocal influences at multiple levels of analysis. It can help us to understand how personal transformations facilitate the creation of alternative settings whose community narratives challenge existing dominant cultural narratives. The role SA's founder played in shaping the community narrative of SA is an example of this. A narrative approach allows us to understand recovery from serious mental illness as an interaction of individual, community, and cultural experiences.

Another important contribution of narrative research is that it is well-suited to reflect the diversity of human experience, as it allows individuals to tell their own stories. This helps to guard against our tendency to frame questions and interpret data within the framework of the dominant cultural narrative and gives voice to the perspectives of minority, marginalized, and stigmatized groups. Interestingly, in our analysis of personal stories, although there was diversity in the sample (57% women, 85% White, age range of 22 to 74 years old), differences did not emerge in the experiences of members from different demographic groups. In this context, it appears that the shared experience of having schizophrenia may be a more powerful referent group than other aspects of identity. As expressed by one member:

> Then everybody went around and told their story and I told my story, too. And when I left, I had this great feeling of relief, you know. Everything's gonna be OK. There are more people like me ... I had something in common with them, that I had with nobody else in my life.
>
> (Weaver Randall & Salem, 2005, p. 190)

We have also found support for the importance of this sense of identification in our quantitative research with SA. In survey research with both Michigan and national samples of SA participants, we have found that SA members' sense of identification with fellow participants (i.e., referent power) was predictive of members' perceptions that SA was helpful to them (Salem, Reischl, Gallacher, & Weaver Randall, 2000) and of their engagement in the different phases of recovery (Beeble & Salem, 2010). In this context, the unheard voices that a narrative approach helped to amplify were those of individuals living with the shame and social stigma of having schizophrenia.

The use of a narrative approach has allowed us to understand what is unique about SA as an organization and to give voice to members' personal stories of recovery. As with any methodology, however, its greatest strengths are also the source of its limitations (McGrath, 1981). Focusing on narratives and stories that are specific to one context can limit the utility and generalizability of our findings for the creation, support, and transformation of settings where those with serious mental illness seek to make meaning of their experiences. The understandings gained from this approach can provide a starting point for contextually sensitive quantitative research and evaluation. We have begun this work within SA by constructing a quantitative measure of recovery based on the four phases identified and using this measure to study change mechanisms in a national sample of SA groups. Our findings suggest that the utilization of context-specific recovery indices provides a more nuanced understanding of how settings facilitate recovery (Beeble & Salem, 2010). A next step includes exploring whether the recovery process identified in SA is generalizable to other consumer-run settings that share key elements of SA's community narrative.

FUTURE RESEARCH DIRECTIONS

We have already learned a great deal about how consumers experience recovery from serious mental illness. Their stories have both uncovered the negative impact of professional and cultural narratives about recovery and provided a new, more hopeful way of viewing the experience. Past research has focused on identifying common models of recovery across individuals. One important direction for future work is the identification of how personal stories of recovery vary in different settings, depending on the meaning-making resources available in those settings.

At the setting level, research that articulates the community narratives of the contexts in which consumers make meaning of their experience is clearly needed. Identification of community narratives helps to increase the access to, creation of, and influence of settings that promote positive stories of recovery. It also helps us to identify the changes that need to be made in many traditional settings to make them compatible with consumer experiences of recovery.

In our efforts to make alternative narratives available to consumers and to transform the narratives of traditional settings, we must understand how these narratives are supported within their settings. Research exploring the structures and processes of settings that support different aspects of a recovery narrative is needed. For example, some settings or processes within settings may be better suited to promoting early phases of recovery (e.g., acceptance), whereas others may support the development of new meanings or attainment of desired goals.

Increasing our understanding of how consumers develop positive recovery stories also requires exploration of how the different community narratives that individuals are exposed to across the settings they inhabit are consistent with, complementary to, or in conflict with one another and how individuals choose among them, integrate them, or apply them selectively in different contexts. Finally, across levels of analysis, we must attend to how individuals manage conflicting community and cultural narratives. For example, what allows individuals to adopt a positive story of recovery and maintain it in a culture that does not support it? In what circumstances does an alternative community narrative act as an effective antidote to the dominant cultural narrative and in what instances is it overwhelmed by that narrative? What processes enhance the capacity of the personal stories of individuals and the community narratives of settings to influence the dominant cultural narrative? What factors influence whether a particular individual will engage in a setting and what aspects of person–environment fit are most important to the adoption of positive personal stories? The answers to these and related questions will help to promote the personal and social change the consumer movement has already set in motion.

CONCLUSION

We started our collaboration with SA hoping to answer two "separate" questions—How does SA help its members? How does it expand and develop in its efforts to reach out to new members? Initially, we viewed these as separate questions with distinct methodologies and guiding theories. Each involved explanation and identification of constructs at multiple levels of analysis. Julian Rappaport's articulation of a narrative approach assisted us in reconceptualizing our efforts to understand SA. By applying a narrative framework, the complex became parsimonious. SA's community narrative emerged as a higher-level representation of the founders' personal story. The personal stories of members became adaptations of the community narrative. Key structures and processes emerged as the glue that binds these together into a holistic experience. The influence of narratives across levels of analysis became evident. The influence of traditional dominant cultural narratives and the community narratives of traditional organizations and institutions helped to explain the successes, frustrations, and changes SA experienced when it worked in and with more traditional contexts to reach individuals experiencing schizophrenia.

SA clearly provides its members with an alternative community narrative that challenges the dominant cultural narrative about recovery from serious mental illness. The organization is structured to support members in the challenging process of adopting this narrative and integrating it into their own personal stories. The stories of recovery we heard as a result of this surely describe personal transformations from tales filled with terror to tales that contain joy.

AUTHOR'S NOTE

I would like to gratefully acknowledge the contributions of Joanne Verbanic, Eric Hufnagel, The National Schizophrenia Foundation, and the leaders and members of Schizophrenics Anonymous who contributed to this work, as well as my collaborators, Tom Reischl, Katie Weaver Randall, Barbara Hughes, and Marisa Beeble. Funding for much of the work described in this manuscript came from the Ethel and James Flinn Foundation.

REFERENCES

Andresen, R., Oades, L., & Caputi, P. (2003). The experience of recovery from schizophrenia: Towards an empirically validated stage model. *Australia and New Zealand Journal of Psychiatry, 37,* 586–594.

Anthony, W. A. (1993). Recovery from mental illness: A guiding vision of the mental health service system in the 1990s. *Psychosocial Rehabilitation Journal, 16,* 11–23.

Anthony, W. A. (2000). A recovery oriented service system: Settting some system level standards. *Psychiatric Rehabilitation Journal, 24,* 159–168.

Arntson, P. & Droge, D. (1987). Social support in self-help groups: The role of communication in enabling perceptions of control. In *Communicating social support.* Albrecht, T. L. & Adelman, M. B. (Eds.), Beverly Hills, CA: Sage Publications.

Bandura, A. (1986). Social foundations of thought and action: A social cognitive theory. Englewood Cliffs, NJ: Prentice-Hall.

Baxter, E. A. & Diehl, S. (1998). Emotional Stages: Consumers and family members recovering from the trauma of mental illness. *Psychiatric Rehabilitation Journal, 21,* 349–355.

Beeble, M. A., & Salem, D. A. (2010). Understanding the phases of recovery from serious mental illness: The roles of referent and expert power in a mutual-help setting. *Journal of Community Psychology 37,* 249–267.

Borkman, T. (1976). Experiential knowledge: A new concept for analysis of self-help groups. *Social Science Review, 50,* 445–456.

Borkman, T. J. (1990). Experiential, professional and lay frames of reference. In T. J. Powell (Ed.), *Working with self help.* Silver Spring, MD: NASW Press.

Borkman, T. (1999). *Understanding self-help/mutual aid: Experiential learning in the commons.* New Brunswick: Rutgers University Press.

Chamberlin, J. (1990). *On our own: Patient controlled alternatives to the mental health system.* New York: McGraw-Hill.

Corrigan, P. W., & Ralph, R. O. (2005). Introduction: Recovery as consumer vision and research paradigm. In R. O. Ralph & P. W. Corrigan (Eds.), *Recovery in mental illness: Broadening our understanding of wellness* (pp. 3–18). Washington, DC: American Psychological Association.

Davidson, L., Sells, D., Sangster, S., & O'Connell, M. (2005). Qualitative studies of recovery: What we can learn from the person. In R. O. Ralph & P. W. Corrigan (Eds.), *Recovery in mental illness: Broadening our understanding of wellness* (pp. 147–170). Washington, DC: American Psychological Association.

Deegan, P. E. (1988). Recovery: The lived experience of rehabilitation. *Psychosocial Rehabilitation Journal, 11,* 11–19.

Deegan, P. E. (1993). Recovering our sense of value after being labeled mentally ill. *Journal of Psychosocial Nursing, 31,* 7–11.

Deegan, P. (1996). Recovery as a journey of the heart. *Psychiatric Rehabilitation Journal, 19,* 91–97.

Deegan, P. (1997). Recovery and empowerment for people with psychiatric disabilities. *Social Work in Health Care, 25,* 11–24.

DeSisto, M. J., Harding, C. M., McCormick, R. V., Ashikaga, T., & Brooks, G. W. (1995). The Maine and Vermont three-decade studies of serious mental illness: II. Longitudinal course comparisons. *British Journal of Psychiatry, 167,* 338–481.

Fraser, M. E. (1994). Educating the public about mental illness: What will it take to get the job done? *Innovations and Research, 3,* 29–31.

Harding, C. M., Brooks, G. W., Ashikaga, T, Strauss, T. S., & Breier, A. (1987). The Vermont longitudinal study of persons with severe mental illness: II. Long term outcomes of subjects who retrospectively met DSM-III criteria for schizophrenia. *American Journal of Psychiatry, 144,* 727–735.

Harding, C. M. & Zahniser, J. H. (1994). Empirical correction of seven myths about schizophrenia with implications for treatment. *Acta Psychiatrica Scandanavica, 90* (Suppl 384), 140–146.

Harding, C. M., Zubin, J., & Strauss, J. S. (1987). Chronicity in schizophrenia: Fact, partial fact or artifact? *Hospital and Community Psychiatry, 38,* 477–486.

Hughes, B. (2004). *Consumer perspectives on the role of self-help and traditional services in the lives of people with schizophrenia.* Unpublished doctoral dissertation, Michigan State University, East Lansing, MI.

Jacobsen, N., & Curtis, L. (2000). Recovery as policy in mental health services: Strategies emerging from states. *Psychiatric Rehabilitation Journal, 23,* 333–341.

Katz, A. H. (1993). *Self help in America. A social movement perspective.* New York: Twayne Publishers.

Kloos, B. (1999). *Cultivating identity: Meaning making in the context of residential treatment settings for persons with histories of psychological disorder.*

Unpublished doctoral dissertation, University of Illinois at Urbana-Champaign, Champaign, IL.

Levine, M. (1988). An analysis of mutual assistance. *American Journal of Community Psychology, 16,* 167–183.

Lieberman, R. P., & Kopelowicz, A. (2005). Recovery from schizophrenia: A criterion based definition. In R. O. Ralph & P. W. Corrigan (Eds.), *Recovery in mental illness: Broadening our understanding of wellness* (pp. 101–130). Washington, DC: American Psychological Association.

Loveland, D, Weaver Randall, K., & Corrigan, P. W. (2005) *Research methods for exploring and assessing recovery.* In R. O. Ralph & P. W. Corrigan (Eds.), *Recovery in mental illness: Broadening our understanding of wellness* (pp.19–59). Washington, DC: American Psychological Association.

Lincoln, Y. S., & Guba, E. G. (1989). *Fourth generation evaluation.* Newbury Park, CA: Sage.

Maton, K. I., & Salem, D. A. (1995). Organizational characteristics of empowering community settings: A multiple case study approach. *American Journal of Community Psychology, 23,* 631–656.

McGrath, J. E. (1981). Dilemmatics: The study of research choices and dilemmas. *American Behavioral Scientist, 25,* 154–179.

Miles, M. B., & Huberman, M. A. (1994). *Qualitative analysis: An expanded sourcebook.* Thousands Oaks, CA: Sage Publications.

Oliver, C. (1991). Strategic response to institutional processes. *Academy of Management* Review, *16,* 145–179.

Perlick, D. A., Rosenheck, R. A., Clarkin, J. F., Sirey, J. A., Salahi, J., Streuning, E. L., & Link, B. G. (2001). Stigma as a barrier to recovery: Adverse effects of perceived stigma on social adaptation of persons diagnosed with bipolar affective disorder. *Psychiatric Services, 52,* 1627–1632.

Petite, D., & Triolo, A. M. (1999). Illness as evolution: The search for identity and meaning in the recovery process. *Psychiatric Rehabilitation Journal, 22,* 255–262.

Pfeffer, J., & Salanick, G. R. (1978). *The external control of organizations.* New York: Harper Collins.

Quirk, M. P., Strosahl, K., Fitzpatrick, W., Casey, M. T., Hennessey, S., & Simon, G. (1995). Quality and customers: Type 2 changes in mental health delivery within health care reform. *The Journal of Mental Health Administration, 22,* 441–445.

Rappaport, J. (1993). Narrative studies, personal stories, and identity transformation in the mutual help context. *Journal of Applied Behavioral Science, 29,* 230–256.

Rappaport, J. (1995). Empowerment meets narrative: Listening to stories and creating settings. *American Journal of Community Psychology, 23,* 795–807.

Rappaport, J. (1998). The art of social change: Community narratives as re-
    sources for individual and collective identity. In X. B. Arriaga &
    S. Oskamp (Eds.), *Addressing community problems: Psychosocial research
    and intervention* (pp. 225–246). Thousand Oaks, CA: Sage.

Rappaport, J. (2000). Community narratives: Tales of terror and joy. *American
    Journal of Community Psychology, 28,* 1–24.

Riessman, F. (1965). The "helper" therapy principle. *Social Work, 10,* 27–32.

Salem, D. A., Foster-Fishman, P. G., & Goodkind, J. R. (2002). Adoption of
    innovation in collective advocacy organizations. *American Journal of
    Community Psychology, 30,* 681–710.

Salem, D. A., Gant, L., & Campbell, R. (1998). The introduction of mutual-
    help groups in group homes for the mentally ill: Barriers to participation.
    Community Mental Health Journal, 34, 419–429.

Salem, D. A., & Hughes, B. (2003, June). *The development of SA groups in
    forensic settings.* Paper presented at the ninth biennial conference on
    Community Research and Action, Las Vegas, New Mexico.

Salem, D. A., Reischl, T. M., Gallacher, F., & Weaver Randall, K. (2000). The
    role of referent and expert power in mutual help. *American Journal of
    Community Psychology, 28 (3),* 303–323.

Salem, D. A., Reischl, T., & Weaver Randall, K. (2008). The impact of profes-
    sional partnership on the development of a mutual-help organization.
    American Journal of Community Psychology, *42,* 179–191.

Salem, D. A., Reischl, T. M., & Weaver Randall, K. (2000). *Schizophrenics
    Anonymous evaluation final report: Member engagement and change.* East
    Lansing, MI: Michigan State University, Department of Psychology.

Schizophrenics Anonymous. (1999). *Schizophrenics Anonymous: A self-help
    support* group. Southfield, MI: Mental Health Association in Michigan.

Schizophrenics Anonymous. (2003). Retrieved June 6, 2003 from http://
    www.sanonymous.org.

Schizophrenics Anonymous. (2005). Retrieved May 14, 2005, from http://
    www.nsfoundation.org/sa.

Scott, W. R. (1995). *Institutions and organizations.* Thousand Oaks, CA: Sage.

Spaniol, L., Gagne, C., & Koehler, M. (1997). Recovery from serious mental
    illness: What is it and how to assist people in their recovery. *Continuum,
    4,* 3–15.

Spaniol, L. S., Wewiorski, N. J., Gagne, C., & Anthony, W. A. (2002). The pro-
    cess of recovery from schizophrenia. *International Journal of Psychiatry,
    14,* 327–336.

Sullivan, W. P. (1994). A long and winding road: The process of recovery
    from severe mental illness. *Innovations and Research, 3,* 19–27.

Torgalsboen, A., & Rund, B. R. (2002). Lessons learned from three studies of recovery from schizophrenia. *International Review of Psychiatry, 14,* 312–317.

Weaver Randall, K. (2000). *Understanding recovery from schizophrenia in a mutual help setting.* Unpublished masters thesis, Michigan State University, East Lansing, MI.

Weaver Randall, K., & Salem, D. A. (2005). Mutual help groups and recovery: The influence of setting on participants' experience of recovery. In R. O. Ralph & P. W. Corrigan (Eds.), *Recovery in mental illness: Broadening our understanding of wellness* (pp. 173–206). Washington, DC: American Psychological Association.

Young, S. L., & Ensing, D. S. (1999). Exploring recovery from the perspective of people with psychiatric disabilities. *Psychiatric Rehabilitation Journal, 22,* 219–231.

Zimmerman, M. (2000). Empowerment theory. In J. Rappaport & E. Seidman (Eds.), *Handbook of community psychology* (pp. 43–63), New York: Klewer.

7

"I Came to Tell You of My Life": Narrative Expositions of "Mental Health" in an American Indian Community

Joseph P. Gone

In the summer of 1994, I inaugurated a series of scholarly investigations concerning the relationship between culture and mental health among my own people, the Gros Ventre of the Fort Belknap Indian reservation in north central Montana.[1] Since then, whether formulating Gros Ventre cultural identity in distinctively Gros Ventre terms (J. P. Gone, 1996, 1999, 2006b; J. P. Gone, Miller, & Rappaport, 1999) or comparing Gros Ventre community discourse with dominant professional discourse regarding psychological distress and its amelioration (J. P. Gone, 2004a, 2006c, 2007, 2008b), narrative representations of self, identity, social relations, community history, and persistent spirituality have figured centrally in my endeavor to "give voice" to an indigenous tradition. Moreover, it is crucial to recognize that this tradition—my community's tradition, my own tradition—was all but decimated by Euro-American colonization. Thus, the significance of recovering our collective voice and making it resound on the northern Plains once more lies in the transformative power of self-expression. For it is self-expression,

1 These investigations proceeded in the context of several years of superlative mentorship offered by Julian Rappaport in his capacity as my graduate advisor at the University of Illinois. My other formal graduate advisor, the developmental cultural psychologist Peggy J. Miller, similarly played an extremely significant role in shaping and directing these investigations.

as just one manifestation of self-determination, that retains the power to refashion coherence in the plan and purpose of a people, to rebuild connectedness between community members and with outsiders, and to rechart lines of cultural continuity to an indigenous way of life across the colonial abyss of history. Insofar as the epidemic of distress, despair, and demoralization that afflicts so many in my community emerged in the wake of a strategic extermination of the bison, a punishing confinement to our reservation, and a coerced assimilation to Euro-American values and beliefs, some of us audaciously imagine that our restoration to wellness will occur through processes of "decolonization" (Wilson & Yellow Bird, 2005). Decolonization is simply the reflective, intentional, and collective self-examination undertaken by a formerly colonized people that actively sustains their reassertion of continuity with the pre-colonial past toward a distinctive and purposeful post-colonial future.

As one contribution to the decolonization effort, this chapter will literally recover the voice of one of our people's most influential 19th-century ritual leaders. In doing so, I intend to recapture the contours of social, psychological, and spiritual experience that once constituted distinctive kinds of Gros Ventre subjectivity (i.e., lived and felt engagements with the world) and that might today inspire the formulation of therapeutic practices and processes uniquely suited for our vibrant restoration to wellness. More specifically, in this chapter I will first recount an extended vignette concerning the final days of our most accomplished Gros Ventre medicine person, Buffalo Bull Lodge. Next, I will undertake a cultural analysis of one genre of Gros Ventre narrative exemplified by the final words of Bull Lodge— namely, the recounting of war stories as a particular instance of the narrative recirculation of *vitality*. In doing so, I will contextualize such *communications of vitality* in terms of several features of Gros Ventre cosmology and associated ethnopsychology, some of which persist among contemporary Gros Ventres today. Subsequently, I will explore how a proper appreciation of this indigenous ethnopsychology might give rise to an alternative construal of the "therapeutic" among mental health professionals and related service providers who work in our community. Finally, I will conclude with a few general observations regarding the promise of community psychology— especially in its recognition and celebration of narrative and empowerment— for assisting contemporary Native American communities in their efforts toward collective decolonization and communal healing.

CONFRONTING DEATH: THE FINAL WORDS OF BULL LODGE

In the winter of 1886, the prominent Gros Ventre leader Bull Lodge (ca. 1802–1886) was informed in a dream that his "time here on this earth" had ended, that he had but 8 days of life remaining, and that he should put his affairs in order (F. P. Gone, 1942). On the night that he was to die, Bull Lodge gathered his family in his lodge, nestled his infant granddaughters on the bed beside him, and began to talk (*see* J. P. Gone, 2006a, for an extended treatment). According to his favorite daughter, Water Snake, "he told many stories of his escapades and the many thrilling experiences he encountered during his past …, as if reviewing his life." To be sure, there would be many thrills to recount in a "review" of his remarkable journey, including perhaps how Bull Lodge was reared in poverty but nevertheless sought to advance his station through childhood devotion to the community's sacred Feathered Pipe. He was "first contacted by the supernatural" at the age of 12 years and obtained assurance that he would be "powerful on this earth," only later to receive instruction at the age of 17 years to begin fasting, praying, and sacrificing atop seven buttes for gifts of "supernatural" power. At the age of 30 years, he was directed to lead a series of war parties that established his renowned military record, and at the age of 40 years he was inspired by compassion (or "pity") to "doctor" a relative using the ceremony gifted him by the Butte Beings. At this stage of his life, he was recognized as one of the most powerful medicine persons on the northern Plains, able even to control the weather. In his later years, he was appointed as the ritual Keeper of the sacred Pipe to which he had devoted himself as a boy. It was not until closer to the end of his life, however, that he was gifted with the ritual knowledge to ensure his own resurrection. Finally, at the age of 84 years, he was notified that he would travel to the Big Sand (i.e., pass away) before daybreak 8 days later. Even among the Gros Ventre, these were thrilling experiences indeed.

From a contemporary perspective it is tempting to conclude that Bull Lodge, in these final hours of his earthly existence, undertook these narrative excursions to celebrate his distinguished achievements in life, to summarize his life's "experiences" for the sake of his assembled progeny, or to consolidate his diverse "escapades" into a coherent account one last time. Elsewhere, I have expressed my reservations about these potential motivations (J. P. Gone, 2006a), at least to the degree that they emerge from and depend on forms of selfhood grounded in modernity. That is, I find it unlikely that this remarkable "narrative event" (Jakobson, 1971, as cited in Bauman, 1986) was the simple expression of what might be called the autobiographical impulse, a modern rhetorical formation involving the desire and obligation of the individual to reflexively represent self and experience in accordance with the aesthetics of consistency, comprehensiveness, and continuity. Instead, Bull Lodge hailed from a society in which the path to status—living "like a man," in words attributed to him—required almost relentless public consideration (and ultimate ratification) of one's actions and achievements. Indeed, within pre-reservation Gros Ventre society there was little differentiation between the public and private domains of life (which has become a hallmark of modernity). Thus, there would appear to have been little need within this close-knit community for the crafting of one's autobiographical narrative to summarize in reflexive terms a personal history of self-relevant events. As an alternative, I have suggested that this final event of narration served the instrumental purpose of extending good health and long life for his loved ones. I believe the key to understanding the generative power of this sort of narrative will become readily apparent through careful consideration of the actual stories that Bull Lodge was reported to have recounted.

Once the family had assembled on the final evening before his appointed death, Water Snake explained that her father first related a story in which his long-time rival (or "enemy-friend"), Sits Like A Woman, had led Bull Lodge and some other Gros Ventre warriors on several days' journey across the Montana prairies to raid the Crow people to the southeast. This war party had yet to encounter the enemy, and so had hidden in a coulee for a night's rest. As apparently recounted by Bull Lodge, the story described how an owl—a harbinger of death among many Plains peoples—warned the party of imminent danger (and here, for the sake of concrete illustration of the kinds of narrative with which we are here concerned, I will quote words attributed to Bull Lodge rather extensively):

> We had already settled for the night, and had made a temporary shelter out of dead falls of small poles and brush and rye grass, and had a fire going, when out of the near brush we heard an owl hoot. This owl would say my name, then would hoot, and after the owl had repeated this two or three times, I told the party, "That owl you hear is saying my name." So Sits Like [A] Woman called a retreat. He said, "Get your things together, and we'll get out of here. That owl ain't doing that for nothing." So we got ready, and all went out as careful as we can without making much noise. And the night was cloudy and exceptionally dark, so in order that no one would stray off, he ordered us to hold one another's hands. We had camped on a small stream some distance away from the mountains. So he, Sits Like [A] Woman, was on the lead, and he led us to the mountains. When we reached them we came to a cliff of rock. So we looked around and found a nice secluded spot, and sat down to wait for early dawn.
>
> As we sat there for a little while, we noticed dirt and small rocks rolling down on us. So one of the men said, "I'll look around." He went along the cliff a ways, and pretty soon he shot [his rifle]. After he shot, we could hear something rolling down near where we sat. And [it] rolled on down past us. No one moved or paid any attention to it. The man returned and sat down. And when

daylight was so we could see pretty good, one of the men went to the spot where we heard [that] the rolling thing [had] stopped. He called and said, "It's a mountain goat." By then, the light was good enough so we could see quite a ways. Then we heard a commotion at the spot where we were early that night and [had] left from. Shots could be heard, and war cries, and yells. And all of a sudden the noise stopped. It must have been when [the enemy] found out [that] there was no one there. As we watched, we seen them ride away from there, and we could recognize them as Crow Indians. After the Crow Indians had gone their way, we butchered the mountain goat and had a big feed.

(F. P. Gone, 1942, pp. 8–10)

At the conclusion of this narrative, Bull Lodge ordered a meal for everyone and then requested fresh attire for his infant granddaughters so he could receive and kiss them. Calling them by name—an unusual formality, as kinship terms were the customary form of address—he carefully arranged them upon his own pillow before proceeding. It was then, with his grandbabies beside him, that Bull Lodge recounted his "escapades." Curiously, however, the story that Water Snake later recalled in the greatest detail from that night barely involved her father but focused instead on the heroic tenacity of a Gros Ventre warrior named Bobtail Horse, who joined a raiding party against the Piegan people to the west. Following an act of almost reckless courage, Bobtail Horse—left for dead by his companions—barely escaped from the Piegan, only to spend the next several weeks making his way on foot (and, eventually, on hands and knees) across an ocean of prairie to the Gros Ventre camps. Three revenge raids later (making four engagements in total), Bobtail Horse was killed in battle. Interesting. Here was unquestionably another "thrilling experience" related by Bull Lodge to his family, but this particular "escapade"—comprising nearly half of what Water Snake later reported when recalling her father's final words—contained very little self-referential content. Instead, what seems to fuse these particular "narrated events" (Bauman, 1986) into a recognizable speech genre is their characterization not as representations of reflexivity but as communications of vitality.

COMMUNICATING LIFE: AN EXPLORATION OF ETHNOPSYCHOLOGY

The extended historical vignette just reviewed affords the opportunity to explore and to systematize the genre of Gros Ventre narrative that I characterize as the *communication of vitality*. Moreover, nuanced appreciation of this genre requires analytical attention to 19th-century Gros Ventre cosmology and (for my purposes here) aspects of an attending ethnopsychology of vitality. The English word *vitality* is not really adequate here. Indeed, English-speaking Gros Ventres actually invented an adjective more than a century ago for the concept I mean to denote: "moose" (which has nothing to do with the animal). This adjective denotes that quality of experience in which difficulty, hardship, and overwhelming odds are met head-on with gusto, talent, energy, and ambition, such that individual agency ultimately prevails. Not surprisingly, the metaphor for such triumphant agency is drawn from the battlefield and exemplified by a "fierce" warrior charging into the enemy despite being outnumbered; it was this ascribed ferocity that the word "moose" was intended to preserve once the Gros Ventre language began its abrupt decline in the face of strategic Euro-American suppression. I choose here to tentatively translate this notion as *vitality* rather than *ferocity* because the former connotes less in terms of violence than it does in terms of *animus*. To fully appreciate what Bull Lodge was up to in choosing to recount exploits of war to his assembled family during their final gathering, I must first attempt to explicate the cultural significance of animus or vitality—and its communication—within historical Gros Ventre experience. The reader should note, however, that I am necessarily summarizing, synthesizing, interpolating, and extrapolating from my first-hand experience in the community as well as the extant ethnographic record in an effort to reconstruct the largely implicit philosophical and religious underpinnings of pre-reservation Gros Ventre life—I am aware of no other source (whether living or departed) or resource (whether oral or written) that has addressed these questions at this level of abstraction and in summary format.[2]

The Eruption of Liveliness

Vitality then is that agentic quality of persons that is demonstrated through distinctive acts of courage, tenacity, aspiration, and industry—it is the eruption of liveliness that prevails over frightful ordeal or bitter circumstance. Among the Gros Ventres there was no more revered personal attribute, and rank and status within the community depended on publicly ratified expressions of such vitality (as accompanied by habitual practices of generosity and redistribution; for more detail, *see* Cooper, 1957; Flannery, 1953; Fowler, 1987; and J. P. Gone & Alcántara, 2010). More specifically, Gros Ventres recognized three distinct means to uncommon expressions of vitality: ability,

---

2 My attempts to systematize and consolidate these rather abstract relations within Gros Ventre cosmology are inspired and influenced by the important work of Jeff Anderson (2001) concerning knowledge and "life movement" among our tribal kin, the Northern Arapaho.

prayer, and power (Cooper, 1957). Ability was simply an individual's inherent strengths, skills, and talents as perfected through exercise and attention.
Prayer was the relatively routine personal expression of desires and requests
to the Supreme Being, the One Above, Who maintained active influence in
human affairs. Power was the means by which human persons might exercise
extraordinary—that is, superhuman—prowess in war, doctoring, gambling, or
seduction, usually as the result of extraordinary gifts of ritual knowledge to
individuals from other-than-human Persons (Who were all ultimately
accountable to the One Above). Ideal expressions of vitality depended principally on ability, as augmented by the efficacy of prayer. Power as a means
for expressing vitality and realizing ambition was frequently sought but (as
we shall soon see) entailed a rather undesirable consequence.

If *expressions* of vitality were the means to rank and status among the
Gros Ventre people, they also signified by implication the most coveted gift
of all: *extensions* of vitality, or long and prosperous lives. All tribal ceremonies
included petitions for long, abundant lives for members of the community;
personal devotions were just as likely to involve such entreaties. The Supreme
Being, the One Above, the "Owner of Life," actively determined how long
individuals would live, deciding to "cut off" life for those who transgressed
the moral order or to extend life on behalf of those for whom He felt compassion (or "pity"). According to one of my ancestors, a former Pipe Keeper
named Lame Bull, "a man lives, not his own life, but according to what is
given and wished by [the Supreme Being]; a man has what he has by the
wish of the One Above" (Cooper, 1957, p. 6). Thus, life is not endogenous to
humans—we do not possess even our own lives—but life is gifted by the One
Above, the Original Vitality, if you will. Furthermore, the means of life's
allocation to humans is the Supreme Being's *wish*. That is, the Original
Vitality distributes life through the exercise of will or thought; not surprisingly, then, the Owner of Life was also known to the Gros Ventres as the
"One Who Controls All By Thought." And although this instrumental quality
of "thought," "will," or "wish" clearly originates with the Supreme Being (perhaps as the Prime Thinker and Archetypal Agent), it similarly applies to
human thought or wish, albeit to a much less potent degree. In sum, life itself
is controlled, distributed, and sustained by wish of the Prime Thinker. The
essence of power, then, is the efficacious concentration of thought or will or
wish for either generative or destructive purposes in the world.

The Power of Thought

Within the philosophical explications of elderly Gros Ventres who reflected
on their "old way of life" in the mid-20th century (Cooper, 1957, p. v), there

remained evident ambiguity regarding whether this instrumental power of thought, when exercised by humans, was properly characterized as a form of action or a form of supplication. Certainly, Gros Ventres acknowledged instances of association between the two, as when a young man in this age-graded society would, in tears, approach very old individuals with the gift of a pipe and receive in return these elders' especially powerful prayers to the Supreme Being for long life on the young person's behalf. These elders' prayers were deemed unusually efficacious because their own long lives—their uncommon vitality—attested to their knowledge of how best to move the Owner of Life to grant extensions of vitality. Here, then, is an example of human wish or thought, channeled to the One Above through prayer on behalf of another, that could effect *a redistribution of life itself.* In contrast, Keepers of the sacred Pipes (such as Lame Bull or Bull Lodge), who by virtue of their specialized ritual knowledge regularly interacted with powerful other-than-human Persons, were admonished upon their selection to these high offices to strictly control their thoughts and words so as not to *inadvertently* harm others who might give relatively innocuous offense. As ritual authorities, these most knowledgeable of humans were deemed potentially dangerous because their facility with power—that is, with the efficacious concentration of thought for instrumental purposes—might amplify their otherwise commonplace annoyance, resentment, or jealousy into "bad luck" for others. In this instance, at least, it seems unlikely that inadvertent harm wrought by the power of undisciplined thought would involve direct supplication of other-then-human Persons as such.

In the end, what seems indisputable is that Gros Ventres recognized thought or wish as *instrumental*—that is, potentially generative or destructive—in the lives of humans, depending on *how it was exercised* and *by whom.* Allow me to suggest that the *how* of such efficacious activity is explained in part by *who* was understood to exercise the power of thought most potently. The identification of Pipe Keepers and elders as especially influential in their thoughts and prayers for others indexes a hierarchy of social relations in which certain humans enjoyed greater facility with the instrumental power of thought than others. This facility was most closely associated with age, owing to the specialized knowledge—especially ritual knowledge—that was required for the activities and responsibilities that characterized later life in this age-graded society (comprised of seven ranks for males). Nevertheless, within this hierarchy of social relations, human beings as a group occupied the lowest orders of efficacy or influence in the cosmos, whereas the Prime Thinker ranked highest in the hierarchy, and a host of other-than-human Persons—the Four Holy Old Men, the Sun, the Thunder Being, and so on—ranked in-between. This ordering of beings by their agentic influence implies certain normative principles of interpersonal interaction: relatively less knowledgeable (and therefore less potent) persons (especially humans, particularly the young) must demonstrate *respect* (through deference, supplication, sacrifice, ritual obligation, and so forth) to more powerful others (including older, more knowledgeable humans, but especially the much more knowledgeable other-than-human Persons), who in turn respond with *pity* (that is, compassion accompanied by the obligation to give) (*see* Anderson, 2001). Expressions of pity thus involve gifts of knowledge—often ritual knowledge—to those who otherwise lack adequate means for amplifying thought or wish for generative (or destructive) purposes. In sum, social relations throughout the cosmos are determined by rank in accordance with agentic potency (or power of will)—respect is properly conveyed upward through this graduated hierarchy, whereas pity is expressed downward, resulting in the redistribution of knowledge to humans for achieving increased agentic efficacy.

The Role of Ritual

If this hierarchy of agentic efficacy structures social relations within the cosmos and explains who is best positioned to exercise the power of thought, how is it that such thought might be most potently exercised by relatively powerless humans for instrumental purposes in the world? I suspect that the means are by now self-evident. Because unaided human thought is limited in its instrumental efficacy, individual efforts typically require amplification to most reliably influence everyday affairs. Such amplification occurs most effectively through the application of specialized knowledge in the form of ritual practice. Such practice was central to Gros Ventre life, particularly in the annual rites and ceremonies involving the two sacred Pipes (known as the "Flat Pipe" and the "Feathered Pipe," respectively). As a result of the routine respect shown these Pipes through devotion and ritual by their knowledgeable Keepers as well as the community more generally, these other-than-human Persons, gifted to the Gros Ventres by the One Above and the Thunder Being respectively, helped to ensure the longevity, abundance, and vitality of the community. Additional rituals were gifted to the community for similar purposes, including the Sacrifice Lodge (or so-called Sundance), the six men's lodges that structured the age-grades, the Old Women's Lodge, and so on (Cooper, 1957).

Beyond these officially sanctioned ceremonies, and owing principally to the ethos of pursuing ambition and expressing vitality, many Gros Ventres independently sought personal gifts of specialized knowledge from other-than-human Persons to get ahead in life (whether by doctoring ability, gambling luck, romantic influence, or war honors). Not surprisingly, these less conventional solicitations of ritual knowledge for personal (and perhaps even "selfish") achievement (after the manner of Bull Lodge's vision quests) were actively admonished among the Gros Ventres, for although knowledge obtained in this fashion might lead to the efficacious amplification of thought toward esteemed achievements of various kinds, such endeavors also represented a compromise of vitality, a crutch (so to speak) that Gros Ventres believed might literally shorten one's lifespan. This is the deleterious consequence I alluded to earlier—namely, that power is dangerous, even life-threatening, precisely because it requires such sophisticated knowledge to manage appropriately. In this regard, Lame Bull observed, "It is not good to ask that kind of career. It would be a life misspent and would be dearly paid for. Man's dearest possession is life, and this would be cut off" (Cooper, 1957, p. 266). Evidently, then, it is important to distinguish between two prospects for the amplification of thought. On one hand, amplifications of thought through applications of authorized knowledge formally gifted by the One Above were consistently generative of life itself. On the other hand, the extra-conventional (and perhaps self-focused or selfishly obtained) knowledge individually solicited from a variety of other-than-human Persons, although temporarily useful to its human "owners," was corrosive to life itself.

And yet, this efficacious amplification of human thought or wish was not *solely* the product of high ceremony or applied ritual knowledge. As we have already seen, the prayers of more knowledgeable people—that is, older people—to the One Above were seen to be efficacious in obtaining blessings, especially long life. In addition, personal devotion and supplication to the One Above was also valued in this regard. Furthermore, *collective* thought against an individual might be potently instrumental. According to Lamebull's son, The Boy, "If a man does something of which the people disapprove very much, their *thought* is against him. They *think* badly of him. Against this mass thinking, his own thinking cannot stand" (Cooper, 1957, p. 366, italics in the original). Lamebull's grandson, Thomas Main, added, "The Gros Ventres thought the psychological effect of public opinion is so great and intense on the one on whom it was trained that it shortened his life… . It was definitely known by the Gros Ventres that they actually thought people to death" (p. 367). Clearly then, human thought did not require ritual amplification to achieve instrumental purposes. Even The Boy acknowledged that "two people may have a battle of thinking; the outcome will depend on how each is developed in his thinking, on their respective powers of thought" (p. 366). Thus, although ritual amplification of human thought may have been the most potent method for ensuring its instrumental effects in the world, practiced or disciplined human wish might realize its potential through other means of expression as well.

The Communication of Vitality

As the vignette of Bull Lodge's death illustrates, one such alternative means of expression appears to have been the previously described communications of vitality—that is, narratives of agentic triumph in which thought or wish or will had become *instrumentally manifest in human action*. This genre of speech was best exemplified in the "war story." The occasions in Gros Ventre life that required the recitation of war stories were so numerous that those without such honors necessarily receded to the shadows of society (Flannery, 1953)—indeed, the prominent man was one whose "wrist would be made slim" from being pulled to his feet in gatherings to recount his experiences in battle. War experiences were recounted when men returned from successful raids to a jubilant community; when scouts returned from their dangerous expeditions with news of the enemy; when men's societies publicly competed with one another for attention or accolades; when the large tree chosen as the center pole for the Sacrifice Lodge was felled; when a new lodge was erected for the first time; when an individual, in contravention of protocol, desired to take unconsumed food from a Pipe Keeper's lodge; when names were first bestowed or changed; and when children's ears were first pierced. Common to many of these occasions was the neutralization of potentially destructive power (e.g., in the encounter of war dangers, such as the felling of the center pole for the Sacrifice Lodge, which symbolized the killing of an enemy) or the dispensation of potentially generative power (e.g., the naming of a child, which was accompanied by prayers for long, abundant life). Above all, as commemorations of triumphant agency in which mortal danger had been neutralized by overwhelming vitality, such narrative events retained some capacity to circulate and redistribute to the assembled audience *at least some measure of that same vitality*—the generative manifestation of thought or wish—that had made possible the very actions portrayed in the narrated events themselves. So it was that among the Gros Ventre, certain kinds of narratives—and the efficacious power of thought these tellings simultaneously commemorate and express— *literally imparted life.*

Returning then to that remarkable winter night in 1886, occasioned by the fading vitality of an unusually knowledgeable human being, I suspect it now seems evident why in the intimacy of his family lodge, Buffalo Bull Lodge, would—mere hours before he was to die—assemble his relatives, place his grandbabies beside him on his bed, and recount tales distinguished not by their reflexivity but by their vitality. Indeed, as communications of vitality, these tellings both collapse and transcend the distinction between semantics and pragmatics by concurrently *(1)* representing specific historical events, *(2)* inspiring his beloved kin to similar acts of triumphant agency, and *(3)* enlivening or empowering his cherished relatives for an abundant and accomplished longevity. In this light, we must recognize that Bull Lodge himself had been the prior recipient of so generative a gift.

More specifically, Water Snake reported that her father had earlier received "supernatural" instructions for conducting ceremonies that his followers could use to achieve his resurrection from the dead:

> One night my Father had a vision in his sleep. He saw an old man standing at a distance on the horizon of a low hill.... Then the old man spoke, saying, "I came to tell you of my life. I give it to you. You will live until you die of old age, but before that [appointed] time you will [first] pass away in order that you may demonstrate the [superhuman] power which I am giving you, the power to arise after you have passed away [to then live out your allotted lifespan]."
>
> (F. P. Gone, 1942, pp. 2–3)

In this resurrection vision, it is significant that the old Person Who appeared to Bull Lodge expressly stated: "I came to tell you of my life. I give it to you. You will live until you die of old age." Here we see that *telling equals giving*. This then is the essence of such communications (in both senses of the word): *expressions* of vitality, recounted in narrative form in the presence of others, yield *extensions* of vitality for them as well. Moreover, the cultural residue of this speech genre—reflecting both its cosmological and ethnopsychological underpinnings—endures among some contemporary Gros Ventres and suggests important possibilities for collective decolonization and communal healing today.

COMMENCING REVITALIZATION: CONTEMPORARY MENTAL HEALTH CONSIDERATIONS

The thrust of the preceding cultural analysis was to demonstrate how nuanced scholarly attention to facets of indigenous ethnopsychology can be seen to necessitate an alternative construal of the therapeutic project within the context of broader decolonization efforts. To be sure, it would be difficult to *over*emphasize the havoc wreaked among the Gros Ventre by processes of Euro-American colonization.

The Demise of a Cultural Legacy?

Subsequent to his account of the heroic saga of Bobtail Horse on that historic night, Bull Lodge shifted his talk to the revelation of disturbing news. According to Water Snake, "When my Father ... got done telling this story, he began talking about the Feathered Pipe" (F. P. Gone, 1942, p. 14). Recall that Bull Lodge had achieved his remarkable status among the Gros Ventre owing to his childhood devotion to the Feathered Pipe, one of two ritual Person-objects entrusted to the community from Above. It was the Person of the Feathered Pipe Who first appeared to Bull Lodge in his youth and assured him that he would indeed be "powerful on this earth." Moreover, Bull Lodge's power for war and doctoring was closely associated with the rainbow, just one manifestation of the Thunder Being Who had originally gifted the Feathered Pipe to the Gros Ventre. Later in life, Bull Lodge became the ritual Keeper of the Feathered Pipe and to this day he continues to signify the power of this Pipe more than any other Gros Ventre leader in tribal memory (Cooper, 1957; F. P. Gone, 1942; J. P. Gone, 1999). As a result, the final words of Bull Lodge were unusually privileged—and therefore unusually distressing—for he was reported to have said:

> The Feathered Pipe—and Its purpose among the tribe—has run its course, and It's now all gone. I was the last to receive those powers, and there will be no more supernatural powers attached to it.
> I pity [i.e., feel and act compassionately toward] it, my Son, the Feathered Pipe. Its days are finished. It shall change hands not more than two or three times after me.
>
> (p. 15)

Following this pronouncement, Bull Lodge bade farewell to his kin person by person, sent them away to their own lodges, and died.

Of course, the reader may recall that Bull Lodge had been gifted with the knowledge to achieve his own resurrection. That is, upon his death in 1886, he could expect to rise again to live out his full allotment of life so long as the necessary rituals were conducted appropriately. Unfortunately, by then, American pacification of the Plains tribes was nearly complete, with the last vestiges of the great northern bison herd having been exterminated by 1884. Because Gros Ventres had not seen a buffalo in years, the materials for the resurrection ritual could not be obtained. Some whispered that Bull Lodge's extra-conventional pursuit of power, or even his misuse of such power, had resulted in this tragic "cutting off" of his life. Whichever interpretation one adopted, all who looked for the revitalization of Bull Lodge were forlorn. But worse was yet to come.

My great grandfather, Frederick P. Gone, who was born in the year of Bull Lodge's death, and who later made it his business to salvage this extraordinary life story "in order to explain what those supernatural powers [of the Feathered Pipe] were and how they worked" (p. 1), interviewed Water Snake and composed *Bull Lodge's Life* in the early 1940s.[3] Not long thereafter, Fred Gone was hastily summoned to the cabin of old Iron Man, where this contemporary "caretaker" of the Feathered Pipe bundle (who had been charged with this duty by the last official Keeper of the bundle, Bull Lodge's son Curly Head) confirmed with evident distress that "the Feathered Pipe Itself was gone" (J. P. Gone, 1999, p. 423). In response, Fred Gone attempted to comfort this anguished elder with an inspired explanation for the disappearance of the Pipe:

> Being as the Supreme Being gave us this Pipe in a supernatural
> way to protect, guide, and take care of us all of these years since
> we got It, why shouldn't He take It back when He thinks we don't
> need It anymore? You know yourself [that] It's an orphan. It didn't
> leave a successor to Bull Lodge. Ever since Bull Lodge died, this
> Pipe's been an orphan.... So, it stands to reason that the Great
> Spirit came and got his Child.
>
> (pp. 425–426)

This acknowledgment of radical discontinuity with ancestral Gros Ventre ritual tradition—the "taking back" of one of the community's most sacred ritual Person-objects—was precipitated by the coercive conversion of most Gros Ventres to the Roman Catholic faith (and the accompanying criminalization of indigenous ceremonial practice). In sum, it testifies to the existential magnitude of the cultural devastation wrought by the colonial encounter.

Today, at the dawn of a new millennium, many Gros Ventres still struggle to put the pieces together. Our tribal community reels from an epidemic amalgamation of demoralization, dysfunction, drinking, depression, dependency, and domestic violence, together sedimented in protracted poverty. Within the professional discourse of "mental health"—an altogether foreign concept that emerges from the Cartesian legacy of the West—a large proportion of us lack it. But the professional clinicians who appear in our midst with talk of "genetic predispositions" and "chemical imbalances" and

---

3 F. P. Gone's manuscript was later edited for publication by tribal member George Horse Capture (F. P. Gone, 1980). Throughout this chapter, I quote material from the earlier manuscript in order to retain fidelity to F. P. Gone's original English entextualization of Water Snake's oral narratives concerning Bull Lodge's life.

"posttraumatic stress reactions" and "poor parenting skills" generally fail to get it: our problems are primarily existential and spiritual in origin, not biological or behavioral—they result from over a century of thwarted ambition and depleted vitality. Indeed, even the most sincere efforts by such professionals, steeped in Western therapeutic discourse and bound to the "rule of the tool" (or Kaplan's [1964] "Law of the Instrument" as cited by Caplan and Nelson [1973]) threaten to inadvertently displace what remnants of indigenous subjectivity we might still celebrate as "traditional."

Nevertheless, given the visibility of such radical change within just a few generations, it is in fact quite remarkable what has persisted in terms of historical Gros Ventre subjectivity. For example, sometime in the 1990s, a community member recounted the following to me:

> I guess I see myself as righteous, giving with no ulterior motive,
> and with high expectations of those I know (and [that I] am
> involved with enough to know). And [I am] very afraid of God or
> the One Above. These traits [that characterize me are] based upon
> that fear. One time I was very angry, and spoke of the person I was
> angry with in [my son's] presence, and [I] said I *wished* [italics
> added] that person would die (in some form or another). He told
> me it was a moral wrong. Just that, stated it matter-of-factly. Yet,
> his opinion brought all the fears I had to a head and I realized
> how wrong I was.

And so, even today, recognition of the potent power of human wish or thought to alter the world—for good or for ill—remains in evidence. It is well beyond the scope of this chapter to articulate a *contemporary* Gros Ventre ethnopsychology, and indeed, such would require systematic empirical inquiry beyond my own previous experiences and investigations. Nevertheless, to address briefly the clinical practices of mental health providers as they intersect with modern Gros Ventre lives, allow me to elucidate a few facets of contemporary subjectivity among many Gros Ventres that necessitate, I think, an alternative construal of the therapeutic endeavor.

The Revitalization of a Cultural Legacy?

For the present-day Gros Ventre community to secure a truly post-colonial recovery, it remains crucial that therapeutic efforts within our midst reinforce, rather than subvert, enduring ethnopsychological phenomena (for more on the ideological dangers of mental health services for Native American communities, *see* J. P Gone, 2003, 2004a, 2004b, 2007, 2008a, 2008b, 2008c,

2009, 2010; J. P. Gone & Alcántara, 2007). I will tentatively offer here four implications of this commitment for the therapeutic endeavor. First, a Gros Ventre person's social status within the community may more significantly shape their subjectivity than the idiographic psychological attributes that are characteristically considered by mental health professionals. Several sources of intratribal diversity—including age, gender, generation, kinship relations, familial reputation, and ritual participation—may reveal more about a person's hopes, expectations, and prospects than individual personality factors, developmental history, or avowed goals or intentions. In sum, contemporary Gros Ventre subjectivity may be less "open" to the individualistic fashioning of the self that many middle-class Euro-Americans take for granted. Thus, in this context, the therapeutic endeavor would benefit from a more searching contextualization of individual "client" lives as formulated within larger semiotic frameworks by which community members structure social meaning.

Second, a Gros Ventre person's communicative expressions may be much more carefully circumscribed than the cathartic self-expressions that are regularly observed or actively elicited in the workaday practice of psychotherapy. The power of thought, will, or wish may well persist in an emphasis on positive thinking, an aversion toward rumination on the painful, ugly, or distressing, and the reluctance to give voice to strong "negative" emotion in the therapeutic setting (especially within a face-to-face community in which virtually no word or deed ever remains truly "private" or "confidential"). In sum, contemporary Gros Ventre subjectivity involves tremendous care in regulating what is said at all. Thus, in this context, the therapeutic endeavor would benefit from a decided shift away from a requirement or expectation that talk—especially talk between community members and non-Native therapists—will be the chief means for healing or recovery.

Third, a Gros Ventre person's success in life may depend a great deal more on respectful beseechings of more knowledgeable others—both human or other-than-human—for guidance, direction, assistance, and knowledge than the mere individualistic exercise of innate talent or creativity that might be clinically encouraged. These beseechings—that is, *prayers*—follow from a recognition that human beings are themselves inadequate for realizing their ambitions absent guidance and direction from powerful Others. In sum, contemporary Gros Ventre subjectivity often entails the routine petitioning of God, "Our Heavenly Father," the "One Above," the "Grandfather Spirits," and family and community elders for guidance and blessings. Thus, in this context, the therapeutic endeavor would benefit from (and may actually require) the facilitation of sacred encounters (rather than secular self-actualization), which are seen to be the source of vitality, longevity, and prosperity.

Finally, a Gros Ventre person's well-being is likely to depend a great deal on the competitive realization of personal ambitions that resonate more with longstanding community values of honorable achievement than with idio-syncratically adopted ideals or (especially) Euro-American indices of success (Gone & Alcántara, 2010). Competition with others is likely to be pursued with relish and valued as an essential means to demonstrating one's vitality and realizing one's wishes, though such wishes might be more closely tied to local reputation, familial honor, and the ability to be extravagantly generous with non-kin community members (as opposed to accumulating great wealth). In sum, contemporary Gros Ventre subjectivity depends on the eruption of liveliness in a variety of modern venues that continues to prove the efficacy of agentic expression in an uncertain world. Thus, in this context, the therapeutic endeavor would benefit from the identification—or even the creation—of circumstances wherein community members might competi-tively exercise their talents and abilities toward pro-social outcomes that simultaneously accrue honor to the individual even as they em-power or en-liven the community.

CONCLUDING REFLECTIONS: THE PROMISE OF COMMUNITY PSYCHOLOGY

The therapeutic alternatives just described emerge from and depend on specific facets of a distinctive Gros Ventre ethnopsychology. This ethnopsy-chology gave rise to and renders intelligible the speech acts attributed to our most famous medicine person in his dying hours some 125 years ago. Vestiges of this ethnopsychology persist today among contemporary Gros Ventres. As a clinical psychologist by training, I have proposed that these vestigial facets of Gros Ventre ethnopsychology—particularly in the context of collec-tive decolonization and communal healing efforts—require an alternative construal of the therapeutic project relative to the clinical services provided by mental health professionals at Fort Belknap today. Moreover, I have sug-gested that an alternative therapeutic approach committed to reinforcing rather than subverting enduring Gros Ventre subjectivity probably requires the contextualization of client lives within enduring local semiotic frame-works, the abandonment of therapeutic talk as the principal means to healing and recovery, the facilitation of sacred encounters for obtaining guidance and blessings, and the identification (and possible creation) of modern cir-cumstances for pro-social competitive expression. On the off-chance that the full implications of these alternatives have been obscured, allow me to clarify that *none* of these approaches routinely appears in the job descriptions of health service providers even among the psychological and counseling professions. Not surprisingly, then, as I have elsewhere observed, in order to heal our community requires "a great deal more of the kinds of professional mental health services that do not yet exist" (J. P. Gone, 2003, p. 228).

What I have in mind is a radical programmatic alternative based on the very concepts that Julian Rappaport reviewed for us over three decades ago, namely, the reframing of professional roles and relationships in alignment with the principles of contextualization, collaboration, diversity, empowerment, relativity, accessibility, prevention, and (above all) critique of the status quo (Rappaport, 1977). Additionally, Rappaport's (1995, 2000) more recent emphasis on narrative extends this able assemblage of guiding precepts toward a community psychology that is ideally suited for advancing the causes of liberating self-expression and empowering self-determination for marginalized communities. More specifically, attention by community psychologists to the narrative practices of such cultural collectivities will help to ensure that collaboratively designed programs, services, and interventions designed to facilitate communal well-being might avoid the subtle but pervasive "West-is-best" cultural assumptions that structure the human services more generally (Gone, 2008a). In the case of the Gros Ventre, examination of the final act of narration evidenced by Bull Lodge among his gathered kin afforded insight into the distinctive genre of Gros Ventre speech in which the recounting of extraordinary expressions of vitality literally imparted extensions of vitality for those who hear such accounts. The means by which words literally realize prosperity and longevity for others depend on the instrumental power of thought—whether human or other-than-human—throughout the cosmos. Thus, it follows that "giving voice" to this particular narrative tradition may effect empowerment for the modern Gros Ventre community in multiple ways.

The most obvious form of empowerment achieved by "giving voice" to Gros Ventre narrative tradition is the now widespread (and increasingly co-opted) notion of facilitating oppressed people's experience of and success with the escalating exercise of autonomy and self-determination. The assumption, of course, is that a people exercising greater control over its own destiny is more likely to improve its material situation and to experience the "good life" as a byproduct of living a purposeful and valued existence. In this sense, there can be little doubt that Euro-American recognition of and regard for a distinctive and persisting Gros Ventre voice relative to our understanding and negotiation of the world would greatly assist in the project of collective decolonization and communal healing. The material consequences of such recognition and regard might even include a radical reconfiguration of the local "helping services" on the reservation in response to a visionary and autonomous exercise of local self-determination. Beyond the escalating exercise of autonomy that is contingent on "giving voice" to indigenous Gros Ventre tradition, however, lies a more compelling sense of empowerment—namely, the potential for a revitalization of ancestral ritual practice that might once again convey our communal respect to Those Above and efficaciously amplify our collective thoughts in service to a renewed recirculation of longevity, abundance, and vitality among our people. In this latter sense, attention to ancestral Gros Ventre voices might literally empower community members to realize our shared wishes for a viable and prosperous future.

In closing, I take solace in the fact that the ritual bundle that originally contained the Feathered Pipe, once "kept" or maintained by Bull Lodge but long abandoned in a dilapidated shack belonging to old Iron Man, was retrieved by his son in the mid-1990s. In fact, during the summer of 2005, Joe Iron Man hosted a community gathering in which the Feathered Pipe bundle was ceremonially rewrapped. Certainly, as I have shown, the potential for a revitalization of Gros Ventre ritual tradition harbors the possibility for a profound subversion of conventional mental health principles and practices. More importantly, such revitalization heralds a greater hope for transforming my community's historical "tale of terror" into a future "tale of joy" (Rappaport, 2000), for actively rekindling Gros Ventre vitality and rediscovering our place in the cosmos. For now, I return to the words of Julian Rappaport (1995), who once observed that in our academic telling of stories about people, "we do not often hear their actual voices. The voices of the people we claim to represent," he wrote, "often remain in the background" (p. 800). In hope of ameliorating such omissions, and with faith that some residual vitality might yet be circulated in their telling, I offer these words—their words, our words—in commemoration of Julian.

ACKNOWLEDGMENTS

This chapter was revised during the author's tenure as the Katrin H. Lamon Fellow at the School for Advanced Research on the Human Experience in Santa Fe, New Mexico. I thank Jeffrey D. Anderson at Colby College for his incisive review of an earlier version of this manuscript.

REFERENCES

Anderson, J. D. (2001). *The four hills of life: Northern Arapaho knowledge and life movement*. Lincoln, NE: University of Nebraska.

Bauman, R. (1986). *Story, performance, and event: Contextual studies of oral narrative*. Cambridge: Cambridge University.

Caplan, N., & Nelson, S. D. (1973). On being useful: The nature and consequences of psychological research on social problems. *American Psychologist, 28*(3), 199–211.

Cooper, J. M. (1957). *The Gros Ventres of Montana: Part II—Religion and ritual* (R. Flannery, Ed.). Washington, DC: Catholic University of America.

Flannery, R. (1953). *The Gros Ventres of Montana: Part I—Social life.* Washington, DC: Catholic University of America.

Fowler, L. (1987). *Shared symbols, contested meanings: Gros Ventre culture and history, 1778–1984.* Ithaca, NY: Cornell University.

Gone, F. P. (1942). *Bull Lodge's life.* Unpublished manuscript.

Gone, F. P. (1980). *The seven visions of Bull Lodge, as told to his daughter, Garter Snake* (G. Horse Capture, Ed.). Lincoln, NE: University of Nebraska.

Gone, J. P. (1996). *Gros Ventre cultural identity as normative self: A case study.* Unpublished master's thesis, University of Illinois, Champaign, IL.

Gone, J. P. (1999). "We were through as Keepers of it": The "Missing Pipe Narrative" and Gros Ventre cultural identity. *Ethos, 27*(4), 415–440.

Gone, J. P. (2003). American Indian mental health service delivery: Persistent challenges and future prospects. In J. S. Mio & G. Y. Iwamasa (Eds.), *Culturally diverse mental health: The challenges of research and resistance* (pp. 211–229). New York: Brunner-Routledge.

Gone, J. P. (2004a). Keeping culture in mind: Transforming academic training in professional psychology for Indian country. In D. A. Mihesuah & A. Cavender Wilson (Eds.), *Indigenizing the academy: Transforming scholarship and empowering communities* (pp. 124–142). Lincoln, NE: University of Nebraska Press.

Gone, J. P. (2004b). Mental health services for Native Americans in the 21st century United States. *Professional Psychology: Research and Practice, 35*(1), 10–18.

Gone, J. P. (2006a). "As if reviewing his life": Bull Lodge's narrative and the mediation of self-representation. *American Indian Culture and Research Journal, 30*(1), 67–86.

Gone, J. P. (2006b). Mental health, wellness, and the quest for an authentic American Indian identity. In T. Witko (Ed.), *Mental health care for urban Indians: Clinical insights from Native practitioners* (pp. 55–80). Washington, DC: American Psychological Association.

Gone, J. P. (2006c). Research reservations: Response and responsibility in an American Indian community. *American Journal of Community Psychology, 37*(3–4), 333–340.

Gone, J. P. (2007). "We never was happy living like a Whiteman": Mental health disparities and the postcolonial predicament in American Indian communities. *American Journal of Community Psychology, 40*(3–4), 290–300.

Gone, J. P. (2008a). Introduction: Mental health discourse as Western cultural proselytization. *Ethos, 36*(3), 310–315.

Gone, J. P. (2008b). "So I can be like a Whiteman": The cultural psychology of space and place in American Indian mental health. *Culture & Psychology, 14*(3), 369–399.

Gone, J. P. (2008c). The Pisimweyapiy Counselling Centre: Paving the red road to wellness in northern Manitoba. In J. B. Waldram (Ed.), *Aboriginal healing in Canada: Studies in therapeutic meaning and practice* (pp. 131–203). Ottawa, Ontario: Aboriginal Healing Foundation.

Gone, J. P. (2009). Encountering professional psychology: Re-envisioning mental health services for Native North America. In L. J. Kirmayer & G. Valaskakis (Eds.), *Healing traditions: The mental health of Aboriginal peoples* (pp. 419-439). Vancouver: University of British Columbia.

Gone, J. P. (2010). Psychotherapy and traditional healing for American Indians: Exploring the prospects for therapeutic integration. *The Counseling Psychologist, 38*(2), 166–235.

Gone, J. P., & Alcántara, C. (2007). Identifying effective mental health interventions for American Indians and Alaska Natives: A review of the literature. *Cultural Diversity & Ethnic Minority Psychology, 13*(4), 356–363.

Gone, J. P., & Alcántara, C. (2010). The Ethnographically Contextualized Case Study Method: Exploring ambitious achievement in an American Indian community. *Cultural Diversity & Ethnic Minority Psychology, 16*(2), 159-168.

Gone, J. P., Miller, P. J., & Rappaport, J. (1999). Conceptual self as normatively oriented: The suitability of past personal narrative for the study of cultural identity. *Culture & Psychology, 5*(4), 371–398.

Jakobson, R. (1971). Shifters, verbal categories, and the Russian verb. In *Roman Jakobson: Selected writings* (Vol. 2, pp. 130–147). The Hague: Mouton.

Kaplan, A. (1964). *The conduct of inquiry.* San Francisco: Chandler.

Rappaport, J. (1977). *Community psychology: Values, research, and action.* Fort Worth, TX: Holt, Rinehart, and Winston.

Rappaport, J. (1995). Empowerment meets narrative: Listening to stories and creating settings. *American Journal of Community Psychology, 23*(5), 795–807.

Rappaport, J. (2000). Community narratives: Tales of terror and joy. *American Journal of Community Psychology, 28*(1), 1–24.

Rappaport, J. (2005). Community psychology is (thank God) more than science. *American Journal of Community Psychology, 35*(3–4), 231–238.

Wilson, W. A. W., & Yellow Bird, M. (Eds.). (2005). *For indigenous eyes only: A decolonization handbook.* Santa Fe, NM: School of American Research.

8   Tales of Terror from Juvenile Justice and Education

N. Dickon Reppucci, Jessica R. Meyer and Jessica Owen Kostelnik

"The mission of the community psychologist/social
scientist can be understood as a calling to use our tools
(methods, critical observation and analysis, scholarship,
social influence) to assist others in the job of turning
tales of terror into tales of joy."

(Rappaport, 2000, p. 7)

Edward Humes, a journalist/writer, provides a powerful and upsetting portrait of the juvenile court and its inhabitants—the youth, the lawyers, the probation workers, the judges, and others—in his 1996 book, *No Matter How Loud I Shout*. It tells a tale of a system that neither protects us from dangerous children nor saves our children in danger. It is a world of chaos, heartbreak, caring, and disinterest that is truly overwhelming to all. For the past several years, this book has been very important to my teaching about Children, Law, Juvenile Justice, and Violence. One reason is that it totally captures the imagination and interest of my students regarding the juvenile justice system. It paints a realistic picture of the kids as being truly scary but also upsettingly pathetic, often callous and dangerous but just as often lonely, unloved, and unwanted. Another reason is that its plaintive title, taken from a writing assignment by one of the youth, appears to capture the feelings of so many juveniles entrapped within this often debilitating system. These children have grown up in a world that neither listens to nor cares about their pain and living conditions. As one incarcerated boy said about being a foster care kid, a category that exemplifies many of them, "You always think it's your fault. You always wonder if you could have been a better kid, then maybe it would never have happened—maybe they would never have taken you away" (p.230). Many have committed heinous crimes but all are provided with a humanity that is lacking in the abstract. They are hard to ignore, but ignore them we do, thus helping to create the community and family conditions that contribute to a childhood of poverty and crime. We (see also, Meyer, Reppucci, & Owen, 2006) argue in this chapter that both this system and the educational system with its now widely accepted "zero-tolerance" policies are actually criminalizing childhood.

The juvenile justice system had its origins in this country a century ago and represents one of the largest preventive interventions for youth ever devised (Reppucci, 1999). Its goal was to rehabilitate and nurture wayward and delinquent youth with kind and loving care, and no stigma was to be attached to any youth who entered into it. The fact that these goals were not accomplished was crystallized in the 1967 Supreme Court decision, *In re Gault*, which empowered juveniles with due process rights as an antidote to the repressive system that had developed. Again the goal was to protect and enhance juveniles' well-being. However, the establishment of these rights, in large part, had the paradoxical effect of ushering in an even more punitive reform period. Public and legal policy changes within the past few decades, exacerbated by fear engendered from sensational media reports and misinformed public perceptions of increasing juvenile crime rates, have dissipated much of what remained of a juvenile court based on a developmentally oriented understanding of childhood. Cultural conceptions of youth as naïve innocents have morphed into impressions of youth as "superpredators" who commit adult crimes. Young people are now less likely to be viewed as malleable individuals deserving protection and rehabilitation. Rather the focus is on holding them accountable for their individual behavior via punishment. This shift in the public's view from troubled youth as misguided and impressionable to youth as dangerous and equally culpable and responsible as adults for their conduct has been accomplished with little discussion or understanding of the vast majority of delinquent youth. Public perceptions of these juveniles are largely based on non-representative, headline-grabbing cases of truly egregious crimes (Merlo & Benekos, 2000; Scott, Reppucci, Antonishak, & DeGennaro, 2006).

Moreover, the fear and moral outrage that has fueled these changes has carried over into our schools. The spate of highly dramatized school shootings, which reached their zenith with the 1999 Columbine tragedy, has resulted in a public that believes their children are not safe in their schools. The fact that a child is more likely to die from being hit by lightning than by an assault in school has made no difference (Center on Juvenile and Criminal Justice, 1998). Mulvey and Cauffman's (2001) *American Psychologist* article pointed out the impossibility of detecting and preventing all school shootings no matter what protective steps might be taken. However, the main "answer" to alleviating the problem of violence had already been found in what has been called "zero- tolerance" policies that have resulted in unbendable rules that are ridiculous at best and exceptionally harmful at worst—for example, *(1)* the 8-year-old who was suspended a few years ago because he pointed a McDonald's chicken McNugget at another student and said, "Bang, bang, you're dead!"; *(2)* the Utah boy who was suspended in 2007 for giving his cousin a cold pill prescribed to both students; *(3)* the 6-year-old in Bedford, Massachusetts, who in 2006 was suspended from classes for sexual harassment because he touched a female classmate on her belt while playing; or *(4)* the high school student in Providence, Rhode Island, who submitted to the yearbook a photograph of himself dressed as a knight with a medieval looking sword and had it rejected because of the school's zero-tolerance policy against weapons (Associated Press, 2007).

The goal of this chapter is first to provide an overview of patterns of juvenile crime and school violence in the United States and then to provide brief narrative histories of *(1)* the development and impact of zero-tolerance policies in our schools, and *(2)* the conception and establishment of a reha-bilitative juvenile justice system that today has become largely adversarial and punitive. These narrative histories or, as Rappaport (2000) might call them, "tales of terror," are used to illuminate the loss of focus on individual-ized justice and accountability to the suppression of youth—especially lower socio-economic, ethnic minority youth! The question raised is "Why do we not hear the anguished cries of many of our most vulnerable citizens no matter how loud they shout?"

PATTERNS OF JUVENILE CRIME AND SCHOOL VIOLENCE

Concerns about juvenile crime have surfaced and resurfaced over the past century. Most recently, between 1980 and 1996, the juvenile (under age 18 years) arrest rate for violent crime increased 58% (FBI, 1996; FBI, 1997). Between 1986 and 1995, homicide arrests of juveniles increased an astonish-ing 89.9%, whereas the homicide arrest rate for adults actually declined 0.3% (FBI, 1996). Such statistics demanded that attention and resources be geared toward the prevention and reduction of youth violence.

However, contrary to popular belief, the *overall* rate of juvenile crime did not increase substantially during the 1990s. Rather, juvenile arrests for violent crimes peaked in 1994, paralleling a more general pattern of diminishing overall crime arrests between 1993 and 2002 (Sickmund, Snyder, & Poe-Yamagata, 1997; FBI, 2003). Moreover, juvenile violent crimes in 2002 were 25.9% below the 1993 figure (FBI, 2003). By 2005, youth accounted for only 12.0% of arrestees for violent crime (Snyder, 2007)—not a percentage to be dismissed lightly but also not an indication of a spiraling problem. In fact, the violent juvenile crime rate today is actually slightly lower than it was in the early 1980s. Nevertheless, nearly 62% of poll respondents falsely believed that juvenile crime was on the increase (Center on Juvenile and Criminal Justice, 2000).

A similar misconception about the frequency of youth violence *within school environments* exists. From 1997 to 1999, a few highly publicized school shootings—most notably the 1999 Columbine High School massacre in Littleton, Colorado, in which 13 students and 1 teacher were killed—generated frightening media images of assaulted children and grief-stricken peers and parents. Leading news sources suggested that violent juvenile crime was soaring in the mid-1990s (Cornell, 2003), and considerable fear was generated about school violence in the general public. Seven out of 10 Americans reported that they believed a shooting was likely in their school system, and Americans were 49% more likely to express fears of violence in their schools in 1999 than in 1998 (Center on Juvenile and Criminal Justice, 2000).

Contrary to these public perceptions, frequency of school violence has been decreasing and has always been relatively rare. Overall crime in schools has declined dramatically since 1994 (National Crime Victimization Survey, 2003), and even homicides in schools declined during the 1990s (National School Safety Center, 2003). Although the number of student homicides on school property ranged from 23 to 35 for the 3-year period (1997–1999), in the following 4 years throughout the entire United States, there was an average of only 5.75 student homicides on school property (http://youth-violence.edschool.virginia.edu/violence-in-schools/school-shootings.html). Similarly, the overall percentage of students who reported being threatened or injured with a weapon at school has remained relatively stable since 1993 Youth Risk Behavior Survey, 2003). Furthermore, statistics indicated that in 1999, there was a 1 in 2 million chance of being killed in one of America's schools (Center on Juvenile and Criminal Justice, 2000). Indeed, more children die of the flu and pneumonia than are killed at school (National Vital Statistics Report, 1998). Schools remain one of the safer environments for young people in the community. Less than 1% of homicides and suicides among school-age children occur in or around school grounds

(Kachur et al., 1996), and the rate of crimes committed by youth is low during actual school hours (Snyder & Sickmund, 1999). None of these statistics appear to have changed the perception of the general public that schools are unsafe.

ZERO-TOLERANCE POLICIES

To promote safety in schools, Congress passed the *Federal Gun-Free Schools Act* (1994), which required that all school districts that received federal funding adopt a gun-free policy and expel students who carry a gun to school for 1 year. Subsequent legislation by states and localities has involved increasingly harsh penalties for school violence, but many states have also extended these policies to a broad range of conduct, including other types of weapons, possession or use of drugs, and less frequently for habitual profanity or defiant/disruptive behavior (Advancement Project and the Civil Rights Project [APCRP], 2000). "Weapons" have included paper clips, nail files, scissors, and plastic knives found in a child's lunchbox, and "drugs" now include aspirin, Certs, Midol, and even Scope, because of its alcohol content. These policies usually oblige administrators to sanction suspension or expulsion to students for the commission of such acts, without regard to legitimate explanations. As a response to perceptions of disorder and chaos within the schools, the implementation of these strategies has received widespread support; zero-tolerance procedures are widely implemented across the nation's schools, and in the year 2000, the vast majority (87%) of Americans favored their use (Rose & Gallup, 2000).

However, others have harshly criticized zero-tolerance policies as punitive and intransigent (Merlo & Benekos, 2003). The American Bar Association stated that zero tolerance treats all threats of violence as equally dangerous and deserving of the same punishments and fails to provide flexibility for school administrators to consider the seriousness of threats or degree of risk (Cornell, 2003). Unfortunately, the bearers of such predetermined punishment are all too often students, ranging in age from 6 to 17 years, who have committed minor infractions and pose no danger to others. The following examples from Webb and Kritsonis' 2006 report are illustrative. Kindergarten students as young as age 6 years have been suspended for bringing to school a nail clipper or toy axe as part of a Halloween costume. A 12-year-old boy diagnosed with hyperactive disorder was suspended for 2 days for telling his friends in a food line that "I'm gonna get you" if they ate all the potatoes; moreover, this boy was then charged by the police with making "terroristic threats" and was incarcerated for 2 weeks while awaiting trial (Claiborne, 1999). Other students have been expelled for accidentally bringing a pocketknife (which was packed in the bag for an earlier Boy Scouts trip) or sparklers to school, and an 11-year-old girl who brought a knife to school in her lunch box to cut her chicken was removed from the school in a police car (APCRP, 2000). A 17-year-old student in Chicago was arrested and later expelled for shooting a paper clip with a rubber band. Similarly, students have been suspended or expelled for "drug-related activity" such as wearing one pants leg up, sniffing white-out in class (APCRP, 2000), or giving another youth two lemon cough drops. Clearly, zero-tolerance policies allow limited, if any, opportunity to consider the context and meaning of threats or actions by students.

Webb and Kritsonis (2006) report that many urban schools, by adopting zero-tolerance policies because of perceived public concerns about school safety, have increased the vulnerability of girls being arrested for assault offenses that include both physical confrontations and threats that occur in or near school grounds. In fact, they argue that before the advent of zero-tolerance preventive measures, most of the students who are now being arrested would have been handled as school disciplinary problems (*see also* Rimer, 2004). This net-widening in school arrests has disproportionately escalated for girls being arrested for violent crimes usually involving minor physical confrontations or verbal threats, frequently with another girl, that previously would have been ignored or dealt with in a less formal fashion (Hall, 2004).

Given the inflexibility of predetermined responses to perceived threats of school violence, disciplinary actions under the zero-tolerance philosophy have been undertaken even when school administrators and others involved recognized that the targeted students intended no harm. One particularly telling case in Virginia involved an eighth-grade boy, Benjamin Ratner, who was suspended for possessing a knife on school grounds in violation of the school's policy. The facts of the case were that the 13-year-old had taken a binder containing the knife from a female friend who had expressed thoughts of suicide and put the binder in his locker without notifying school authorities. When he was later summoned by the Dean of the school, Mrs. Kellogg, and asked about the knife, he readily admitted having it and turned it over to her. "Kellogg acknowledged that she believed Ratner acted in what he saw as the girl's best interest and at no time did Ratner pose a threat to harm anyone with the knife" (*Ratner v Loudoun County Public Schools*, 2001). Even so, Ratner was suspended for the remainder of the school term by the Superintendent under the district's zero-tolerance policy.

In another case in Mississippi, five high school students threw peanuts while on the school bus and accidentally hit the bus driver. The young men were arrested for felony assault, which carries a maximum penalty of 5 years in prison. They also lost their bus privileges and suspension was recommended.

Although community support aided in the dismissal of the charges, all of the students dropped out of school because they lacked a substitute means of transportation to school (APCRP, 2000).

The rigidity of zero-tolerance policies as seen in these tales of terror has also significantly affected the treatment of disabled children. Despite the *Individuals with Disabilities Education Act* (1997), which prohibited school administrators from disciplining students with special needs as they would discipline students without disabilities, administrators respond to disabled students with standard zero-tolerance approaches. For example, an autistic child was expelled and charged with battery for kicking a teacher, and a young child with ADHD was charged with battery for kicking an aide (APCRP, 2000).

Clearly, the strict sanctions of zero-tolerance policies include, erroneously, students who neither intend to nor actually commit any harm. In attempting to curb violence in the schools, an admirable goal for sure, these policies have the inherent weakness of any one-size-fits-all model. Combined with the fact that violent behavior committed by youth is a rare event and extremely difficult to detect reliably, predictive strategies identify an exceptionally large number of false-positives (Mulvey & Cauffman, 2001). This is not a small problem, as millions of children have been denied educational opportunities as a result of being a false-positive identified by zero tolerance.

Approximately 3.1 million students in America, or nearly 6.8% of all students, were suspended or expelled from school in 1997. This was up from 3.7% of students in 1974 (Center on Juvenile and Criminal Justice, 2000) and appears to be related to increased suspension rates when zero-tolerance sanctions are employed (APCRP, 2000). Unfortunately, many students who receive exclusionary punishments become alienated from the educational process and experience short- or long-term deprivation of education. Moreover, suspension is a moderate to strong predictor of a student dropping out of school and may accelerate the process of delinquency by providing at-risk youth with little parental supervision and more time to associate with deviant peers (Skiba & Peterson, 1999).

Perhaps even more alarming, zero-tolerance policies have led to a growing number of criminal charges filed against children for their conduct in school. For example, in January, 2005, in Ocala, Florida, two special education male students, ages 9 and 10 years, were charged with felonies and taken away from school in handcuffs, accused of making violent drawings of stick figures. There are 43 states that mandate a report of a commission of a crime on school property to law enforcement agencies. School administrators may interpret these laws differently, and sometimes youth are reported for behavior that would not be considered a criminal act in the community.

Students subjected to zero-tolerance sanctions have frequently been charged with assault or battery for kicking, hitting, or fist fights. Although the law requires serious bodily injury in most criminal charges of aggravated assault, the severity of the behavior in the school system often goes unnoticed. Therefore, students engaging in typical childhood/adolescent behavior may now become enmeshed in the juvenile justice system. Given the increasingly harsh way that youth are treated in this system, it is critical to examine the repercussions of entangling children in it for infractions committed in the school environment.

Indeed, returning to school is especially problematic for youth who have had criminal charges filed against them for their conduct in school. According to a report by the Office of Juvenile Justice and Delinquency Prevention (2000), youth exiting juvenile correctional facilities may "become lost in a tangle of bureaucratic agencies that too often share only limited information with each other, resulting in fragmented assistance. In most cases, no single agency or advocate 'looks after' the needs of an adjudicated youth" (p. 3). The lack of a clear definition of roles often leads to duplication of services or to "guess[ing]" by educators supplied with inadequate information as to the services the youth received while in detention. "The time it takes to obtain all the information," the OJJDP report states, "often leads to unnecessary referrals, duplicate services, inaccurate information, and service delays." (p. 3). For many children, re-enrollment involves participation in an "alternative school" for students labeled as having disciplinary problems (Tobin & Sprague, 2000), which may exacerbate engagement in the undesirable behaviors. Finally, zero-tolerance policies often make it difficult—if not impossible—to admit or re-admit any youth labeled as a juvenile offender (Altschuler & Brash, 2004). These issues lead us to the juvenile justice system itself.

HISTORICAL CONTEXT AND TRANSFORMATION OF THE JUVENILE JUSTICE SYSTEM

Before the 1900s, children under the age of 7 years were considered incapable of engaging in criminal activity, youth between 7 and 14 years could be treated as adults if courts determined that they acted as adults, and all individuals 14 years and older were considered to be adults in the judicial system (Reppucci, 1999). Reformers of the era were enraged that children as young as 7 years could be tried and punished as adults (Levine & Levine, 1992), and they were influential in establishing the first juvenile courts at the turn of the century. Juvenile courts were created to pursue the "best interests" of the child with the state serving as *parens patriae*, a surrogate parent, and their goal was to offer children rehabilitative intervention rather than

punitive sanctions. An underlying principle was that because of their immaturity, youth do not bear the same culpability as adults for committing crimes.
Thus, judicial proceedings were informal in orderto care for youth and to
consider individual circumstances when making determinations of whether
to incarcerate them. Records and proceedings were kept confidential to prevent the attachment of stigma to youth, and if incarcerated, juveniles were
separated from adult criminals in prison (Reppucci, 1999). To maintain the
informality, due process rights, such as the right to counsel and the privilege
against self-incrimination, were precluded from judicial proceedings.

As the ideals of the court slowly morphed into a more punishment-
oriented system, the lack of due process rights became the focus of major
criticism in the 1960s, because many poor and minority youth were being
incarcerated who may not have been if they had been afforded such rights.
Moreover, the paternalistic juvenile court was failing to rehabilitate young
criminals or reduce juvenile crime (Dean & Reppucci, 1974; Levine & Levine,
1992). In essence, youth were neither receiving procedural safeguards nor
effective rehabilitative efforts. In response, the Supreme Court, in the landmark case, *In re Gault* (1967) granted juveniles due process rights, including
the right to counsel and privilege against self-incrimination. Accordingly,
conceptual and procedural differences between the social control of youth
and adults began to erode. The *Gault* case highlighted a fundamental shift
from treating juveniles as children toward treating them as adults. In this one
sphere, youth, who committed criminal acts, were empowered by giving
them rights similar to adults. However, by empowering them, whether it was
intended or not, the *Gault* decision also legitimated policy changes over the
next several decades that have resulted in the imposition of harsher sanctions
on these misbehaving youth. (For a detailed discussion of this issue, *see*
Manfredi, 1998.)

The need to dictate less punishment to juveniles because of their developmental immaturity remained during the *Gault* era (Scott & Grisso, 1997)
and was explicitly demonstrated in Supreme Court rulings that considered
the culpability and constitutionality of sentencing young offenders. In *Lockett
v. Ohio* (438 U.S. 586, 604 [1978]), the Supreme Court ruled that a sentencing court must consider a youth's age as a mitigating factor. *Eddings v.
Oklahoma* (455 U.S. 104 at 116 [1982]) noted that age, mental and emotional development, and background must be considered in sentencing and
ruled that youth "deserve less punishment because (they) may have less
capacity to control their conduct and to think in long-range terms than adults"
(455 U.S. at 115 n 11). Similarly, in *Thompson v. Oklahoma* (486 U.S. 815
[1988]), which concerned capital punishment for a 15-year-old, the court
ruled that a young person's culpability is not equal to that of an adult's, and
therefore youth are not deserving of the same punishment (i.e., death penalty).

The *Thompson* court also declared that "adolescents as a class are less mature and responsible than adults . . . minors often lack the experience, perspective, and judgment expected of adults . . . inexperience, less education, and less intelligence make the teenager less able to evaluate the consequences of his or her conduct while at the same time he or she is much more apt to be motivated by mere emotion or peer pressure than is an adult." (487 U.S. at 834).

However, *Stanford v. Kentucky* (492 U.S. 361 [1989]) rejected the culpability analysis of the *Thompson* (1988) ruling and declined to prohibit capital punishment for 16- and 17-year-olds. The *Stanford* and *Thompson* rulings, although only 1 year apart, parallel the shift from the paternalistic, rehabilitative view of youth to the view of youth as adult-like predators that has occurred over the past few decades. Although the goal of blending the best interests of the child (social welfare) and the demand for community protection (social control) into a single institution, the juvenile court, has always been difficult (Worrell, 1985), recent changes within the juvenile justice system now threaten to mask developmental differences between children and adults.

The aforementioned media depictions solidified the view that juvenile crime was out of control (Males, 1996). Today's juvenile courts embody more procedural formality, waive serious young offenders to the adult criminal system for a large array of violent and nonviolent crimes—especially those involving drugs—and tend to emphasize punishment instead of rehabilitation (Scott & Grisso, 2005) These changes largely result from a de-emphasis on individualized treatment of the juvenile offender and are justified by the offender's empowerment with due process rights. Paternalistic, rehabilitative ideals aimed at gaining a fuller understanding of a juvenile's character and circumstances to meet his/her needs have largely disappeared. Although rehabilitation is still listed as a goal of the juvenile system, juvenile and criminal court systems have converged, with punishment as the first priority.

The mechanisms to facilitate youth's prosecution under adult criminal laws are commonly known as *waiver* or *transfer laws* (Reppucci, Michel, & Kostelnik (2009). The waiver of juveniles to adult court has been an option of judges since the inception of the juvenile court. However, juvenile waivers were based largely on individual differences in adolescents' dangerousness, sophistication-maturity, and amenability to treatment (Salekin, 2002) and were seldom invoked regardless of crime. This practice has changed significantly over the last 20 years; transfers have increasingly become automatic—especially for older youth—and judicial review on a case-by-case basis has been restricted. Within a 5-year period in the early 1990s, nearly every state amended its waiver laws in response to real or perceived escalation of urban youth violence (Feld, 1999). Although states have limited waiver to felony offenses and usually establish a minimum age of 14 years, a few states have lowered the age of transfer to 13, 10, or even 8 years, and some have no restrictions on age of transfer at all (Snyder & Sickmund, 1995). In addition, states have extended the number of crimes that youth can be transferred for without hearings; in fact, federal crime statistics suggest that more youth are transferred for drug and property crimes than for violent ones (Reppucci, 1999). As a result, there was a 71% increase in juvenile cases transferred to adult courts between 1985 and 1994 and a 100% increase from 1994 to 1998 (Salekin, 2002).

Once a youth is waived, the likelihood of diminished responsibility and immaturity being recognized is slim (Feld, 1999). Several studies (McNulty, 1996; Podkopacz & Feld, 1996; Rudman, Hartstone, Fagan, & Moore, 1986) show that criminal courts imprison youth more often and with longer sentences than juvenile courts do. A 1993 California Department of Corrections study found juveniles were consistently confined for 60% *longer* than adults for the same crimes (Males, 1996). Nearly all states confine juveniles sentenced in criminal court to adult correctional facilities either with young adult offenders or in the general prison population (Torbet, Gable, Hurst, Montgomery, Szymanski, & Thomas, 1996). Moreover, and perhaps most importantly, using a sophisticated experimental design, Lanza-Kaduce, Lane, Bishop, & Frazier (2005) investigated a large sample of Florida youth matched for crime committed and either transferred to adult court or prosecuted in the juvenile system and found that adult sanctions were more often linked to recidivism than were juvenile sanctions in the analysis of paired comparisons. In addition, waived youth as young as 13, 14, and 15 years of age have been sentenced to life without parole, and several 16- or 17-year-olds were sentenced to death. Although customary international law has explicitly prohibited the execution of juvenile offenders for years, the United States was the only country in the world that proclaimed its legal right to do so (Amnesty International, 2004; Streib, 2002). Only in March 2005 was this practice changed by the Supreme Court in a controversial 5–4 decision that proclaimed it "cruel and unusual punishment" to execute anyone under the age of 18 years (*Roper v. Simmons*, 124S.Ct. 2198 [2005]). Although this decision and the more recent Graham v. Florida, 560 U.S.___ [2010] decision that the Constitution does not permit a juvenile offender to be sentenced to life in prison without parole for a non-homicide offense may be seen as steps toward restoring a special status to juveniles, mandatory life sentences for juveniles who commit homicides remain an option and embody a cultural judgment that youth are as culpable and blameworthy as adults and thus should be held as equally accountable.

CONCLUSION

In both the case of zero tolerance in schools and the more punitive approach to juvenile justice, the explicit goal has been the protection of the public. Almost two decades later, however, there is no evidence that this goal has been met; in fact, there is evidence that the public is less safe as indicated by the increased recidivism rates for those youth tried as adults (Lanza-Kaduce et al., 2005) and the distinct lack of any positive results from zero tolerance policies. Rather, the major outcome seems to have been the creation of a group of "throw-away" children, whom the public views as dangerous, deserving of punishment, and not worthy of either caring or rehabilitation. "Old enough to do the crime; old enough to do the time" has become the mantra of our age for these youth. The fact that the vast majority of these youth have grown up in poverty ("the biggest single risk factor for the welfare of young people") (Feld, 1999, p. 333) and in dysfunctional families no longer seems to invoke the altruistic goal of helping them; rather, public opinion and law seems to believe that these juveniles, a disproportional number of whom are ethnic minorities (Feld, 1999; Giroux, 2003), should know better and deserve to be punished severely. As William Raspberry, the columnist, stated several years ago, "[When children, with many risk factors] get in trouble, we act as though their behavior is the simple result of free will and moral choice. We would never deprive a child of schooling and then, at age 18, throw him in jail for illiteracy. But isn't that what we're doing with kids who grow up unsocialized in middle-class values and then act out?" (p. A8).

Several of the youth in Humes' book have engaged in terrible acts that cannot be ignored, although the youth, themselves, were usually ignored by family and community helping agencies until they had committed an act that truly demanded negative sanctions. However, as we have seen in the discussion of zero-tolerance policies, the youth who have been impacted by these policies have all too often been punished in a manner that neither fits the crime (if there even was a crime) nor helps them become better people. We seem to believe that children are as competent, mature, and culpable as we expect adults to be, unless, of course, the children in question are our own. If ours, they deserve guidance, second chances, and help; if theirs, they should be punished for our safety and because they are bad! Unfortunately, the methods employed seldom have any linkage to our safety or their rehabilitation. At best, they exclude youth from school and/or incarcerate them in an adult or juvenile correctional facility for a period of time with little serious education or treatment. At worst, when the youth do rejoin society, they are embittered, have few skills, are behind in their education, often not allowed to re-enroll in school, and are unable to secure meaningful jobs.

Their most likely path is to engage in more crime. No one has heard their cry for help!

In this chapter, we have discussed two tales of terror, with little attention to tales of joy. We wish it uthwere otherwise. However, we believe that the public policies of the past few decades have had the result of criminalizing childhood for many youth. These policies appear to have been adopted to alleviate the public's fear of violent youth, exacerbated by exaggerated depictions from the mass media of heinous juvenile crimes and school shootings. We do not refute the seriousness of juvenile crime or a need for sanctions, but we do believe that the emphasis should be to turn these tales of terror into tales of joy by developing innovative approaches to help, not to excoriate, these youth. *In re Gault (1967)* empowered youth with due process rights but had the paradoxical effect of also depriving many of these youth of their rights to nurturance as juveniles. Youth are now trapped in the situation that because they have been empowered with these rights, they are viewed by the legal system as not needing the protections that resulted from a philosophical stance about their immaturity of judgment and decision making. Yet in all realms except for crime-related activities, they are still considered too immature to exercise their supposed autonomy. Criminal policies for public protection should be grounded in reality; they should not be ineffective policies that make us feel better and pray on our fears but do nothing to protect us or rehabilitate these youth. Redding (2006) concluded that transferring youth for trial and sentencing in adult court has not been a deterrent to future crimes; rather, it has "produced the unintended effect of increasing recidivism" (p. 8). Like the reformers who developed the juvenile justice system, we believe that the facilitation of the rehabilitation of youth and their successful transition to adulthood will be the most effective way to protect the public. This is not done by considering them as autonomous "bad kids" when they engage in delinquent acts but immature and lacking autonomy in every other decision-making situation. As the authors (Owen-Kostelnik, Reppucci, & Meyer, 2006) have argued in regard to interrogation contexts, "kids are kids" whether they are considered victims or perpetrators, and they need to be treated as juveniles. Just saying they are different, does not make them so!

By blaming the youth, themselves, and punishing them severely, we avoid having to address the many flaws in society, such as an ever increasing number of children raised in poverty (Males, 1996), vast discrepancies in resources allocated to schools in lower SES communities that result in less qualified teachers in these poorer school systems (Tuerk, 2005) and a mass culture that glorifies violence, guns, and consumer materialism (Reppucci, Fried, & Schmidt, 2002). We focus the blame on poor and minority youth and their families, as though we as a society have had no input into their situation. This is wrong! Criminalizing childhood by introducing zero-tolerance policies in the schools and treating youth as adults in our justice system may make us feel safer, but it is not an answer that will result in a tale of joy.

Author's Note

I (Dick Reppucci) met Julian Rappaport in 1975 at the Austin Conference on Community Psychology. A mutual acquaintance had told each of us that we each reminded him of the other. After all, we both had a Siberian husky—Nikita and Natasha, respectively—and from our graduate student days in the 1960s, we both had a similar commitment to the emerging field of community psychology—Julian knowingly, because of his mentorship from Emory Cowen; me unknowingly, but knowing that I was dissatisfied with the sorts of therapeutic interventions that were the standard fare of the time. In Austin, Julian had a major positive impact on me both for his content and style of presentation. Here was a person of my own cohort, with whom I wanted to discuss issues and become friends. I discovered that we had both been on the job market in 1968 and that he had decided not to pursue the position at Yale, for which I have been grateful ever since because it enabled me rather than him to work with Seymour Sarason for 8 years! Since Austin, we have had many discussions, become very good friends, biennially gone on a men's "activity" trip for the past two decades and agreed that, above all else, our written work should not be "boring." I am not at all sure that I have managed to adhere to this admonition, but I do know that Julian has. His papers are always anticipated with joy and savoured by those of us who never fail to be impressed by the enlightened metaphors and stories he employs to make salient concepts usable both in action and theory. He has been using community narratives throughout his career with astoundingly positive impact. Therefore, it was no surprise to see that in 2000 he provided us with a theory of community narratives or as he calls them—"Tales of Terror and Joy"—in which he asserts that, "the mission of the community psychologist/social scientist can be understood as a calling to use our tools (methods, critical observation and analysis, scholarship, social influence) to assist others in the job of turning tales of terror into tales of joy" (Rappaport, 2000, p. 7). Throughout his career, he has continuously practiced what he preaches, and we are the better for it. Community Psychology as a field has benefited from his many theoretical contributions and insights, his students have had a wonderful mentor, and I am happy and proud that he is my friend.

REFERENCES

Advancement Project and the Civil Rights Project (APCRP) (2000) Opportunities suspended: The devastating consequences of zero tolerance and school discipline policies. Boston, MA: Harvard Civil Rights Project, Retrieved from: http://www.law.harvard.edu/civilrights/conferences/zero/zt_report.html

Altschuler, D. M., & Brash, R. (2004). Adolescent and teenage offenders confronting the challenges and opportunities of reentry, *Youth Violence and Juvenile Justice, 2*(1), 72–87.

Amnesty International (2004). Stop child executions! Ending the death penalty for child offenders. Retrieved from: http://www.amnestyusa.org/abolish/juveniles/.

Associated Press (June 15, 2007) Has "zero tolerance" in schools gone too far? Center on Juvenile and Criminal Justice (2000). School house hype: Two years later. Washington, DC: Retrieved from: http://www.cjcj.org/pubs.schoolhouse/shh2pr.html

Center on Juvenile and Criminal Justice (1998). School house hype: The school shootings, and the real risk kids face in America. Washington, DC: Retrieved from: http://www.cjcj.org/pubs/shooting/shootings.html

Claiborne, W. (December 17, 1999). Disparity in school discipline found:\; Blacks disproportionately penalized under get-tough policies, study says. *Washington Post,* pp. A3.

Cornell, D. G. (2003). Guidelines for responding to student threats of violence. *Journal of Educational Administration, 41,* 705–719.

Dean, C., and Reppucci, N. D. (1974) Juvenile correctional institutions. In D. Glaser (Ed.), *The handbook of criminology* (pp. 865–895). Chicago: Rand McNally.

Eddings v. *Oklahoma* 455 U.S. 104 (1982).

Federal Bureau of Investigation (FBI). (2003) *Uniform Crime Reports.* Washington, DC: U.S. Department of Justice.

Federal Bureau of Investigation (FBI). (1997). *Uniform Crime Reports.* Washington, DC: U.S. Department of Justice.

Federal Bureau of Investigation (FBI). (1996). *Uniform Crime Reports.* Washington, DC: U.S. Department of Justice.

Federal Guns-Free Schools Act, 20 U.S.C. 8921 (1994).

Feld, B. C. (*1999*). *Bad kids: Race and the transformation of the juvenile court.* New York: Oxford University Press.

Giroux, H. (2003). Racial injustice and disposable youth in the age of zero tolerance, *International Journal of Qualitative Studies in Education, 16–4,* 553–565.

Graham v. Florida, 560 U.S. ___2010.

Hall, W. (April,21,2004). Violence among girls on upswing. *The Patriot News*, pp. A1, A8.

In re Gault, 387U.S.1 [*1967*].

Individuals with Disabilities Education Act, 20 U.S.C. 1400 (1997).

Kachur, S. P., Stennies, G., Powell, K., et al. (1996). School-associated deaths in the United States, 1992–1994. *JAMA, 275*, 1729–1733.

Lanza-Kaduce, L., Lane, J., Bishop, D. M., & Frazier, C. E. (2002). Juvenile offenders and adult felony recidivism: The impact of transfer. *Journal of Crime and Justice, 28*, 59–77.

Levine, M., & Levine, A. (1992) *Helping children: A social history*. New York: Oxford University Press.

Lockett v. Ohio 438 U.S. 586 (1978).

Males, M. A. (1996) *The scapegoat generation: America's war on adolescents*. Monroe, ME: Common Courage Press.

Manfredi, C. P. (1998). *The Supreme Court and Juvenile Justice*, Lawrence, K. S: University Press of Kansas.

McNulty, E. W. (1996). The transfer of juvenile offenders to adult court: Panacea or problem? *Law and Policy, 18*, 61–76.

Meyer, J., Reppucci, N. D., & Owen, J. (2006). Criminalizing childhood, In K. Freeark & W. Davidson (Ed.) *The Crisis in Youth Mental Health: Critical Issues and Effective Programs, Vol. 3: Issues for Families, Schools and Communities*, New York: Praeger Publications.

Merlo, A. V., & Benekos, P. J. (2000). *What's wrong with the criminal justice system? Ideology, politics, and the media*. Cincinnati, OH: Anderson.

Merlo, A. V., & Benekos, P. J. (2003). Defining juvenile justice in the 21st century. *Youth Violence and Juvenile Justice, (1)*3, 276–288.

Mulvey, E. P. & Cauffman, E. (2001). The inherent limits of predicting school violence, *American Psychologist, 56*(10), 797–802.

National Crime Victimization Survey (NCVS) (2003). Bureau of Justice Statistics, U.S. Department of Justice. Retrieved from: http://youthviolence.edschool.virginia.edu/violence-in-schools/national-statistics.html.

National School Safety Center (2003). *School associated with violent deaths*. Westlake Village, CA: Retrieved from: www.nssc1.org.

National Vital Statistics Report (1998). Washington, DC: National Center for Health Statistics.

Owen-Kostelnik, J., Reppucci, N. D., & Meyer, J. (2006). Testimony and interrogation of juveniles: Assumptions of maturity and morality": *American Psychologist, 61*, 286–304.

Podkopacz, M. R., & Field, B. C. (1996). The end of the line: An empirical study of judicial waiver. *Journal of Criminal law and Criminology, 86*, 449–492.

Rappaport, J. (2000) Community narratives: Tales of terror and joy, *American Journal of Community Psychology, 289,* 1–24.

Raspberry, W. (February, 22, 1999). *The Daily Progress,* Charlottesville, Virginia, p. A8.

Redding, R. E. (2006). Juvenile transfer laws: An effective deterrent to delinquency? *Juvenile Justice Bulletin,* Office of Juvenile Justice and Delinquency Prevention.

Reppucci, N. D. (1999). Adolescent development and juvenile justice. *Amerian Journal of Community Psychology, 27*(3), 307–326.

Reppucci, N. D., Fried, C. S., & Schmidt, M. G. (2002). Youth violence: Risk and protective factors. In R. Corrado, R. Roesch, & S. Hart (Eds.) *Multi-Problem Youth: A Foundation for Comparative Research on Needs, Interventions, and Outcomes,* Amsterdam: ISO Press.

Reppucci, N. D., Michel, J., & Kostelnik, J. O. (2009) Challenging juvenile transfer: faulty assumptions and misguided policy. In B. L. Bottoms, C. J. Najdowski, & G. L. Goodman (Eds.), Children as Victims, Witnesses and Offenders: *Psychological Science and the Law,* New York: Guilford Press.

Rimer, S. (January 4, 2004). Unruly students facing arrest, not detention. *New York Times,* p. 15A.

Roper v. *Simmons,* 124 S.Ct. 2198 (2005).

Rose, L. C., & Gallup, A. M. (2000). The 32nd annual Phi Delta Kappa/ Gallup poll of the public's attitudes toward the public schools. *Phi Delta Kappan, 86*(1), 41–52.

Rudman, C., Hartstone, E., Fagan, J., & Moore, M. (1986). Violent youth in adult court: Process and punishment. *Crime & Delinquency, 36,* 75–96.

Salekin, R. T. (2002). Juvenile transfer to adult court. In Bottoms, B. L., Kovera, M. B., & McAuliff, B. D (Eds). *Children, social science, and the law* (pp. 203–232). Cambridge, UK: Cambridge University Press.

Scott, E., & Grisso, T. (1997). The evolution of adolescence: A developmental perspective on juvenile justice reform. *Journal of Criminal Law and Criminology, 88,* 137–189.

Scott, E., & Grisso, T. (2005). Developmental incompetence, due process and juvenile justice policy. *North Carolina Law Review. 83,* 101–147.

Scott, E. S., Reppucci, N. D., Antonishak, J., & DeGennaro, J. T. (2006). Public attitudes about culpability and punishment of young offenders. *Behavioral Sciences and the Law. 24,* 815–832.

Sickmund, M., Synder, H. N., & Poe-Yamagata, E. (1997). *Juvenile offenders and victims: 1997 update on violence.* Washington, DC: Office of Juvenile and Delinquency Prevention.

Skiba, R., & Peterson, R. (1999). The dark side of zero tolerance: Can punishment lead to safe schools? *Phi Delta Kappan, 80*(5), 372–376.

Snyder, H. (2007). *Juvenile arrests 2005. OJJDP Juvenile Justice Bulletin.* Washington, DC: U.S. Department of Justice.

Snyder, H., & Sickmund, M. (1995). *Juvenile offenders and victims: A focus on violence.* U.S. Department of Justice, Office of Juvenile Justice and Delinquency Prevention.

Stanford v. *Kentucky,* 492 U.S. 361 (1989).

Streib, V. L. (2002). Gendering the death penalty: Countering sex bias in a masculine sanctuary. *Ohio State Law Journal, 63.* 433.

Thompson v. *Oklahoma,* 487 U.S. 815 (1988).

Tobin, T., & Sprague, J. (2000). Alternative education strategies: Reducing violence in school and the community. *Journal of Emotional and Behavioral Disroders, 8,* 177–186.

Torbet, P., Gable, R., Hurst, H., Montgomery, I., Szymanski, L., Thomas, D. (1996). *State responses to serious and violent juvenile crime: Research report.* Washington, DC: U.S. Department of Justice, Office of Juvenile and Delinquency Prevention.

Tuerk, P. W. (2005). Research in the high stakes era: Achievement, resources, and No Child Left Behind. *Psychological Sciences. 16,* 419–425.

Webb, P. & Kritsonis, W. A. (2006). Zero-tolerance policies and youth: Protection or profiling? *Doctoral Forum: National Journal for Publishing and Mentoring Doctoral Student Research, 3*(1), 1–8.

Worrell, C. (1985) Pretrial detention of juveniles: Denial of equal protection masked as the Parens Patriae doctrine. *Yale Law journal, 95,* 174–193.

Youth Risk Behavior Survey (2003). Washington, DC: National Center for Disease and Prevention and Health Promotion, Bureau of Justice Statistics, Retrieved from: http://youthviolence.edschool.virginia.edu/violence-in-schools/national-statistics.html.

9 The Neglected Role of Community Narratives in Culturally Anchored Prevention and Public Policy

Hirokazu Yoshikawa and
Maria A. Ramos Olazagasti

Rappaport and colleagues' recent work (Mankowski & Rappaport, 1995; Rappaport, 1995, 2000) challenges us as community psychologists to find "tales of terror" and turn them into tales of joy. As always, Rappaport provides sage and thought-provoking advice to the field in ways that both embody core principles of community psychology and extend them. The steps in this process of identifying and transforming narratives include the following. First, uncover societal, community- and setting-level stories. This is a hermeneutic process, one that requires interpretation of not only oral narratives but visual, behavioral, and spatial ones. Second, examine what the stories reveal about patterns of oppression (terror). What do they reveal about successful responses to oppression (joy)? Third, assist communities in turning their tales of oppression into tales of empowerment.

The narrative project in community psychology is one that reflects several aspects of Rappaport's work that have inspired the field for years. The first is the optimism of community psychology. The faith, so well-described in his textbook of 1977 (Rappaport, 1977), that community psychology can imagine a new psychology with respect for ecological and cultural diversity, is still present in his work on narratives. The second is the emphasis on oppression and empowerment. Since at least the seminal article in 1981 on empowerment, Rappaport has urged us to identify instances where communities are fighting oppression and taking mastery over their lives (Rappaport, 1981, 1987). The narrative project is a recasting of this goal, with attention to the stories that communities tell to themselves and to the world. The third is the emphasis on ecology. One of the strengths of his narrative theory is its insistence that narratives occur not only at the individual level but at the levels of social settings, communities, and society (Rappaport, 1995).

The narrative approach to community psychology has tremendous potential to inform culturally anchored research and action in the field. As many have noted (Hughes & Seidman, 2002; French & D'Augelli, 2002; Trickett, 2002), diversity and cultural relevance are continuing challenges and areas of growth for community psychology. In this chapter, we outline some of the ways in which a community narrative perspective can enrich culturally anchored work, using examples from three studies related to HIV prevention, welfare-to-work policies, and immigrants' use of public benefits. For each study, we describe recent data and discuss how the narrative perspective is reflected in the work, challenges it, and provides guidelines for future research and action.

COMMUNITY NARRATIVES AND CULTURALLY ANCHORED PREVENTION

Mainstream prevention research, as exemplified by the Preventive Intervention Research Cycle (Institute of Medicine, 1994; O'Connell, Boat, & Warner, 2009), is based on stories as much as any other human endeavor. In this field, stories are the behavioral theories from which prevention approaches are best thought to be developed. Mainstream prevention research continues to rely on stories that are assumed to hold across variation in culture, immigration, race, and ethnicity. They are typically written for—not by—the communities they aim to help (Rappaport, 1981). Theories of social cognition, reasoned action, or health behaviors are just three stories that aim to describe human behavior across contexts. These stories all assume universal psychological or cognitive processes that work just as well in immigrant Laotian communities as in White middle-class ones. Kegeles (2003), who developed with her colleagues an exemplar community-level HIV prevention program for young gay men, reported a tale of terror from mainstream prevention research. She reported that members of a National Institutes of Health (NIH) review panel simply did not understand why a grant would be needed to alter a program, first found successful with White gay men, to make it applicable to Black gay men.

How does the universal storytelling of mainstream prevention research limit the field? Miller and Shinn (2005), among many others (Feinberg, Greenberg, & Osgood, 2004; Rapkin, 2002; Schorr, 1988; Torrey et al., 2001; Yoshikawa, Wilson, Peterson, & Shinn, 2005), point out the ways. Dissemination, effectiveness research, and scaling-up are all phrases that describe the most ignored phase of prevention research, the take-up and implementation of prevention programs in community settings.

As many have advocated, why not turn the prevention research cycle on its head? Start with naturally occurring prevention efforts in community settings, bring them into public view, and encourage their influence on mainstream prevention research and on other community efforts. This, of course, is what Rappaport (1981, 1987) advocated in his work outlining a theory of empowerment for community psychology. But this message continues to be lost in the bulk of grant-funded prevention research in the United States. The vast expertise of community organizations—both formal and informal—working with communities of color tends to be ignored. Instead they are encouraged through policy and funding incentives to use empirically proven prevention models.

The community narrative approach could be vital in the process of furthering culturally anchored prevention. This approach is diametrically opposed to the usual "tailoring" approach by which a prevention program, found effective with one population, is then altered to fit the cultural norms of another. The tailoring approach assumes that core components of a prevention program predict behavior change and that they need to be retained for the prevention program to succeed with a new population. According to this model, implementation of those components may require changes when targeting the new group. The narrative approach, on the other hand, is a bottom-up approach to identifying culturally anchored, successful prevention models. Here we would start with the experience of local community efforts—both formal and informal—to prevent problematic outcomes and promote health. No tailoring is necessary if local efforts are culturally grounded in the daily routines and social contexts of community members.

In a recent study, we used this approach to identify promising approaches to HIV prevention in Asian and Pacific Islander (A&PI) communities (Yoshikawa et al., 2003). Our research stemmed from this dilemma: No culturally specific behavioral theories exist to guide HIV prevention in A&PI populations in the United States. Instead of using behavioral theories derived from prior research as our model, we used a sample of front-line peer educators in a large community-based health organization serving A&PI's. The peer educators were of Bangladeshi, Cambodian, Chinese, Filipino, Indian, Japanese, Korean, Malaysian, Okinawan, Pakistani, Thai, and Vietnamese backgrounds. Through focus group interviews (conducted in English and in

Bengali), we asked a straightforward set of questions: In your work, what are the strategies that have been successful in changing the health behaviors of A&PI's? Then we asked follow-up questions: For whom were these effective (under what conditions and in what settings)? How did the process of behavior change occur? What strategies were not effective? These are questions that guide much of mainstream prevention science; however, they are usually asked of researchers, not of practitioners.

First, we found that individual-level strategies for change were perceived nearly unanimously as unsuccessful. The predominant form of individual-level HIV prevention and education conducted by CBO's in U.S. cities is still street outreach, in which peer educators talk to individuals in community settings about HIV/AIDS and hand out information, often with condoms. These strategies were seen as ineffective by the peer educators for multiple cultural reasons, including taboos against accepting gifts from strangers in public spaces and discussing sexual matters with strangers, and norms equating condom use with promiscuity. Although they described modifications to these strategies to make them somewhat more effective (e.g., wrapping condoms in red-and-gold packaging, associated with good luck in Chinese immigrant communities), the overall assessment of the street outreach approach was a grim one of tedium on the part of peer educators and lack of response on the part of their target population.

In contrast, prevention strategies targeting change at social network, social setting, and community levels were perceived as successful. Social networks of South Asian immigrant women, for example, were targeted in one prevention effort:

> PARTICIPANT: We set up an appointment. For instance, let's say
> [Ms. A] calls one person and she's going to call me saying
> [Ms. B] we have to go to this person's house. So we make a
> group, and we go there so [Ms. A] knows someone and that lady
> brings other friends, her friends, at her house. First we come in.
> We don't suddenly start. We talk about different issues going on
> in family, we relax and get hospitable. They offer us tea. And
> then we get on with discussing about HIV and AIDS and they
> ask us questions and then we talk about their own personal lives
> that affect them, immigration issues, sexuality issues.

Social networks were also targeted in work conducted by the CBO with other A&PI populations, including sex workers and gay men. Many have noted the relatively high levels of social capital in immigrant enclave communities (e.g., Portes, 1998). That literature, together with these data, suggested the potential benefit of using diffusion of innovation methods (Rogers, 1995) in naturally occurring social networks in HIV prevention with

Asian and other immigrant communities. Social networks seemed to be more powerful channels of influence on health behaviors in A&PI communities than formal service providers or media. In further work on social networks, in a separate study of Asian gay men, we found further evidence of the importance of social networks in HIV risk behavior. In a survey study of Asian gay men, we explored whether talking about discrimination with social network members buffered the negative influence of discrimination on HIV risk for this group. We found, indeed, that conversations with family members as well as with friendship networks about discrimination protected these men from the otherwise positive correlation between experiences of racism, homophobia, and anti-immigrant discrimination and rates of unprotected sex (Yoshikawa, Wilson, Chae, & Cheng, 2004). Narrating tales of discrimination in conversations with one's family and friends appeared to be associated with protective health behaviors.

Setting-level change is another relatively neglected area of prevention science (Linney, 2000; Maton & Salem, 1995; Seidman & Tseng, 2005; Tseng & Seidman, 2007; Shinn, 1987; Shinn & Yoshikawa, 2008). Some prevention efforts conducted by the CBO in the focus group study appeared to alter social regularities (Seidman, 2002) in settings of particular relevance for A&PI immigrants at risk for HIV. In one neighborhood with a high concentration of recent Bangladeshi immigrants, for example, a peer educator worked with a network of grocery store owners to help distribute condoms and HIV information. These grocery stores serve as informal social centers for recently immigrated Bangladeshi adults. The owners were the opinion leaders in these settings. By working with the owners, resulting in the distribution of condoms and HIV information, this particular peer educator harnessed the power of existing social regularities in settings of relevance to this particular immigrant community:

> MALE PARTICIPANT: Reason is, they are scared from their friends, their relatives, their society, so they don't like to take the condoms in open. That's why I put some condoms in different stores so they are taking from the owners. The condoms I put in [the street], one grocery store, and I put in ten condoms, and yesterday I went over there and I find only one condom.
> FACILITATOR: So, you educated the owners first?
> PARTICIPANT: Yes. First I'm going in the different stores and asking the owners and, the same time, who are coming to buy materials, goods, shopping.

Some of the peer educators spoke about the match between setting-level goals of social contexts important to A&PI's, on the one hand, and the peers' own prevention goals, on the other. They reported more successful efforts when there was a match; the choice of these particular settings for outreach overcame some of the barriers of stigma that make street outreach extremely difficult for A&PI communities. A peer educator spoke of targeting pharmacies in Chinatown for outreach activities, because of the particular cultural meanings pharmacies hold for those in the Chinese immigrant community:

> I use the outreach and first of all, I have to talk about, it really depends on the environment. It could be a pharmacy store in Chinatown would be different from the grocery store in Chinatown because, the pharmacy, the people come in with tendency to rely on the pharmacist because they have a tendency to come to the pharmacist needing some kind of medication. So if you're doing outreach in front of the pharmacy or inside, people pay much more attention than if you do it in the grocery store.

The CBO peer educators also perceived community-level prevention strategies as some of the most successful in their work. One coalition-building effort brought together artists, activists, and peer educators to design an HIV-prevention media campaign to be unveiled at Gay Pride in New York City. The campaign targeted A&PI LGBT people. This quote illustrates how involvement in this coalition changed one peer educator's sense of what HIV prevention can do:

> PARTICIPANT: So this group of people came together, and we tried to figure out a time that we could meet. And we had long meetings. It was basically just a thinking group, and we would come together and put issues on the table and work through them and figure out what we wanted SLAAAP to do and what we, what holes we felt there were in the kind of education that was being done amongst queer Asians. And what we discovered was that HIV, we felt, was just one of many issues. And that there were all these other things that kept people from thinking about HIV, you know, that it can't be a concern, for example, if your immigration status is in the way or it can't be a concern if you're really really upset about breaking up with someone at that time. You know, that all these other things had to be addressed. And I think the way SLAAAP was most productive for me was that that whole process changed the way I thought about doing HIV prevention outreach.

These examples illustrate how narratives of change at setting and community levels can inform theory and practice in HIV prevention for communities of color. As community psychologists, we have the responsibility of using our resources to provide opportunities for people to voice their individual and collective narratives, to help them transform those narratives into positive stories, and to develop setting that are responsive to those stories. This is in essence an empowerment process, with the ultimate goal to prevent HIV infection. By uncovering the neglected expertise of front-line CBO staff, theories of change and concrete prevention strategies can be derived that are grounded in the cultural norms of diverse populations. Although narrative theory is often used as a justification for using qualitative methods, that does not mean that quantitative methods do not have anything to contribute to the understanding of the function and structure of narratives (Rappaport, 1995). For example, theories of change and prevention strategies developed based on community narratives can further be tested using traditional methods suited to causal inference, such as experiments and quasi-experiments. An integrated approach to empowerment and prevention can thus also integrate, from a research perspective, qualitative and quantitative methods (Yoshikawa, Weisner, Kalil, & Way, 2008). The field of prevention science might have fewer struggles with effectiveness, replication, and dissemination in diverse communities if it integrated to a greater degree empowerment processes that elicited community-member expertise and narratives in developing prevention programs.

COMMUNITY NARRATIVES AND CULTURALLY ANCHORED PUBLIC POLICY

Public policy analysis, perhaps even more than prevention research, is grounded in narratives that are assumed to be universal in scope and relevance. Why? Public policy by definition is a form of intervention that affects public goods and rights, and access to them, among entire populations (Bardach, 2000). In addition, the principal discipline informing policy analytic methods is economics, a social science wherein most celebrated behavioral theories, like those in psychology, are assumed to be universal. Finally, a traditionally weak area in public policy analysis is implementation research. The ecological level at which policy is experienced by the people whom it targets—the "street level," in front-line settings where implementation occurs—is where one would find the greatest variation in social regularities depending on the cultural background of the policy worker and target population. That is precisely the level at which research is most neglected.

Elmore noted this more than 25 years ago in his landmark article on backward mapping (Elmore, 1980); the point is still relevant today, as is obvious if one attends a typical annual meeting of the Association for Public Policy Analysis and Management (the most prominent regular meeting of policy analysts in the United States). Despite the fact that successful public policy is assumed to be responsive to the public (Bardach, 2000), too little research examines diversity in the public's daily experiences in settings affected by public policy (Yoshikawa & Hsueh, 2001; Yoshikawa et al., 2010).

How can a narrative approach address these shortcomings of policy analysis? We will discuss two examples, from evaluations of welfare and antipoverty policy. One addresses how the culture of welfare offices, as embodied in the interactions of front-line caseworkers with their clients, can be explored through narrative methods. Another concerns how immigrant parents experience U.S. program and policy contexts.

In the 1990s, profound policy changes affected welfare policies in the United States. Stereotypes associating welfare use with Black "welfare queens" getting rich off the dole, coupled with more objective concern about rising rates of AFDC use, resulted in the greatest changes to American welfare policy since the 1930s, when Aid to Dependent Children and Social Security were first established. State-level policy changes in the early 1990s tried a variety of more stringent requirements to work, such as time limits, coupled with (in some cases) more generous work support services. These culminated in the Personal Responsibility and Work Opportunity Reconciliation Act of 1996, which did away with cash welfare as an entitlement, instituted work requirements, and replaced AFDC with time-limited support provided at states' discretion. Meyers conducted a study evaluating change in welfare offices brought about by California's efforts to reform welfare in the 1990s (the GAIN program). She examined how front-line caseworkers' work was or was not reflecting the intended shift from checking eligibility to facilitating work (Meyers, Glaser, & Macdonald, 1998). By taping interviews between caseworkers and parents in welfare offices in California, she was able to examine just how the new reforms in California's GAIN program were experienced by the targets of the policy change. What she found was sobering: Little change in the culture of welfare offices occurred. Workers essentially continued to check for eligibility for welfare, without offering the work referral and support services that the GAIN program intended. This study showed how difficult changing the culture of welfare offices can be. More recent work on welfare policy implementation has shown how office-level caseworker support for welfare to work transitions is indeed associated with faster rates of increase in earnings and income and faster rates of decrease in welfare use (Godfrey, Yoshikawa, in press).

A second example of the promise of narrative methods in informing culturally anchored public policy concerns welfare policy for immigrants in the United States. The rights of legal immigrants to receive federal means-tested benefits were curtailed sharply in the 1996 federal welfare reform legislation. Since then, a "chilling" effect has been observed, such that even among immigrants still eligible, rates of use of federal programs such as Food Stamps or Medicaid have plunged (Capps, Ku, & Fix, 2002). However, little research has examined the concerns of immigrant parents about consequences of benefit use or how they make decisions about use of government assistance, post-1996. Therefore, theory about how to intervene to increase immigrants' access to vital supports like Food Stamps is lacking an evidentiary base. Here again, narrative methods can prove useful in grounding changes in public policy in detailed information from diverse populations.

In a recent study using multiple qualitative methods, we uncovered not only "tales of terror" about the consequences of benefit use among immigrant parents but also information about how such tales are told and important instances of silence, or tales not being told (Yoshikawa, Lugo-Gil, Chaudry, & Tamis-LeMonda, 2005; Yoshikawa, in press). We conducted a qualitative study with a sample of Mexican, Dominican, Chinese, Puerto Rican, and Black low-income parents in New York City. Fieldworkers visited these parents 12 times over the course of 8 to 10 months, in an intensive, multimethod study.[1] Visits alternated between semi-structured interviews and participant observation. Our data consisted of complete interview transcripts (in many cases transcribed and then translated from Chinese or Spanish into English) and extensive field notes written immediately after each visit.

Most of our Mexican, Dominican, and Chinese parents were first-generation immigrant parents. Our research questions about U.S. programs and policies for low-income families included the following: How do immigrant parents learn about the full range of federal programs and policies for low-income families? What kinds of attitudes do they express about these programs (both negative attitudes, like those resulting from stigma, and positive ones, like those resulting from network members' reports of helpfulness of programs)? How do they make decisions about utilization of these programs? Through these questions, we aimed to shed light on the way the "chilling" of immigrants' access to public benefits actually took place in immigrant communities.

We found, first of all, that immigrant parents overwhelmingly rely on their informal social networks, rather than formal service providers, for information about government assistance. This was true even of a population that

---

1 This study constituted the initial phase of work of the NYU Center for Research on Culture, Development, and Education. The study was aimed to inform the development of two large-scale, multimethod cohort studies of immigrant and ethnically diverse families.

was recruited from community agencies. A field worker reported about a Mexican immigrant mother:

> This friend took her to sign up—and told her it was a program for children where they would be taught things because sometimes as parents you don't know where to take your children. Here they would be taught things that you don't teach them at home—like colors or names of fruits.

Similarly, a Chinese mother said in an interview, "I do not know much about the help. I just heard some from my friends and did as they told me to apply for it. Or sometimes I would call them for information if needed." Second-generation and other U.S.-born mothers, in contrast, reported many sources of information that included not only informal network members but also formal service providers. For many of these mothers, the sources of information were too numerous to pinpoint.

The immigrant parents in our sample also related tales of literal terror about the consequences of benefit use for their citizenship. This occurred, as one might expect, among undocumented mothers concerned about potential amnesty or transitions to legal permanent resident (LPR) status. One Mexican mother hid her benefit use from her own husband:

> Xenia's[2] husband is applying for residency and he thinks that the government would look down upon him if they find that his family receives assistance. She therefore receives assistance, but doesn't tell her husband. She hides her benefits card from her husband, and often offers to go shopping by herself so that he's not suspicious of money.

Among the undocumented group, those in mixed-status families often expressed concerns that led them not to apply for benefits that their children were eligible for.[3] One field worker wrote in her field notes:

> Consuela, a Mexican mother, and her husband decided not to ask for benefits other than food. They believe that if amnesty comes through one day, they will lose their chances of getting it because they have been a burden for the country. She knows

---

2 All names in the qualitative data presented from this study are pseudonyms.

3 Mixed-status families are those that include undocumented parents with U.S.-born citizen children. These families are now a sizable percentage of immigrant families in the U.S. (Jasso, 1995).

that U.S-born children qualify for some cash and housing benefits, but they have decided not to request them. They do not want to take benefits for themselves that are based on their U.S-born children's eligibility. They are trying to do everything possible (including paying taxes) to demonstrate that they have not been a burden to the country in hoping that they get amnesty one day.

These narratives suggest that children in mixed-status families are just as much at risk of not receiving benefits that could help them as children who are themselves undocumented.

In data new to the literature, we found avoidance of government assistance not only among the undocumented mothers but also among LPR mothers concerned about transitions to citizenship. One Chinese mother "knows about it [Food Stamps] but they dare not apply ... because they are in the process of applying for their citizenship. She said she didn't want to hurt the application." Another Chinese mother, who wanted to start a storefront- or buffet-type Chinese restaurant (as did many of our Chinese parents from Fujian province, currently the largest sending province in China), "felt that if her family got help from the government, they would run into problems in the future when they wanted to start the business."

Are these immigrants' fears founded in current government policy regarding consequences of benefit use for citizenship applications? The ICE's most recent guidance of 1999 stated that, with the exception of two very unusual circumstances, immigrants who are LPRs are not subject to "public charge" tests based on use of federal means-tested benefit programs (Fremstad, 2000).[4] For immigrants who are not LPRs, in contrast, the Immigration and Customs Enforcement agency (ICE) can take into account Supplemental Security Income (SSI), Temporary Assistance for Needy Families (TANF), and General Assistance receipt as evidence contributing to an assessment of "public charge." However, they cannot account for other forms of benefit receipt, including Food Stamps, childcare, health-related benefits (except for long-term care in nursing homes) such as Medicaid or the State Children's Health Insurance Program (SCHIP), school lunch, or housing benefits. As for mixed-status families such as Consuela's, with a noncitizen parent and a citizen child, the ICE guidance states that receipt of cash benefits by an immigrant's citizen family member does not influence public charge determination unless the family is reliant on the benefits as its sole financial means of support.

---

4 "Public charge" tests can potentially deny someone citizenship because they have been shown to be a "drain" on government benefit programs.

Some of the fears of the parents expressed in our study were well-founded in ICE policy, and some were not. Xenia's belief that receipt of cash assistance might threaten her husband's application for legal permanent residency does have a basis in the ICE guidance. Consuela's distinction between food and other forms of assistance, similarly, does have some basis in the guidance (although she may not be aware that many other forms of in-kind assistance, besides Food Stamps, would also not be permissible in a public charge determination).

In contrast, none of the Chinese mothers' fears about consequences of assistance for progression from LPR status to citizenship status, or for future businesses, are founded in the language of the current ICE guidance. Consuela's fear that her U.S.-born children's receipt of assistance would count against them in a public charge determination would only be true if those benefits were the family's only form of financial support. However, the information in the ICE guidance is complex and nuanced and most likely not communicated consistently and accurately by sources of information such as service providers, let alone members of informal social networks. Therefore, the decision by these parents to forgo receipt of many benefits may be an adaptive choice, given uncertainty about the government's regulations and future intent.

The data from our sample about sources of knowledge about public assistance, as well as concerns about the consequences of use for citizenship, have implications for the design of interventions to address the "chilling" effect. In particular, informal social settings such as personal networks appeared to serve as important conduits of information linking the policy level to the individual level. The importance of informal social networks in the dissemination of knowledge among immigrant populations suggests that what Rappaport might term the dominant cultural narrative of public policy is interpreted by networks, which in turn transmit messages to their individual members. Thus, even an assumed universal message, such as one imposed by public policy, assumes great diversity at the level of the target behavior (Elmore, 1980).

Furthermore, the role of social networks uncovered through the immigrant parents' narratives suggests that current outreach efforts to educate the public about benefits, such as media campaigns and training of service providers to inform immigrant populations of programs like Food Stamps, may be barking up the wrong tree. In public health, interventions using diffusion of innovation methods have long used existing social networks to disseminate information and bring about behavior change (Rogers, 1995). Such methods, relying on opinion leaders and natural communication channels, may be particularly suited to the task of informing low-income immigrant populations about forms of government and community assistance for food, housing, childcare, and work. These forms of intervention, used for this purpose, have never been evaluated. Yet, individual stories—particularly those from leaders in the community—have the potential to create and shape the groups' narratives (Mankowski & Rappaport, 1995).

Addressing fears of consequences of benefit use may be more challenging. In the current policy climate toward immigrants in the United States, service providers may be aware of ICE guidelines but may still caution immigrant parents of LPR status or those in mixed-status families not to use public assistance, to be on the safe side. Such cautions likely also travel through informal social networks in immigrant communities. Allaying such fears would take considerable societal change in not only this area of immigrant policy but other related areas such as naturalization and border policies.

We also found some evidence of silence in narratives about government policy told to us by the immigrant mothers in our study. We asked our sample how they felt government assistance was different in the United States compared to their countries of origin. Perhaps in part because of our sampling from countries with weaker safety nets than the United States (Mexico, the Dominican Republic, and poorer areas of mainland China), immigrant parents overwhelmingly felt that the United States was more generous. This was not particularly surprising. What struck us, however, was the complete lack of statements from the immigrant parents about not being eligible for many forms of government assistance. Many were in fact not eligible because of their post-1996 arrival as legal immigrants or their undocumented status. Silence in this instance was just as telling as the stories the parents told us. In fact, the group in our sample that other studies in New York suggest have the highest proportions of undocumented parents—Mexicans—reported significantly higher levels of system justification, or perceptions that society is fair (Godfrey, 2008), than U.S.-born Blacks or Dominicans. Freire, among others, relates how silence about oppression may indicate potential for raising it to conscious awareness, through pedagogical and collaborative efforts (Freire, 1972; Serrano-Garcia & Bond, 1994). In this case, working with advocates to educate immigrant parents about how government policies treat them may address some of the worrisome silences that we heard.

There is a lot to learn from the communities that we serve, and it is our responsibility to expose, rather than hide, stories of terror. By doing so, we move a step forward in helping reconstruct narratives in ways that liberate and empower, rather than oppress (Rappaport, 2000). "Top-down" approaches in which communities are seen as passive recipients of policies have little to contribute to the development of policies and evaluations that are culturally relevant. In contrast, "bottom-up" approaches in which communities are seen as competent and knowledgeable and capable of informing policy development and evaluation have a more optimistic future in informing policy work that is relevant to the diverse populations that we serve. Narrative methods show promise in informing true backward mapping efforts to develop and evaluate policies using "bottom-up" rather than "top-down" methods. Instead of evaluating policies' intended effects by examining changes in desired outcomes across populations, narrative methods can uncover the immediate proximal factors that influence decision making and behaviors of particular target populations. These methods can help us get closer to the source of policy problems, thereby allowing us to focus on the delivery-level mechanisms that might produce change. Information about the individual and setting-level factors that influence the behaviors of particular groups, including cultural norms in networks, modes of communication, and particular attitudes about public policies, can then be used to craft a new generation of policies with better knowledge of how to restructure settings of policy implementation.

The value of narrative methods is not limited to their potential to inform true "bottom-up" approaches to policy creation and evaluation that are relevant to the population under study. Narrative methods are also an important empowerment tool for community psychologists. Helping people give voice to a collective narrative that cherishes their own personal life stories and developing settings that make such activities possible embraces the goals of empowerment (Rappaport, 1995). Empowerment is a collaborative community process involving mutual respect and participation where people who lack valuable resources not only obtain access to these but gain control over such resources (Cornell University Empowerment Group, 1989). Giving people the opportunity to communicate their own stories and to influence their collective stories is an invaluable and empowering resource (Rappaport, 1995).

There are, however, some limitations of narrative methods. First, collecting and analyzing narrative data demands a considerable amount of time and effort. Second, because it is so time-consuming, the sample size for such studies tends to be relatively small, and data often have greater limits regarding generalizability than larger-scale quantitative studies. Third, limitations resulting from imposing researchers' interpretation and meaning on individuals' experience afflicts qualitative research as much as quantitative (Yoshikawa, Weisner, Kalil, & Way, 2008).

These issues can be addressed, however, through several strategies. First, data transcription and analysis can be focused on the subset of themes relevant to a particular study. Second, generalizability issues can be addressed by paying careful attention to sampling in qualitative studies. Finally, relying solely on researcher perspectives can be avoided by involving community stakeholders in all aspects of the research and intervention development process, including conceptualization, protocol and measure development, data analysis, and interpretation.

CONCLUSION

Julian Rappaport's challenge to community psychology, to incorporate narrative methods in efforts to bring about social change, is part of a recent shift in the field to better employ qualitative methods in the service of action (AJCP special issue on qualitative methods, "Qualitative research," 1998; Yoshikawa et al., 2008). In this chapter, we have argued that narrative methods can also bring a more culturally anchored perspective, long neglected, to prevention research and public policy analysis. In addition, we have outlined how such methods can be integrated with quantitative methods of evaluation and causal inference to strengthen work in both prevention and public policy.

Rappaport's first step of uncovering community narratives contrasts in both method and ecological level of analysis with the generative phase in prevention science and policy analysis. In prevention research, risk and protective factors that are associated with a negative outcome are first identified, often without much regard to the ecological level through which these factors operate or aggregate. In top-down approaches to policy analysis, the causal impact of a policy's implementation is estimated on the target behavior across a jurisdiction, often without sufficient attention to the intermediate ecological levels—institutional, organizational, community, and network—that affect the quality of implementation. The examples from this chapter from culturally anchored prevention and public policy analysis revealed processes at the setting or contextual level that could inform future prevention and policy. Discrimination faced by Asian immigrants was countered by examples of community organizing and mobilization of social networks. Resistance from family members to accepting help from government sources was countered by examples of use of network referrals to enroll children in early childhood education.

Prevention programs are still most often based on individual-level theories of behavior change or developmental psychopathology. Public policy, similarly, is often based on individual- or, at the most, household-level theories of decision-making, gatekeeping, and resource allocation, across economic, educational, health, or other domains. Community narratives can show the potential of a greater range of social processes in settings, from the network to the organizational, that communities harness to enhance their well-being and counter experiences of discrimination and oppression. Rappaport's emphasis on stories at the societal, community, and setting levels as the first step in his hermeneutic approach ensures this shift in ecological focus, while also prioritizing the richness of multiple observational methods (verbal, visual, and spatial). Such information should be used more often to help ensure that the next generaton of prevention and policy initiatives is more responsive to the settings and contexts in which diverse populations live and work in the United States.

Universal theories of behavior change do not account for the reality that all people do not respond to interventions the same way and that the mechanisms that produce behavioral change for one group might not bring about change for other groups. Past work on prevention research and public policy analysis has often ignored the voices of the people that deliver the services offered by programs and the people that are affected by these programs and policies. Community psychology has been challenged to gather information from the community and bring it to the larger public and to policymakers, as opposed to relying solely on research-based behavioral theories of change. By replacing universal theories of behavior change with local narratives of individuals in the community settings where they live, community psychologists can participate in generating more responsive and culturally specific prevention programs and public policies.

References

Bardach, E. (2000). *A practical guide for policy analysis: The eightfold path to more effective problem solving.* New York: Seven Bridges Press.

Capps, R., Ku, L., & Fix, M. (2002). *How are immigrants faring after welfare reform? Preliminary evidence from Los Angeles and New York City.* Washington, DC: The Urban Institute.

Cornell Empowerment Group. (1989). Empowerment and family support. *Networking Bulletin, 1,* 1–23.

Elmore, R. (1980). Backward mapping: Implementation research and policy decisions. *Political Science Quarterly, 94,* 601–616.

Feinberg, M. E., Greenberg, M. T., & Osgood, D. (2004). Readiness, functioning, and perceived effectiveness in community prevention coalitions: A study of communities that care. *American Journal of Community Psychology, 33,* 163–176.

Freire, P. (1972). *Pedagogy of the oppressed, chapter 1* (pp. 27–56). New York: Seabury.

Fremstad, S. (2000). *The ICE public charge guidance: What does it mean for immigrants who need public assistance?* Washington, DC: Center for Budget and Policy Priorities.

French, S. E., & D'Augelli, A. R. (2002). Diversity in community psychology. In T. A. Revenson, A. D'Augelli, S. E. French, D. Hughes, D. Livert, E. Seidman, M. Shinn, & H. Yoshikawa (Editors). *Ecological research to promote social change: Methodological advnaces from community psychology* (pp. 65–80). New York: Plenum.

Godfrey, E. B. (2008). *Data on system justification among Mexican, Dominican, and African American low-income parents.* Unpublished data.

Godfrey, E. B., & Yoshikawa, H., (in press). Caseworker-recipient interaction: Welfare office differences, economic trajectories and child outcomes. *Child Development.*

Hughes, D.,& Seidman, E. (2002). In pursuit of a culturally anchored methodology. In T. A. Revenson, A. D'Augelli, S. E. French, D. Hughes, D. Livert, E. Seidman, M. Shinn, & H. Yoshikawa (Editors). *Ecological research to promote social change: Methodological advances from community psychology* (pp. 243–256). New York: Plenum.

Institute of Medicine (1994). *Reducing risks for mental disorders: Frontiers of preventive intervention research.* Washington, DC: National Academy Press.

Institute of Medicine (in press). *Report of the Committee on Prevention of Mental Disorders of the Institute of Medicine, National Research Council.* Washington, DC: National Academy Press.

Jasso, G. (2005). *Children of the New Immigrant Survey: Overview and preliminary results based on the Round I survey.* Presented at "One in Five: Addressing Health, Educational, and Socioeconomic Disparities of Children in Immigrant Families," a conference sponsored by the National Institute of Child Health and Human Development, Rockville, MD, May.

Kegeles, S. (2003). *The Mpowerment Project: Lessons from dissemination research.* Presented at the U.S. Conference on AIDS, Atlanta, GA.

Linney, J. A. (2000). Assessing ecological constructs and community context. In J. Rappaport & E. Seidman (Eds.), *Handbook of community psychology* (pp. 647–667). New York: Plenum.

Mankowski, E., & Rappaport, J. (1995). Stories, identity and the psychological sense of community. In R.S. Wyer (Ed.), *Advances in social cognition (Volume 8)*, (pp. 211–236.) Mahwah, NJ: Erlbaum.

Maton, K. I., & Salem, D. A. (1995). Organizational characteristics of empowering community settings: A multiple case study approach. *American Journal of Community Psychology, 23,* 631–656.

Meyers, M. K., Glaser, B., & MacDonald, K. (1998). On the front lines of welfare delivery: Are workers implementing policy reforms? *Journal of Policy Analysis and Management, 17,* 1–22.

Miller, K. E., & Banyard, V. L. (Eds.). (1998). Qualitative research in community psychology [Special issue]. *American Journal of Community Psychology, 26*(4).

Miller, R. L., & Shinn, M. (2005). Learning from communities: Overcoming difficulties in dissemination of prevention and promotion efforts. *American Journal of Community Psychology, 35,* 169.

O'Connell, M. E., Boat, T., & Warner, K. E. (2009). (Eds.). *Preventing mental, emotional and behavioral disorders among young people: Progress and possibilities.* Washington, DC: National Academy Press.

Portes, A. (1998). *The economic sociology of immigration.* New York: Russell Sage Foundation.

Rapkin, B. D. (2002). Ecologically-minded reconstruction of experiments in HIV prevention: Reduce, reuse and recycle. *Journal of Primary Prevention, 23,* 235–250.

Rappaport, J. (1977). *Community psychology: Values, research and action.* New York: Holt, Rinehart, and Winston.

Rappaport, J. (1981). In praise of paradox: A social policy of empowerment over prevention. *American Journal of Community Psychology, 9,* 10–25.

Rappaport, J. (1987). Terms of empowerment/exemplars of prevention: Toward a theory for community psychology. *American Journal of Community Psychology, 15,* 121–145.

Rappaport, J. (1995). Empowerment meets narrative: Listening to stories and creating settings, *American Journal of Community Psychology, 23,* 795–807.

Rappaport, J. (2000). Community narratives: Tales of terror and joy. *American Journal of Community Psychology, 28,* 1–24.

Rogers, E. M. (1995). *Diffusion of innovations* (fourth edition). New York: Free Press.

Schorr, L. B. (1988). *Within our reach: Breaking the cycle of disadvantage.* New York: Anchor Press/Doubleday.

Seidman, E. (2002). Back to the future, community psychology: Unfolding a theory of social intervention. In T. A. Revenson, A. D'Augelli, S. E. French, D. Hughes, D. Livert, E. Seidman, M. Shinn, & H. Yoshikawa (Editors), *A quarter century of community psychology.* (pp. 181–203). New York: Plenum.

Seidman, E., & Tseng, V. (2005). *Social settings: A place to stand for community psychologists.* Presented at the Festschrift for Julian Rappaport, biennial meeting of the Society for Community Research and Action, Urbana-Champaign, IL, June.

Serrano-Garcia, I., & Bond, M. (1994). (Eds.). Empowering the silent ranks [Special Issue]. *American Journal of Community Psychology, 22*(4).

Shinn, M. (1987). Expanding community psychology's domain. *American Journal of Community Psychology,* 15, 555–574.

Shinn, M., & Yoshikawa, H. (Eds.). (2008). *Toward positive youth development: Transforming schools and community programs.* New York: Oxford University Press.

Torrey, W. C., Drake, R. E., Dixon, L., et al. (2001). Implementing evidence-based practices for persons with severe mental illnesses. *Psychiatric Services,* 52, 45–50.

Trickett, E. J. (2002). A future for community psychology: The contexts of diversity and the diversity of contexts. In T. A. Revenson, A. D'Augelli, S. E. French, D. Hughes, D. Livert, E. Seidman, M. Shinn, & H. Yoshikawa (Editors), *A quarter century of community psychology.* (pp. 513–534). New York: Plenum.

Tseng, V. & Seidman, E. (2007). A theoretical framework for understanding social settings: A dynamic systems approach. *American Journal of Community Psychology,* 39, 217–228.

Yoshikawa, H., (in press). *Immigrants raising citizens: Undocumented parents and their young children's development.* New York: Russell Sage.

Yoshikawa, H., & Hsueh, J. (2001). Child development and public policy: Towards a dynamic systems perspective. *Child Development,* 72, 1887–1903.

Yoshikawa, H., Lugo-Gil, J., Chaudry, A., & Tamis-LeMonda, C.S. (2004). *How lower-income immigrant parents in New York City navigate U.S. programs and policies for children.* Paper presented at "The Next Generation: Immigrant Youth and Families in Comparative Perspective," Radcliffe Institute for Advanced Study, Harvard University, Cambridge, MA.

Yoshikawa, H., Gassman-Pines, A., Morris, P. A., Gennetian, L. A., & Godfrey, E. B. (2010). Racial/ethnic differences in effects of welfare policies on school readiness and later school achievement. *Applied Developmental Science. 14*, 137–153.

Yoshikawa, H., Weisner, T. S., Kalil, A., & Way, N. (2008). Mixing qualitative and quantitative research methods in developmental science: Uses and methodological choices. *Developmental Psychology,* 44, 344–354.

Yoshikawa, H., Wilson, P. A., Chae, D. H., & Cheng, J. F. (2004). Do family and friendship networks protect against the influence of discrimination on mental health and HIV risk among Asian and Pacific Islander gay men? *AIDS Education and Prevention: Official Publication of the International Society for AIDS Education, 16*(1), 84–100.

Yoshikawa, H., Wilson, P. A., Hsueh, J., Rosman, E. A., Kim, J., & Chin, J. (2003). What frontline CBO staff can tell us about culturally anchored theories of change in HIV prevention for Asian/Pacific Islanders. *American Journal of Community Psychology, 32,* 143–158.

Yoshikawa, H., Wilson, P. A., Peterson, J. L., & Shinn, M. (2005). Multiple pathways to community-level impacts in HIV prevention: Implications for conceptualization, implementation, and evaluation of interventions. In E. J. Trickett & W. Pequegnat (Eds.), *Community interventions and AIDS* (pp. 28–55). New York: Oxford University Press.

10   On Voice: Difference, Power, Change

J. Eric Stewart

"Narrative is where theory takes place"
                    (Christian, 1987, p. 101).

"About ideas, how can one tell?"
                    (J. Bruner, 1983, p. 126).

Jerome Bruner (1990) argues that we confront the world as "a field of differences" and that we must, in some manner, "adjudicate the different construals of reality that are inevitable in any diverse society" (p. 95). This contrasts with psychology's traditional focus on how to best fit people in some Procrustean way into a standard and inevitable world. Bruner frames the question for psychology as being about the "kind of world needed to make it possible to use mind (or heart!) effectively—what kinds of symbol systems, what kinds of accounts of the past, what arts and sciences?" (Bruner, 1996, p. 9). Similarly, Shweder and Sullivan (1993) emphasize the need for an intellectual climate that questions the "one-sided emphasis on fixed essences, intrinsic features, and universally necessary truths" and call for a revaluation of "processes and constraints that are local, variable, context-dependent, and in some sense made up" (p. 500). Elaborating on narrative theory and the cultural perspective it entails in Bruner's work, Geertz (2000) identifies the implications for psychology in this way:

> To argue that culture is socially and historically constructed, that narrative is a primary, in humans perhaps the primary, mode of

knowing, that we assemble the selves we live in out of materials lying about in the society around us ... that we act not directly on the world but on beliefs we hold about the world, impassioned "meaning makers" in search of plausible stories—such a view amounts to rather more than a midcourse correction. Taken all in all, it amounts to adopting a position that can fairly be called radical, not to say subversive.

(p. 196)

This is more than a call for—or for greater legitimation of—qualitative methods. It is more than "discovering" people's and communities' stories, amplifying or "giving" voice. Rather, a narrative approach can "advance our thinking about the problems and puzzles of community psychology" (Rappaport, 1995, p. 3), placing in the foreground a number of the major dilemmas for the field: top-down versus bottom-up (in the social and power-laden sense), meaning and action, social determinism and unencumbered agency, relativism and universalism, and, "perhaps most fundamentally, difference and commonality" (Geertz, 2000, p. 197).

These are already familiar concerns for many community psychologists, and if narrative theory foregrounds them, it can also provide a useful approach for articulating and confronting them. Narratives simultaneously reflect personal, community, and broader (or dominant) cultural perspectives, practices, and relations: they and we are both constituted by and constitutive of social meanings, contexts, and relationships (e.g., Altman & Rogoff, 1987; Barthes, 1977; Bruner, 1990; Castells, 1997; de Certeau, 1984; Denzin, 1997; Polkinghorne, 1988; Siebers, 1992; Miller & Goodnow, 1995; Yudice, 1990). Narratives and their performance involve and represent communicative practices, institutional structure, complex forms and presentations of agency, and relations of power and knowledge (Denzin, 1997; Frow & Morris, 1993). Plummer (1995) argues that for narratives to be viable, there must be a community to hear, and for "communities to hear, there must be stories which weave together their history, their identity, their politics. The one—community—feeds upon and into the other—story" (p. 87). Narrators strengthen and theorize their communities and themselves through narratives, while also expanding their audience or community of listeners (Chase, 2005; Mankowski & Rappaport, 1995; Rappaport, 1995, 1998, 2000).

In relation to empowerment and social change, critical consciousness about marginalized or oppressed status and identity requires the possibility of articulating shared, general theory on the basis of experience as well as recognizing the ways that that experience differs from that of others. In the context of disability studies, Siebers (2008) articulates the ways that narrative provides a means to satisfy the theoretical, practical, and political requirements of both collective identification and a critical deployment of difference:

> Narratives about disability identity are theoretical because they posit a different experience that clashes with how social existence is usually constructed and recorded. They are practical because they often contain solutions to problems experienced by disabled and nondisabled people alike. They are political because they offer a basis for identity politics, allowing people with different disabilities to tell a story about their common cause. The story of this common cause is also the story of an outsider position that reveals what a given society contains. For example, when a disabled body moves into a social space, the lack of fit exposes the shape of the normative body for which the space was originally designed. Disabled identities make a difference, and in making a difference, they require a story that illuminates the society in which they are found.
>
> (p. 104)

Narrative allows personal experience *and* difference to become common cause in social identification and community, to become practical strategies for being in the world, and, importantly, to become critical theory: narratives of identity and identification contain useful information about how people can make their appearance and negotiate relationships in the world (Alcoff, 2006; Siebers, 1992). Although they possess little social power, disability identities and collective identifications, *"because of their lack of fit, serve as critical frameworks for identifying and questioning complicated ideologies on which social injustice and oppression depend"* (Siebers, 2008, p. 105, emphasis added). Narratives as theory enable communities to "show what society contains," to analyze social and structural reality as theorized, power-laden stories about how things are, should be, or must be.

I think it is important to emphasize that it is only in this *double* exposition—where exposed experiences of "lack of fit," or "tales of terror" (Rappaport, 2000), are taken as critical exposition of oppressive ideologies and institutional regularities—that narrative can meet empowerment, that listening to stories can engender social change (Rappaport, 1995; 1998). Otherwise, "giving voice" tends to really mean appropriating experience, reifying description, or a kind of voyeuristic tourism (Stewart, 2000). If we fail to attend to the implicit or explicit critiques of power relations and cultural/institutional discourses that they pose, then accounts of difference, distress, or, indeed, terror easily become reinscriptions of failure and malad-justment (further tales of terror) or valorizations of our therapeutic enter-prises and policy formations. No joy—just specimens of terror.

For example, Savin-Williams (2008) recently surveyed the psycholog-ical literature on same-sex sexuality since 1995, including some that has appeared in the *American Journal of Community Psychology,* a literature with particular emphasis on youth. Noting that this literature is suffused by a clinical fixation on the problematic, he concludes:

> It is as if same-sex oriented populations are only interesting to
> the extent that they differ in the negative … I am hard pressed to
> identify any data-based positive attribute that characterizes the
> lives of same-sex oriented preadults relative to heterosexuals.
> Can this possibly be true? Although considerable empirical data
> document gay youth as depressed, suicidal, victimized, homeless,
> and HIV+, might it be possible, as suggested by Luthar (2001),
> that experiences of adversity may precipitate not only suicide but
> also significant personal growth through increasing the depth and
> complexity in one's life?
>
> (p. 137)

This literature very rarely interrogates, in a direct and critical way, the contexts and dominant narratives gay (and straight) youth confront, except in an "everybody knows" kind of implicitness. This literature even more rarely presents LGBT or queer youth as critical strategists and theorists with the capacity to illuminate ideological blueprints of society (for an exception, *see* Cohler & Hammack, 2007). So, although in recent decades most of the psychological literature (including that within community psychology and including qualitative, "voice-giving" work) on queer or LGBT youth has adopted a sympathetic, "it's not their fault" perspective on this litany of pathology, it still adds up to the same thing: tragic, self-destructive young homosexuals. I don't imagine that I need to reference Ryan (1971) here to make the point. Even when the implicit, "goes-without-saying" context of that work is that these problems and risk behaviors are the effects of oppres-sion, pathology is the story for LGBTQ youth, albeit sometimes with a (typ-ically individualist) heroic overcoming twist (Cohler & Hammack, 2007). My point is about more than bad science—it is also about bad faith. If the story we mean to tell is a story of oppression, then it seems to me that that story ought to include, ought to catalog and dissect, that which oppresses. Community psychology's commitment to social and setting change, to a strengths-based perspective, and to empowerment would seem to dictate that we should be using the stories of outsider positions to identify and question the "complicated ideologies on which social injustice and oppression depend" (Siebers, 2008, p. 105).

If we solicit and present the terrible tales of misfits, outsiders, the at-risk, the angry, the distressed, the queer, or the crazy—even if we present them as full narrative accounts—but we do not allow them to be or deploy them as explicit and critical illuminations and interrogations of the order of things, then we are reproducing rather than contesting given ideological systems (cf. Scott, 1991). Using qualitative methods and enlisting the participation of understudied populations does not necessarily minimize the risk of reproduction and reinscription of victim-blaming or victim-mongering; In fact, unreflexive work will likely exacerbate the risks (e.g., R.D.G. Kelley, 1997; Stewart, 2000).

The exemplary work represented in the four preceding chapters takes up narrative and voice in ways that demonstrate its applicability and expository power in a variety of contexts, at different levels of analysis, for diverse problems and populations, and as serving a range of goals and strategies. I think that the intertextual relationship here, the relationships between and within the chapters, is demonstrative of the value of voice and narrative to a range of interests and strategies that are central to community psychology. Before I commence to commentary, let me say that these authors and their work speak quite eloquently; I do not (dare not) provide an executive summary or mount an exegetical study here. Rather, I want (idiosyncratically) to draw out some themes and strengths that amplify or problematize the use and deployment of voice and narrative in research and action; and, vice versa, I hope to indicate what voice and narrative can amplify and problematize about research, action, and the social order.

Deborah Salem's (Chapter 6, this volume) long-term (25 years) collaborative work with Schizophrenics Anonymous (SA) illustrates how membership in a mutual-help setting enables resistance to the discourse of individuality and of pathology. Membership in SA provides a context, set of relationships, and meaning-making resources for a re-narration of a "radically different understanding of what it means to recover from an illness like schizophrenia," one based on personal and collective experience. But, as Salem points out, this alternative narrative of self-acceptance, hope, and re-authored life goals meets powerful—if passive—resistance in professional and institutionalized settings, where members' storytelling rights are undermined or overwhelmed by disabling dominant narratives and practices.

Recognizing the practical and historical complications involved, and meaning no criticism either of SA or of Salem's work, I want to offer a critique of the surrounding and interpellating systems of control and subjectification. Namely, I can't help but wonder to what extent the acceptance of a "consumer" identity in relation to a mental health industry (however liberating this may have been in comparison to the "patient" or inmate identity), along with SA's narrative that positively values professional services and accountings, might actually serve to limit the transformative power and possibilities of the group as a collective and of its individual members. This may relate to Salem's finding that this particular aspect of SA's narrative is unevenly accepted by its members. In some ways, it is a narrative that casts members in a set of roles and relationships defined by market ideology, by the commoditized structuring and provision of "services," with a focus on *independence* and *productivity*, terms that also serve perpetually to disqualify many people and communities from citizenship and humanity.

Again, I do not mean to discount the ways that SA has provided a forum and form for the re-authoring of identity and meaning, of relationship to self and others; Salem's work has demonstrated the value and power of SA for its members in that regard. My point is more about how this aspect of the narrative might or might not allow SA and its members to critically engage the systems and ideologies on which social injustice and oppression depend and, in that, allow them to more critically engage with the institutional settings with and within which they must negotiate.

In very different historical and cultural context, Joe Gone's work (Chapter 7, this volume) "gives voice" to a pre- or de-colonized narrative of collective identity, meaning-making, and wellness. Gone "literally recovers" and deploys a Gros Ventre narrative that displaces and exposes—rather than negotiates with—the dominant professional narratives about mental health and therapeutic intervention. What is provided in Gone's chapter is a fully articulated cultural analysis of a particular Gros Ventre narrative genre of *vitality*. What is especially interesting is that he doesn't operate as a "native informant" who lends himself to the purposes of academic and ethnographic information-gathering and evaluation. Rather, in relation to the narrative he recovers and also in developing a *counter-narrative*, Gone works as "an organic intellectual" concerned with producing a critical text of local history, a political *testimonio* (Beverly, 2005). In the excavation of that local history, the "resurrection of subjugated knowledges" (Foucault, 1997), Gone also provides a critical juxtaposition to the practices and assumptions of clinical and counseling psychology. In so doing, he provides an exposition of the ways that the practices and ideology of psychology and mental health systems participate in subjugation and colonization. I am very curious to see where Gone's work goes from here—how, for example, the resurrected narrative becomes responsive to and reflective of contemporary circumstances and relationships, and how it posits practical solutions for the Gros Ventre people (and community psychology).

Working within a modulative, prevention framework, Hiro Yoshikawa and Olga Ramos Olazagasti (Chapter 9, this volume) employ a backward-mapping approach to inform professional and institutional beliefs and practices in three contexts: HIV/AIDS prevention programming, welfare-to-work program evaluations, and research on immigrants' beliefs about government aid programs to low-income families. They demonstrate how a narrative approach can enhance culturally anchored research and culturally resonant programming in diverse domains and in relation to diverse institutions. Although there is no attempt to challenge some of the broader cultural regularities implicated—racism or homophobia, for example, or immigration, labor, or welfare policy—Yoshikawa and Olazagasti do demonstrate the scientific value of engaging in dialogue and engaging the experience, wisdom, and voice of community members, as well as a phenomenology of everyday life. Such strategies can challenge and—more to the point here—*improve* intervention and service-provision practices and policies (as well as funding practices).

Although a number of personal stories are referenced and employed as counterpoint illustrations, N. Dickon Reppucci (Chapter 8, this volume) addresses the fact that the voices (or shouts) of youth are unheard over the sheer volume of the self-feeding cultural narrative of a certain subset of youth as dangerous, irredeemable superpredators. This is a narrative that both undergirds and emanates from other policy narratives—namely, Zero Tolerance. In a kind of feedback loop, these narratives and policies reinforce and are reinforced by a juvenile justice system that has become adversarial and punitive—that is, a juvenile criminalization system. Reppucci analyzes the narrative histories and epistemologies of the Juvenile Justice System and of Zero Tolerance policies in public schools to illuminate something about the narrative possibilities for youth today: how they are storied by others in the culture and in the systems meant (or not) to serve their needs, as well as their options for narrating themselves and their worlds.

These broad, structuring narratives are rarely laid out and articulated in a critical way within psychology; they tend to seem natural or inevitable, and so naturalize a host of policies, practices, and stories. Youth have few opportunities or resources for collective identification in common cause or the development of counter-narratives. In fact, I'd argue most youth-directed systems militate against common cause. The expansive project of pathologizing youth, meanwhile, serves varied—even apparently opposed—political, economic, and professional interests (including those of privatization and school "choice," of No Child Left Behind, or of the prison-industrial complex). Reppucci's exposition of these structured and structuring cultural discourses facilitates identifying and questioning those complicated ideologies that support injustice and oppression. It does so in a way that even an assemblage of the personal stories of individual youth might not be able to. This is not exactly the kind of backward-mapping or bottom-up strategy of empowerment that Rappaport (1981) articulated, but this kind of critical, "topdown" analysis of policy and system narratives and relationships—particularly when juxtaposed with evocative personal stories—can denaturalize what has been made to seem inevitable. Such an analysis can also help expose the ways that numerous communities—those who may not see or even be repelled by the idea of commonality—are in fact simultaneously (if not identically) "terrorized" by these narratives. Thus it can open the ground for greater common cause.

I think the question of if—and how—anybody *will listen* to these voices, even if amplified, is salient in all of the preceding chapters. Furthermore, assuming the voices are heard, I think there are important questions about the terms on which they can speak, on which they will be or *can* be understood and construed. Gayatri Spivak's (1988) essay "Can the subaltern speak?" (1988) directly addresses the problem of voice for the subaltern or (pardon the simplifying gloss) the Other and the terms on which that voice is elicited, interpreted, and used. In an essay that is a pillar of post-colonial studies, Spivak analyzes the power-laden problematic operating in any attempt to apprehend the voice of the cultural other. The analysis can apply as well, I think, to the voice of many marginalized and devalued others, including people designated as seriously mentally ill, welfare recipients, poor people, African Americans, and youth. Beverly (2005) summarizes Spivak's argument as follows:

> If the subaltern could speak—that is, speak in a way that really
> *matters* to us, that we would feel compelled to listen to—then it
> would not be subaltern. Behind the gesture of the ethnographer
> or solidarity activist committed to the cause of the subaltern in
> allowing or enabling the subaltern to speak is the trace of the
> construction of an other who is available to speak to us (with
> whom we *can* speak or with whom we feel comfortable speaking),
> thus neutralizing the force of the reality of difference and
> antagonism to which our relatively privileged position in the global
> system might give rise. She is saying that one of the things being
> subaltern means is not mattering, not being worth listening to,
> or not being understood when one is "heard."
>
> (Beverly, 2005, p. 551)

Even critical ethnographers and solidarity activists may have resistance to hearing when they are disturbed by the Other actually possessing *an agenda*: when rather than giving us their voice they actively attempt to expose and elaborate the workings of hegemony (*see also* Derrida, 1972). We are comfortable with and are valorized by the naïve "native informant," the supplicant, or the authentic yet uncritical representative of a more "natural" culture or community. In a sense, to be heard, to be included in social science or society generally, the subaltern must perform for us—must actually jettison or be relieved of their subalternity in favor of a species of domestication; they must fit into and valorize our (progressive) endeavors and the terms of our narratives (Champagne, 1995). This argument has also been applied, not incidentally, to the terms under which *some* of the culturally marginalized are elevated to the status of "privileged marginals" for inclusion within the academy and so reconstructed as exemplary individuals with "special" knowledges: "artifacts" of a discipline's "canonical objects" (Pease, 1995, pp. xi–xii). Consider our own "special things": special populations, special issues, and special topics (e.g., Plummer, 2005).

When we "give voice"—or, more accurately, when Others *give us* their voices—the speakers lose control of the contexts and interpretive frameworks to which their voices and experience will be taken, how and by whom they will be construed, and for what purposes they will be used. This is related to but is not identical to concerns about the terms on which that voice or story is collected, because even the "native" or the most thoughtful and embedded solidarity activist loses control of the products of her research as they are taken up by different readers. Voice, once taken, may be made to serve a variety of goals and agendas, including reinscriptions and reifications that the giver may not be able to anticipate, let alone control.

Furthermore, there is the tendency in the social sciences to let the voice and experience of the representative stand in metonymically for the voice and experience of the whole of the group or category. Thus, the experience of the subaltern, even when captured as community narrative, can paradoxically be construed as both idiosyncratic *and* general. This applies to the most well-intended efforts, as when we seek to determine and designate, for example, "what disabled people want" (substitute your community of interest), as if there were a universal possibility of answering the question for a diverse population (Snyder & Mitchell, 2006). Such slippages elide the diversity within the communities and populations so designated. These slippages also reinforce a naturalness or foundational reality of categories and types (e.g., Black, gay, disabled, poor, crazy) as something prefiguring or determining cultural and political (or scientific) distinctions and discourses, rather than as products of or responsive strategies to political, cultural, and discursive distinctions and categorizations (e.g., Gergen, 1990; Kincheloe & McClaren, 2005; Plummer, 2005).

That brings me back to the double explication that I have argued for: it is necessary to expose more than voices and narratives of people and communities but also to expose and question the complicated ideologies that undergird and emanate from subjugation. As Snyder and Mitchell (2006) point out in relation to disability (although again I think the argument generalizes):

> This is one reason why merely consulting with disabled people about their own desires is not a remedy to a history of diminished autonomy (Barnes, 2003) Recent trends to consult people on their own desires, such as "emancipatory research" and "client-centered care," do not evade the social problematic at the heart of disability: if disabled people are subject to the internalization of dominant definitions and values of disability just like those who are nondisabled, then asking clients about their personal goals is not a pat solution."
>
> (p. 8)

Simply asking is not a solution, that is, if we are serious about social change and social justice, not solely about better program outcomes or improved psychometrics (Prilleltensky, 2001). Not that those are somehow inherently wrong, but more that they limit us to a rehabilitative, or simply cataloguing and self-affirming enterprise that I believe community psychology means to displace. Neoliberalism, for example, draws us into ways of understanding, of taking as natural or rational beliefs about, say, identity and inequality (e.g., Duggan, 2003), government and care (e.g., Nafstad, Blakar, Carlquist, Phelps, & Rand-Hendriksen, 2009), disability (Snyder & Mitchell, 2006), obesity (Guthman & DuPuis, 2006), minority youth (R.D.G. Kelley, 1997), or queerness (Champagne, 1995). Such ways of knowing and relating are hard to escape, even to identify, when we focus only at the level of individuals or settings (e.g., Fox & Prilleltensky, 1997). These dominant narratives also tend to define the terms and contexts of resistance or protest, thereby preemptively disqualifying or delegitimizing grievances or counter-narratives.

Narratives can offer a means to critically theorize and challenge the order of things and the ideologies that author that order. They provide the wronged the rhetorical form to "argue their case" (Lyotard, 1988). In their attention to practices, experience, and meaning, community narratives can also provide practical solutions to problems in living (Siebers, 2008). But narrative theory allows for more than exposing or redressing wrongs. If many of the problems of society (and of community psychology) are relational in nature and pluralism is in fact a special form of universalism (Shweder & Sullivan, 1993), then I think narrative and voice can enable possibilities for who we are and where we might go from here. For Gamson (2002), storytelling "promotes empathy across different social locations" (p. 189); situated accounts of experience can open *discursive opportunities* in society. Unlike abstract argument or detached analysis, "deliberation and dialogue in a narrative mode lends itself more easily to the expression of moral complexity" (p. 197). The situated, experientially elaborated narrative "facilitates a healthy democratic, public life" (Gamson, 2002, p. 197; *see also* Thomas & Rappaport, 1996).

In this commentary, I aimed to elaborate some of the questions and the possibilities raised by narrative theory and voice in relation to community psychology. Consistent with Rappaport's focus on empowerment as an orienting concept, I wanted to place emphasis on questions of "why should," rather than just "how to," to attend to value choices and ramifications involved in methodological and theoretical choices (Kelly, 2003; Kincheloe & McClaren, 2005; Prilleltensky, 2001). As we go about looking for voices to give, operationalizing narrative theory, cutting and tailoring to specific empirical purposes, I wanted to encourage an expansion of the potential of narrative theory, rather than shrinking it to fit existing measurement requirements, conceptual frames, and methodological forms (Kelly, 2003). Gadamer (1989) cautioned that we ought to be very careful in our endeavors to determine *what is* because those endeavors hold such powerful determinative consequences for how we can conceive *what ought to be*. Consistent with this concern with *critical immanence*—a vision of what could or should be—it is critical to attend to how narratives and voices are collected, understood, and deployed in community psychology. Narrative and voice, like critical immanence, can help us build new forms of relationships across diverse populations and social positions to conceptualize and create better settings and better worlds.

REFERENCES

Alcoff, L. M. (2006). *Visible identities: Race, gender and the self.* New York: Oxford University Press.

Altman, I., & Rogoff, B. (1987). World views in psychology: Trait, interactional, organismic, and transactional perspectives. In D. Stokols and I. Altman (Eds.), *Handbook of environmental psychology* (pp. 7–40). New York: Wiley.

Barnes, C. (2003). What a difference a decade makes: Reflections on doing "emancipatory" disability research. *Disability and Society, 18* (1), 3–17.

Barthes, R. (1977). *Image, music, text* (S. Heath, Trans.). New York: Hill & Wang.

Beverly, J. (2005). Testimonio, subalternity, and narrative authority. In N. K. Denzin & Y. S. Lincoln (Eds.), *The Sage handbook of qualitative research, 3rd Edition* (pp.547–557). Thousand Oaks, CA: Sage.

Bruner, J. (1983). *In search of mind: Essays in autobiography*. New York: Harper and Row.

Bruner, J. (1990). *Acts of meaning*. Cambridge, MA: Harvard University Press.

Bruner, J. (1996). *The culture of education*. Cambridge: Harvard University Press.

Castells, M. (1997). *The power of identity*. Oxford, UK: Blackwell.

Champagne, J. (1995). *The ethics of marginality: A new approach to gay studies*. Minneapolis: University of Minnesota Press.

Chase, S. E. (2005). Narrative inquiry: Multiple lenses, approaches, voices. In N. K. Denzin & Y. S. Lincoln (Eds.), *The Sage handbook of qualitative research, 3rd Edition* (pp. 651–679). Thousand Oaks, CA: Sage.

Christian, B. (1987). The race for theory. *Cultural Critique, 6,* 51–53.

Cohler, B. J., & Hammack, P. L. (2007). The psychological world of the gay teenager: Social change, narrative, and "normality." *Journal of Youth and Adolescence, 36,* 47–59.

de Certeau, M. (1984). *The practice of everyday life*. S. Rendall (Trans.). Berkeley: University of California Press.

Denzin, N. K. (1997). *Interpretive ethnography: Ethnographic practices for the twenty-first century*. Thousand Oaks, CA: Sage.

Derrida, J. (1972). Structure, sign, and play in the discourse of the human sciences. In R. Macksey and E. Donato (Eds.), *The structuralist controversy* (pp. 247–272). Baltimore, MD: The Johns Hopkins University Press.

Duggan, L. (2003). *The twilight of equality: Neoliberalism, cultural politics, and the attack on democracy*. Boston: Beacon Press.

Foucault, M. (1997). January 7, 1976. In *Society must be defended: Lectures at the College de France, 1975–1976*, A.I. Davidson (Ed.), David Macey (Trans.). New York: Picador.

Fox, D. & Prilleltensky, I. (Eds.). (1997). *Critical psychology: An introduction*. Thousand Oaks, CA: Sage.

Frow, J., & Morris, M. (Eds.). (1993). *Australian cultural studies: A reader*. Urbana, IL: University of Illinois Press.

Gadamer, H-G. (1989). *Truth and method*. (J. Weinsheimer & D. G. Marshall, Eds. & Trans.). New York: Crossroads.

Gamson, W. A. (2002). How storytelling can be empowering. In K. A. Cerulo (Ed.), *Culture and mind: Toward a sociology of culture and cognition* (pp. 187–198). New York: Routledge.

Geertz, C. (2000). *Available Light: Anthropological reflections on philosophical topics*. Princeton, NJ: Princeton University Press.

Gergen, K. J. (1990). Social understanding and the inscription of self. In J. Stigler, R. Shweder, & G. Herdt (Eds.), *Cultural psychology* (pp. 569–607). New York: Cambridge University Press.

Guthman, J., & DuPuis, M. (2006). Embodying Neoliberalism: Economy, culture, and the politics of fat. *Environment and Planning: Society and Space, 24*, 427–448.

Kelly, J. G. (2003). Science and community psychology: Social norms for pluralistic inquiry. *American Journal of Community Psychology, 31*, 213–217.

Kelley, R. D. G. (1997). *Yo mama's disfunktional! Fighting the culture wars in urban America.* Boston: Beacon Press.

Kincheloe, J. L. & McClaren, P. (2005). Rethinking critical theory and qualitative research. In N. K. Denzin & Y. S. Lincoln (Eds.), *The Sage handbook of qualitative research, 3rd Edition* (pp.303–342). Thousand Oaks, CA: Sage.

Lyotard, J-F. (1988). *The différend: Phases in dispute.* (G. Van Den Abbeele, Trans.). Minneapolis, MN: University of Minnesota Press.

Mankowski, E., & Rappaport, J. (1995). Stories, identity and the psychological sense of community. In R. S. Wyer, Jr. (Ed.), *Advances in social cognition* Vol. 8 (pp. 211–226). Hillsdale, NJ: Lawrence Erlbaum Associates.

Miller, P. J., & Goodnow, J. J. (1995). Cultural practices: Toward an integration of culture and development. *New Directions in Child Development, 67*, 5–16.

Nafstad, H. E., Blakar, R. M., Carlquist, E., Phelps, J. M., & Rand-Hendriksen, K. (2009). Globalization, neo-liberalism and community psychology. *American Journal of Community Psychology, 43*, 162–175.

Pease, D. (1995). Forward. In J. Champagne, *The ethics of marginality: A new approach to gay studies* (pp. vii–xxii). Minneapolis: University of Minnesota Press.

Plummer, K. (1995). *Telling sexual stories: Power, change, and social worlds.* London: Routledge.

Plummer, K. (2005). Critical Humanism and queer theory: Living with the tensions. In N. K. Denzin & Y. S. Lincoln (Eds.), *The Sage handbook of qualitative research, 3rd Edition* (pp. 357–373). Thousand Oaks, CA: Sage.

Polkinghorne, D. E. (1988). *Narrative knowing in the human sciences.* Albany, NY: State University of New York Press.

Prilleltensky, I. (2001). Value-based praxis in community psychology: Moving toward social justice and social action. *American Journal of Community Psychology, 29*, 747–778.

Rappaport, J. (1981). In praise of paradox: A social policy of empowerment over prevention. *American Journal of Community Psychology, 9*, 1–25.

Rappaport, J. (1995). Empowerment meets narrative: Listening to stories and creating settings. *American Journal of Community Psychology, 23*(5), 795–807.

Rappaport, J. (1998). The art of social change: Community narratives as resources for individual and collective identity. In X. B. Arriaga &

S. Oskamp (Eds.), *Addressing community problems: Psychological research and intervention* (pp. 225–246). Thousand Oaks, CA: Sage.

Rappaport, J. (2000). Community narratives: Tales of terror and joy. *American Journal of Community Psychology, 28*(1), 1–24.

Ryan, W. (1971). *Blaming the victim.* New York: Vintage Books.

Savin-Williams, R. C. (2008). Then and now: Recruitment, definition, diversity and positive attributes of same-sex populations. *Developmental Psychology, 44, 135-138.*

Shweder, R. A., & Sullivan, M. A. (1993). Cultural psychology: Who needs it? *Annual Review of Psychology, 44,* 497–523.

Scott, J. W. (1991). The evidence of experience. *Critical Inquiry, 17,* 773–797.

Siebers, T. (1992). *Morals and stories.* New York: Oxford University Press.

Siebers, T. (2008). *Disability theory.* Ann Arbor, MI: University of Michigan Press.

Snyder, S. L., & Mitchell, D. T. (2006). *Cultural locations of disability.* Chicago: University of Chicago Press.

Spivak, G. C. (1988). Can the subaltern speak? In C. Nelson & L. Grossberg (Eds.), *Marxism and the interpretation of culture* (pp. 280–316). Urbana, IL: University of Illinois Press.

Stewart, E. (2000). Thinking through others: Qualitative research and community psychology. In J. Rappaport & E. Seidman (Eds.), *Handbook of community psychology* (pp. 725–736). New York: Kluwer Academic/Plenum Publishers.

Thomas, R. E., & Rappaport, J. (1996). Art as community narrative: A resource for social change. In M. B. Lykes, R. Liem, A. Banauzizi, & M. Morris (Eds.), *Myths about the powerless: Contesting social inequalities* (pp. 317–336). Philadelphia, PA: Temple University Press.

Yudice, G. (1990). For a practical aesthetics. *Social Text, 25,* 129–145.

11 Contradictions and Consistencies: Rappaport's Contributions to Community Psychology (1968–2007)

Irma Serrano-García

As I focused on writing this chapter, I was aware that not only did I have a challenging task ahead of me but that I would have to delve into my personal and professional relationship with Julian Rappaport. This would be necessary because Rappaport's contributions have touched and shaped all of us who identify as community psychologists (and read English), particularly those of us who know him on a more personal level. His contributions to the organizing themes of this volume will be evident as I examine his *corpus* of work, providing an interesting and valuable lens through which to view the trajectory of thinking in the field on these themes. Along the way, I will be recounting some important aspects of his career, detailing particular contributions, and highlighting specific ways he and his work have shaped my life.

I first "met" Julian Rappaport briefly over the phone in 1977 and personally in 1980 when he visited Puerto Rico to give a 5-day seminar on community psychology. I saw him again that same year at the Tampa Conference. By then I had read and reread the "Bible" (his 1977 textbook) and used it in my course at the undergraduate level. After that I witnessed his *In Praise of Paradox* presentation at APA in 1981 and saw, for the first and last time at an APA Division 27 event, an entire audience rise to its feet in applause. Since then, I have followed his work in publications, attended presentations at SCRA Biennials and APA, and enjoyed dinners, basketball games, and leisurely conversations both with him and his wife, Arlene. This summary is relevant because, as you well know, our personal experience colors our perception and construction of realities just as our historical context colors our individual lives.

CONSISTENCY AND CONTRADICTION

The title of this chapter refers to consistencies and contradictions. According to the New Webster's Dictionary (1981), "consistency" is defined as coherence and firmness. One who is consistent is "not self-contradictory" (p. 217). On the other hand, "contradiction" is "assertion of the contrary or opposite" and "contradictory [implies a] denial of what has been asserted or to be "inconsistent" (p. 221). I have sought to identify and examine consistency and contradiction in Julian's work, over time, between the values he exposed and the activities he pursued, in his presentation of major concepts, and with the directions he has set forth for community psychology.

Examining contradictions and consistencies is important for each of us and for the field and becomes particularly relevant when they refer to central figures who influence the future of the discipline, such as Rappaport. They reflect basic premises, values, and shifts in priorities. They determine the use and emergence or rejection of particular research interests and methodologies. They influence training models and the nature of our interventions and their impact.

Let me clarify that I do not think being consistent is necessarily positive and being contradictory necessarily negative. In my opinion, being consistent is important, particularly as regards values and goals. What we value and what we seek are beacons for what we will do. On the other hand, although evident contradictions over time may indicate confusion or doubts as to values and goals, they can also be a sign of change, of reflection, or of accurate response to changing times.

METHOD

To get to know Julian better, and to be consistent with the title I had chosen for this chapter, I requested a copy of his Vitae and analyzed **only** the publication section to identify consistencies and contradictions as well as omissions or challenges that should be addressed in the future. I did this with regard to three areas of his scholarship—empowerment, research theory and methods, and professional/nonprofessional practice.

I divided his years of productivity into decades because in my own personal experience there are important shifts in my interests more or less every 10 years. I then sought key words or phrases in the titles of his books and articles relative to: *(1)* empowerment, research (methods, instruments, procedures or paradigms), and practice (roles, issues, professional, and nonprofessional interveners); *(2)* populations (underserved, poor, and oppressed) he had focused on; *(3)* emphasis on development of theoretical frameworks or research methods; and *(4)* the disciplinary nature of his publications.

After counting the key words, authors, and journal titles—a summary I will present—I chose at least three articles from each decade—one about research, one about empowerment, and another about practice—focusing on those I had not previously read. I also reread some of his "classics" (*In praise of paradox, Terms of empowerment, Tales of Terror and Joy*, a few chapters from the 1977 book) and a couple of other pieces prompted by the articles I was reading. I read these in chronological order to see how his writings changed across the decades. As a result, I will present quantitative data in figures and will include some of the most illustrative quotes I identified related to the three issues of concern. In sum, I developed a quantitative and qualitative analysis of the publication section of Rappaport's Vitae, and my conclusions reflect the method I have just described.

ANALYSIS

Across Time

Figure 11-1 includes a count of his writings in the three areas on which I was focusing. It also includes bars that refer to articles or books that deal with all subjects (e.g., the 1977 textbook) and articles that deal with other areas (e.g., articles about clinical or educational endeavors). Rappaport has written about the three topics during most of his professional life. His first decade, the '70s, emphasized professional versus nonprofessional practice and "other" areas (he had just finished his clinical psychology degree). In the '80s, he emphasized empowerment and "other," whereas in the '90s, research and empowerment were his dominating themes. From 2000 to 2005 he focused on writings that integrated diverse topics of the discipline. In sum, he has consistently been working on these issues throughout the years.

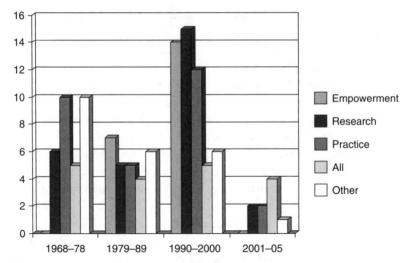

Figure 11.1   Content Areas 1968–2005

Empowerment

As soon as I began to read, I realized that Rappaport selected empowerment (a term he used for the first time in 1981) to label the set of values and goals which he had proposed for Community Psychology and about which he had been writing since 1977. In that year he wrote:

> If social scientists and professionals are to be more than agents of social control, maintainers of the status quo, and rationalizers of the current social order, we will need to turn toward a *collaboration* with local community people in their natural environments.
>
> (1977, p.viii)

> The defining aspects of the perspective [referring to community psychology] are cultural relativity, diversity, and ecology: the fit between persons and environments.
>
> (Rappaport, 1977, p. 1)

> Community psychology is interested in social change.
>
> (1977, p. 3)

> Community psychology must ultimately accept responsibility for human resource development, political activity, and scientific method.
>
> (1977, p. 5)

Community psychology is by its very nature dedicated to the challenge of the status quo.

(1977, p. 29)

The political temper of the times demands control by diverse groups over their own destiny...

(1977, p.52)

[Community psychology] must shift [its] emphasis away from programs for prevention of illness and toward programs... to support strengths of diverse communities...

(p. 125)

In this book, he also devoted a chapter to multilevel interventions and first- and second-order change.

As can be seen in the next set of quotes, this commitment to social change, psychological and political activity, collaboration, resource development, focus on strength versus weakness, and multilevel interventions, all of which require multidisciplinary understanding, continued to express itself consistently throughout the years. Some examples include his articles on empowerment (Rappaport, 1981, 1985, 1987), on collaborative research (Rappaport et al., 1985), and an analysis of social policy (Aber & Rappaport, 1994). It can also be seen in quotes such as:

...advocacy is suggested as a means of focusing intervention efforts on resource stimulation and generation rather than on individual repair.

(Davidson & Rappaport, 1978, pp. 76–77)

Empowerment has both psychological and political components.

(Rappaport, 1985, p. 17)

The nature of the theory [for Community Psychology] must be ecological.

(Rappaport, 1987, p.134)

Community psychology must be concerned with social justice.
(Rappaport, 2003)

His commitment to these values is also evident in his work with groups, usually on the margins of society or in need of particular services, as can be seen in Figure 11–2. It also includes much work with communities and

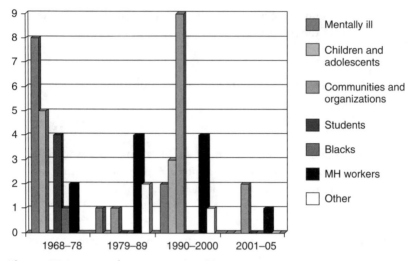

Figure 11.2   Populations 1968–2005

organizations (self-help and mutual-help groups, religious settings, schools) in which he has demonstrated the importance of collaboration.

The journals in which he and his colleagues have published show his commitment to multidisciplinary thinking and action (*see* Fig. 11–3). Although he has published frequently in community psychology journals, he has more publications in journals in other areas or specialties. Within psychology he has published in specialized journals related to clinical and consulting, school, educational, social, genetic, and developmental psychology and in journals that span the field such as *Professional Psychology*, *Psychological Bulletin*, and the *American Psychologist*. Other writings are in journals related to community mental health, juvenile justice, law and human behavior, urban education, and social policy.

Despite these consistencies, there are some interesting contradictions regarding: the definition of power, his thoughts about prevention, and the role of the profession vis-à-vis government or the State. Let us examine these next.

Power

In my readings, I could only identify one occasion in which Rappaport devotes some time to defining power. That is in itself an interesting omission for someone who works with empowerment. In his 1977 book, he assumes Ryan's (1971) definition of the concept. He speaks of power as both

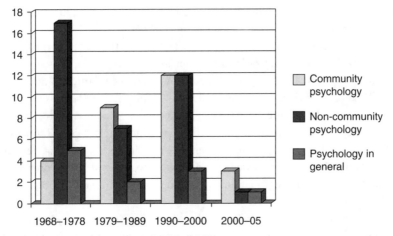

Figure 11.3   Publications 1968–2005

psychological and political—as a resource. He accepts Ryan's analysis that the "primary cause of social problems is powerlessness; its cure is a redistribution of power." In defining it as a resource, he speaks to a limited commodity that some have and some do not, as can be seen in the following quotes:

> ...- we must - develop a language and symbolism that fosters belief in each other rather than in **powerful others.**
>
> (Rappaport, 1985, p.17)

> Empowerment is not something that can be given, it must be taken. What **those who have it** and want to share it can do is to provide the conditions, the language and beliefs that make it possible to be taken by those who are in need of it.
>
> (Rappaport, 1985, p.18)

> [...] that those **who hold power** have the advantage of defining terms such as wellness.
>
> (Rappaport, 2000, p.110)

These quotes stem from a zero/sum vision of power—to the extent that some have it, others will not. However, in other writings, while still thinking of power as a resource, he emphasizes the non-restricted quality of the concept, how we can all be empowered (Rappaport, 1987). He carries this conceptualization on to his own life. In a recent reflection of his life and career, he stated: "I learned ... that shared working relationships and intellectual credit are not limited resources" (Rappaport, 2004, p. 29).

On other occasions, however, sometimes in the same writings, he abandons the conceptualization of power as resource and speaks to power as **relationship**. In 1977, he mentioned "power and economic **relationships**" (p. 52), and in 1987, he mentioned "There is built into the term [empowerment] a quality of **the relationship** between a person and his or her community, environment, or something outside one's self" (Rappaport, 1987, p.30). He also stated more recently, "... I did not realize that personal responsibility can be expressed in opposition to, as well as in congruence with, status quo **power relationships** among people... (Rappaport, 2005, p. 42).

This view is congruent with work on empowering community settings. Maton (2008) indicates that empowering settings simultaneously contribute to individual growth, community improvement, and social change. If power is viewed as centrally dependent on the nature of the relationship between persons and their surroundings, then the possibility of influence for positive change is increased, because resources contributed by all levels are activated through their interaction.

When I finished reading, I was left with the following questions: Does Rappaport consider power a resource? a relationship? Can there be people without power? Does power reside in some places and not in others? Although various authors from other disciplines have spoken to these issues (Clegg, 1989; Gamson, 1968; López & Serrano-García, 1986; Rogers, 1974), these have infrequently been discussed by community psychologists, not excepting Rappaport.

Prevention

Some believe prevention and empowerment are sides of the same coin, whereas others believe they are completely antagonistic concepts. These differences are evident in the distress I have identified in Julian's writings about prevention, as a result of his conscious recognition of his contradictions. In the past 40 years he both rejected and adopted prevention as a guiding concept and as a strategy for the field on different occasions. In 1977, he spoke to the fact that we should not focus on the prevention of illness, and in 1981 he rejected the concept strongly for generating the wrong symbolism and outliving its usefulness. He said:

Prevention and advocacy are one-sided.

(Rappaport, 1981, p. 1)

> ... programs aimed at so-called structural change, when
> framed in terms of prevention, create a metaphor that despite
> intentions, when adopted by our social institutions yields all the
> wrong symbols, images and meta messages.
>
> (Rappaport, 1981, p. 12)

> Many of us have placed our bets on the ideology of
> prevention. It is my contention that this ideology has outlived its
> usefulness and is one-sided at its core. It is a product of our failed
> social history and it creates the wrong symbolism.
>
> (Rappaport, 1981, p. 13)

Then, in 1987, he proposed it as an exemplar for the field, as an intervention strategy. He recanted on the incompatibility between prevention and empowerment.

> I seem to have suggested that adopting the concept of
> empowerment requires rejecting the concept of prevention ...
> I, mistakenly I think, suggested that these two ideas are necessarily
> incompatible. I now believe that although the distinction between
> prevention and empowerment is very important, they are not
> necessarily incompatible. ... empowerment refers to the phenomena
> of interest ... prevention is an exemplar...that is, [a] strategy of
> intervention ... Grasping this difference, and the potentially
> complementary relationship between empowerment and
> prevention is very important to the future development of the field.
>
> (Rappaport, 1987. p. 127)

However, in 1992 and 2000 he again criticized prevention, this time as narrow and circumscribed and as contrary to a social justice agenda.

> The concept of prevention...in the post-community mental health
> era [has] dramatically narrowed. It has come to have a technical
> meaning that is quite circumscribed.
>
> (Rappaport, 1992, p. 97)

> I want to problematize psychological language and metaphor ...
> [P]sychological language is personological, it relies on a variety of
> individualistic metaphors. Because it is a language steeped in
> medical notions of prevention of disease, it is not a language that
> invokes political metaphors essential to a social justice agenda.
>
> (Rappaport, 2000, p. 107)

As recently as in 2005, he again included it as an option for the field.

> Community psychology is one effort to identify and support alternative care, including prevention, mobilization of citizen volunteers, mutual help organization, advocacy and other empowering social policies.
>
> (Rappaport, 2005a, p. 43)

I believe this apparent ambivalence and contradiction is evidenced in "the intersection of autobiography and history," a phrase he suitably coined in 2004. In the early years, Rappaport was searching for new definitions for the field. In his own terms, he was pushing paradox to its limits by promoting a social change model. In the process, I believe he was fighting against his own training. In fact, he recently said, "I learned that I could not spend my life doing psychological testing and psychotherapy..." (Rappaport, 2004, p. 27), and that "The more I learned about clinical psychology the less I liked it" (Rappaport, 2004, p. 29). Thus, he came out with his attack on prevention and community mental health in 1981. However, at the time, primary prevention was, in my opinion, a move in the right direction. Before it was co-opted, prevention was the way to combat the ever-powerful medical model. It was the way to focus on the healthy instead of the ill. It was a way in which psychologists could legitimately use more of their nonclinical knowledge. Thus, continued rejection of prevention would curtail its positive impact in furthering values that needed to be advanced. So, in 1987, I believe he was masterfully bringing the field together, because we had become embroiled in the prevention-empowerment debate perhaps to no good purpose (Felner, 1985; Serrano-García, 1986). After the '80s, prevention was co-opted by both scientists and service providers and is now the purview of those that develop packaged interventions for specific diseases. This must have led to his rejection of this "new" manifestation of the term, perhaps bolstered by his observations of mutual-help and self-help groups empowering their members without help from professionals, and also his awareness that a similar process of cooptation was occurring with empowerment.

This continuous back and forth, this reflection in response to changing times, raises some serious questions for the field. Where do we stand as a field regarding prevention and empowerment? Are they still useful concepts for what we intend to do? Are they compatible at this historical moment? Should we be moving toward concepts such as oppression and liberation? In fact, Rappaport has recently stated that questions related to oppression are central to the field.

> One would do well to ask who are the oppressed people of this time and place and what do we have to learn from them? How can

I collaborate rather than dominate? How does oppression express itself in today's world? Asking such questions is central to the project of community psychology.

(Rappaport, 2005a, p. 43)

These questions have a lot to do with the next issue I have identified as contradictory in Rappaport's writings—that of our role vis-à-vis the State. I will now address the role of community psychologist as intervener.

Interveners and the State

If community psychology is to be committed to empowerment, then our roles must match this goal. Since the '70s, Rappaport has always spoken to the need for new roles for our profession (Rappaport, 1977; Davidson & Rappaport, 1978), given the re-conceptualization of community psychology as a social change effort. He has spoken of community psychology as a social movement and stated that community psychology must avoid professionalization. In that direction, he ardently fought against APA's efforts toward the licensing and credentialing of our field (Rappaport, 1978). He stated:

To the extent that a discipline becomes more a profession and less a social movement its practitioners are likely to become more defensive, conservative and lose their sense of urgency.

(Rappaport, 1981, p.8)

One of the intervention levels he mentions frequently to achieve social change is that of social or public policy. As can be seen in the next set of quotes, his main argument has been that we should identify settings that have been successful in solving the social problems that concern us (e.g., mutual-help groups, religious communities) and make these solutions as public as possible by incorporating them into policies.

[We must] study natural settings that are effective and make them public.

(Rappaport et al., 1985, p. 13)

A national policy aimed at developing mutual help organizations is a promising alternative.

(Rappaport et al., 1985, p. 23)

Locally developed solutions are more empowering than single solutions...

(Rappaport, 1987, p. 141)

One crucial issue is to find ways in which non-professional and self-help initiatives may become a legitimate part of the public health delivery system.

(Salzer, Rappaport, & Segre, 2001, p. 9)

He has stressed that these solutions will be varied and that they will change over time. Repeatedly he has stated that today's solutions will be tomorrow's problems.

Simultaneously, he has warned us about the necessity of independence from "those in power" and asked us to challenge those that finance our work.

...the advocate should be politically and economically independent from potential targets of change. A sound base of support must be established for the advocate.

(Davidson & Rappaport, 1978, p. 80)

To take this seriously [confrontation of paradoxes] means that those who are interested in social change must never allow themselves the privilege of being in the majority, else they run the risk of losing their grasp of the paradox.

(Rappaport, 1981, p. 3)

Prevention programs aimed at so called high-risk populations, especially programs under the auspices of established social institutions can easily become a new arena for colonialization, where people are forced to consume our goods and services, thereby providing us with goods and money.

(Rappaport, 1981, p. 13)

If empowerment is our aim, we will find ourselves questioning both our public policy and our role relationship to dependent people. We will not settle for a public policy of programs designed, operated or packaged for social agencies to use on people...

(Rappaport, 1985, p. 17)

Those interested in primary prevention will accomplish more by challenging the social institutions that keep people powerless than by trying to make their work acceptable to those who view prevention as yet another means for the social control of deviants... Given the reality that prevention ... will always remain marginalized by government, why not go ahead and bite the hand that feeds you?

(Rappaport, 1992, p. 99)

The questions for the field, and particularly for those of us committed to the development of public policy interventions, include: How do we foster public policies that do not immediately become a national effort to impose the same solutions on diverse groups of people? Can projects and policies that are "truly" empowering be funded? At what stage in our careers, and under what circumstances, do we stop caring about our dependence on those in power? Is there a way to really be independent? Is there a way to foster a public policy that will not co-opt independent community efforts and, even worse, not claim success for strategies that have been developed by community members? We should devote serious consideration to the contradictions that Rappaport identifies regarding these issues.

Research Theory and Methods

As we saw in Figure 11–1, research has always been at the forefront of Rappaport's concerns. He has combined his writings in the area with those of theory development, a suitable match (*see* Fig. 11–4). His trajectory reflects a shift from positivistic quantitative research, to positivistic qualitative research, to questioning positivism, incorporating constructionism and promoting alternate criteria for methodological excellence.

Early in his career, his emphasis was on methodological rigor from a positivistic quantitative perspective. This phase is characterized by articles such as one on the evaluation of "accurate empathy ratings" (Chinsky & Rappaport, 1970) and instrument development for the assessment of classroom behavior (Seidman, Linney, Rappaport, Herzberger, Kramer & Alden, 1979). In 1978, as a result of his effort to divert adolescents from the legal

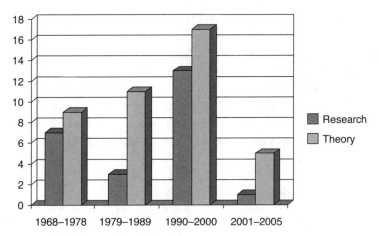

Figure 11.4   Research and Theory

system (Rappaport, Seidman, & Davidson, 1979), he began questioning the congruence between an experimental research model and the values and goals of community psychology, a theme that continues to trouble and motivate him.

In 1985, Rappaport and colleagues (Rappaport et al., 1985) wrote about collaborative research and their experience with GROW. He questioned traditional roles and research processes and proposed alternate relationships in the following statement:

> If we want to reform a social policy of empowerment and develop
> interventions or encourage empowering settings, we may find it
> necessary to become participant-observers rather than
> manipulators, to learn to collaborate and develop trust among
> researchers and people living in their own settings, where the
> researcher is guest rather than host, and where the beneficiaries
> of the setting are those who make the decisions.
>
> (Rappaport et al., 1985, p.15)

Although Rappaport had already begun to engage in qualitative research in the previous decade, in GROW's evaluation its use flourished. The team used multiple qualitative techniques (observation, logs, investigative reporting) to support its findings and to better understand the organization. In 1987, he also stressed the importance of longitudinal research:

> Longitudinal research, or the study of people, organizations and
> policies over time, is seen to be at least desirable, and perhaps
> necessary.
>
> (Rappaport, 1987, p. 140)

In following years, he participated in various studies with varying degrees of combinations of qualitative and quantitative techniques (McFadden, Seidman, & Rappaport, 1992; Salzer, Rappaport, & Segre, 1999, 2001; Toro et al., 1988). Like the previous ones, these were characterized by methodological rigor and the applicability of positivistic standards of good research.

In 1990, he returned to his preoccupation with the match between empowerment, values, and research. Interestingly, within the same article, he made statements that I consider contradictory. On the one hand he stated:

> Although the implications [of an empowerment agenda for
> research] are methodological in nature, they do not specify

particular research designs, measures or data analytic techniques.
They do concern themselves with how to conduct research
(rather than what to research) and could be applied to most
content areas.

(Rappaport, 1990, p. 52)

This statement emphasized the importance of content and the flexibility
of method. The emphasis is on the "what," not the "how."

On the other hand, emphasis is placed on "how" in the statements
that follow:

...a variety of practices that are consistent with empowerment
intentions are by their very nature questionable under currently
popular scientific canons.

(Rappaport, 1990, p. 54)

Research that asserts a strength perspective and that seeks to
give voice to the people of concern may benefit from data
collection and analysis approaches that emphasize description,
multiple perspectives and authentication of those voices that are
often ignored.

(Rappaport, 1990, p. 58)

Statistical procedures may obscure the existence of
paradoxical criteria and so fail to give voice to the people of
concern.

(Rappaport, 1990, p. 60)

Because the latter position is more thoroughly expressed, I conclude
that he believes, as I do, that not only is it important to decide research
themes and content consistent with empowerment, but it is just as important
to select "particular research designs, measures or data analytic techniques"
that foster an empowering agenda and to reject those deleterious to its implementation.

In this same piece, Rappaport presented Lincoln and Guba's (1986)
alternative criteria for research as applicable to an empowerment agenda for
both quantitative and qualitative methods and reiterated their usefulness
at an NIH conference in 1992. These criteria stem from a constructionist
perspective (Berger & Luckmann; 1967; Gergen, 1985; Ibañez, 1994), a perspective that he had mentioned in 1977 and 1987 but did not apply to his
research until recently.

Consistent with these criteria is the belief that we must learn from diverse sources and that science is not the only source of legitimate knowledge. As recently as 2003, he said: "Let us use whatever methods provide information. Science is not concerned with what ought to be" (Rappaport, 2003, p. 9). And recently, in 2005, Rappaport added:

> If I want to understand something, why not use all the means available? If I grasp it from a novel, or a journalist, or a table of numbers, or a story the question remains "Did I learn something and is it useful in describing, explaining or understanding some phenomenon of interest? Who cares if the method has been sanctified as scientific?
>
> (Rappaport, 2005b, pp. 234–235)

Since he arrived at these understandings, he has intensively worked on developing a theory of narratives (Rappaport, 2000; Mankowski & Rappaport, 2000). A cursory glance at the articles of the Special Section that he co-edited on the topic (Mankowski & Rappaport, 2000) shows the application of these new criteria in some of the studies. These articles, as well as his earlier piece on the subject (Rappaport, 2000), also demonstrate the ways in which he has integrated his understanding of method as a social change strategy, which in itself can generate understanding, collaboration, and empowerment.

He states:

> "For those of us interested in social change reading community narratives of our own time differently so that they reveal and expose rather that hide the terror is a step toward helping to recast the narratives in ways that liberate."
>
> (Rappaport, 2000, p. 3)

> Because narratives are resources they may be understood as one of the potential tools for empowerment
>
> (Rappaport, 2000, p. 6).

> ... the mission of the community psychologist/social scientist can be understood as a calling to use our tools (methods, critical observation, and analysis, scholarship, social influence) to assist others in the job of turning tales of terror into tales of joy.
>
> (Rappaport, 2000, p. 7)

These reflections notwithstanding, Rappaport continues to work in projects with both positivistic and constructionist frameworks. Is he incurring in contradiction or is he on the dialectical verge of a new synthesis? Given the authoritative manner in which different authors (Guba, 1990; Gurvitch, 1969) have espoused the impossibility of integrating these approaches, I would ask him to write more about this issue, as I would challenge others to question his stance.

Research and the State

As in the case of interventions, Rappaport has posed serious questions regarding the relationship between researchers and the State. He has posited since 1978 that government defines what content should be studied, by whom, and what methods are legitimate and which are not. He has also explained how the prevailing political stance in government—be it conservative or liberal—influences these decisions. He emphasizes how decisions are predetermined by priority values and economic interests rather than by the use of scientific knowledge that policymakers purport to respect and defend. He also mentions how funding determines our professional prestige and value and the nature and extent of our collaboration with communities. The following statements reflect his position on these issues, on which he has been consistent, if more or less forcefully, throughout the years.

> … as society becomes more politically conservative, we turn to a social science explanation favoring the intrapsychic as opposed to the environmental.
>
> (Rappaport, 1981, p. 13)

> Policy makers and service providers are much more likely to make decisions on socio-political realities and economic self-interest than on considerations of scientific knowledge. Scientists and practitioners need patrons to pay for their research and their services. In the modern world the patron is largely government. In short, government priorities, set by an imperfect relationship between the public, government officials and scientists and practitioners, determine what will be studied and what services will be delivered.
>
> (Rappaport, 1992, p. 96)

Today prevention is understood by NIH as the prevention of specific disorders. The ideal for research is experimental tests of causal models.

(Rappaport, 1992, p. 97)

State sponsored science will eventually circumscribe any social change activity that falls under its mantle.

(Rappaport, 1992, p. 97)

The greatest danger to freedom is not in the union of church and State but in the union of science and State.

(Rappaport, 2003, p. 1)

The obtaining of grants, often from the State, becomes an important index of one's worth as a scientist.

(Rappaport, 2003, p. 3)

… university/community collaboration should not be dependent on time limited grant funds.

(Rappaport, 2004, p. 34)

… there is no reason to assume government sponsored research is a neutral force with respect to the products of that research.

(Rappaport, 2005b, p. 231)

Conventional scientific methods are no guarantee of research agendas free of social control because such methods are themselves representative of current consensual (status quo) ideas about methodology on the one hand and exclusion of social critique on the other.

(Rappaport, 2005b, p. 232)

These messages should lead us all to reflect on our role within this delicate web of forces. What are our values and priorities? Are we aware of the constraints, as well as the benefits, that government funding of our projects entails? Should we be pleased or concerned when NIH begins to accept qualitative techniques and develops calls for proposals on participatory research? Can we maintain a socially critical position while encumbered by governmental norms and guidelines? Is it desirable or even possible to work outside these norms? It is my contention that being aware, creative, daring, and, when necessary, outrageous is one way of maintaining our purpose and goals within this constraining environment.

Professional and Nonprofessional Practice

Of the three areas I chose to examine for this chapter, this is by far the one where Rappaport exhibits the most consistency. Since the very beginning he has championed nonprofessionals, be they students, members of self-help or mutual-help organizations, or members of religious communities—to name but a few. He has argued that they can competently fill the gap between need for services and service provision, that there should be policies that foster professional/nonprofessional collaboration, and furthermore, that we can and should learn from them. In doing so, he has rejected notions of dependence on experts and one-down helper–helpee relationships. To support these contentions, he has directed and participated in research projects to study contributions of students as service providers (Alden, Rappaport, & Seidman, 1975; Rappaport, Chinsky, & Cohen 1971; Seidman & Rappaport, 1974), the relationship between professionals and nonprofessionals (Salzer et al., 1999; 2001; Toro et al., 1988), and differences between self- and mutual-help (McFadden et al., 1992). The following quotes communicate his commitment to these issues:

> Nonprofessionals should be agents of direct-service.
> (Rappaport, 1977, p. 372)

> There are now enough studies of non-professionals ... so
> that even if one is more conservative than to argue that they are
> better than professionals for certain problems...neither can one
> argue that there is better evidence for the effectiveness of
> professionals.
> (Rappaport, 1981, p. 7)

> We must find alternatives to inadequate and unrealistic
> traditional outpatient services and to the dumping of patients
> into the community with no services, no support and no skills. One
> positive alternative, albeit largely unresearched, may be mutual
> help organizations.
> (Rappaport et al., 1985, p. 13)

> If we are to reject a culture of dependency on experts we need
> to use a different vocabulary, to give ourselves a way to express
> new meanings, new beliefs and a new faith in ourselves and one
> another, rather than in experts.
> (Rappaport, 1985, p. 16)

I do not know how many of us have followed this path, but it is definitely one worth traveling.

IMPLICATIONS AND CHALLENGES FOR THE DISCIPLINE: WHAT STILL HAUNTS US?

In conclusion, Rappaport's 40 years of work, from my perspective, point to the following areas of development for community psychology:

1. Development of a theory of power that is congruent with our theorizing about empowerment
2. Examination of the current relationship between prevention and empowerment and the usefulness of these terms for the field. Is it time to move on?
3. Analysis of the relationship between different research paradigms and their implications for community psychology's values and goals
4. Questioning our position vis-à-vis the State in our diverse roles and settings
5. Continuing to foster nonprofessional interventions and an equitable relationship between nonprofessionals and professionals.

Before concluding this chapter, I will take the liberty of boring or challenging you with a couple of stray thoughts.

Stray Thoughts

As I read and reread many of the writings I have quoted, and as I wrote this chapter, I thought of many other things I could say about Julian Rappaport's work. As has probably happened to you when you engage in this type of activity, I discarded some of these ideas as useless or unimportant, and I forced myself to abandon others because, although tempting, they did not fit into the framework I had set for this chapter. There are, however, two ideas I want to briefly mention without going into detailed analysis. One is what I perceive of as the abandonment of cultural diversity and relativity. The other regards our identities as community psychologists.

Despite his monumental contributions, Rappaport has not delved into studies or issues related to culture as much as he has worked on the other subjects I have mentioned. Although he constantly refers to the importance of respecting difference, until his recent narrative work, he has not closely examined issues of cultural expression, cultural stigmatization, cultural norms and values and their interplay with issues such as service delivery, research content and method, nor the nature of our interventions. Even less has he examined international issues, including a focus on culture beyond the United States.

I do not mention this at the end of this chapter to be unduly critical. Rappaport is truly *estadounidense*[1]. In so being he reflects the context of isolationism and national self-centeredness that politically and culturally characterizes the United States (Burnett & Marshall, 2001; Rivera-Ramos, 2001). Despite this milieu, he is aware and has clearly explicated the impact of his socio-economic and family background, religion, and educational formation on what he believes in today (Rappaport, 2005). For me, this is explanation enough of why he has not furthered work on cultural issues. At the same time, it raises the issue of whether we can transcend our formation and backgrounds to examine cultural differences or if, as it usually happens, those who belong to a subculture solely carry the burden and responsibility for the study of, and interventions with, their particular group.

The second issue is that of our identities. Rappaport has frequently stated the need to transcend disciplinary boundaries, examine problems from different perspectives, and collaborate with others with diverse interests and academic backgrounds. However, I dare say he is first and foremost a community psychologist. He has generated theories and methods for the field as few have, and he has beckoned us to follow routes that he sees as particular to our discipline. As recently as 2005, in an *American Journal of Community Psychology* article, he wrote about what makes us distinct. To do as he proposes, if we choose to, requires a clear identity; it requires knowing who we are and what we stand for. Despite our interest in collaboration and disciplinary exchange, we must remain what we are—community psychologists. It is from this vantage point that we see the world differently, create new challenges, and receive from and provide support to those who share our calling.

I want to end where I started, with an anecdote of my relationship to Rappaport. I said initially that I met Julian Rappaport briefly over the phone in 1977. I called him at the behest of Richard Price (one of my mentors at the University of Michigan), because I was deciding whether to pursue a post-doctorate or go back to Puerto Rico to a teaching position I had been offered. Price said I should call Rappaport because he thought our values and ideas about community psychology were similar. So I gathered up all my

---

1 I could not find a suitable translation for this term. Some people may have said American, but that term pertains to all of us who live in the Americas. The translation for *estadounidense* in the New Webster's Dictionary is "citizen of the US" and that does not capture the meaning of being immersed in the nation's culture.

youthful gumption and called Professor Rappaport from my home phone. At the time I thought I was calling an older man. The phone rang, he picked it up, and I was halfway through explaining who I was and why I was calling when suddenly he interrupted me. He wanted to know who was paying for the call. Completely thrown off balance, I said that I was. Then he told me to hang up; I should not pay for the call. He would call me back so we could continue the conversation. He did, and we talked for more than an hour. I will never forget that gesture. With this chapter, I finally had the opportunity to pay for the call.

References

Aber, M. S. & Rappaport, J. (1994). The violence of prediction: The uneasy relationship between social science and social policy. *Applied and Preventive Psychology, 3*, 43–54.

Alden, L., Rappaport, J. & Seidman, E. (1975). College students as interventionists for primary grade youngsters: A comparison of structured academic and companionship programs for children from low-income families. *American Journal of Community Psychology, 3*, 261–271.

Berger, P., & Luckmann, T. (1967). *The social construction of reality.* New York: Doubleday.

Burnett, H. C. & Marshall, B. (2001). *Foreign in a domestic sense: Puerto Rico, American expansion and the constitution.* Durham, NC: Duke University Press.

Chinsky, J. M. & Rappaport, J. (1970) Brief critique of the meaning and reliability of "accurate empathy" ratings. *Psychological Bulletin, 73*, 379–382.

Clegg S. (1989). *Frameworks of power.* Newbury Park, CA: Sage.

Davidson, W. S. & Rappaport, J. (1978). Advocacy and community psychology. In G. H. Weber, & G. J. McCall (Eds.), *Social scientists as advocates: Views from applied disciplines* (pp. 67–97). Beverly Hills, CA: Sage.

Felner, R. (1985). Prevention. *The Community Psychologist, 18* (1), 31–34.

Gamson, W. (1968). *Power and discontent.* Homewood, IL: Dorsey Press.

Gergen, K. (1985). The social constructionist movement in social psychology. *American Psychologist, 40*, 266–275.

Guba, E. (1990). *The paradigm dialog.* Newbury Park, CA: Sage.

Gurvitch, G. (1969). *Los marcos sociales del conocimiento.* Caracas, Venezuela: Monte Avila Eds.

Ibañez, T. (1994). La construcción del conocimiento desde una perspectiva socio-construccionista: *Conocimiento, realidad e ideología. AVEPSO Fascículo 6*, 37–48.

Lincoln, Y. & Guba, E. (1986). But is it rigorous? Trustworthiness and aunthenticity in naturalistic inquiry. *New Directions for Program Evaluation, 30*, 73–84.

López, G. & Serrano-García, I. (1986). El poder: Posesión, capacidad o relación. *Revista de Ciencias Sociales, XXV* (1–2), 121–148.

Mankowski, E. & Rappaport, J. (2000). (Eds.) Qualitative research on the narratives of spiritually-based communities. *Journal of Community Psychology (Special Section), 28*, 479–534.

Maton, K. (2008). Empowering community settings: Agents of individual development, community betterment and positive social change. *American Journal of Community Psychology, 41* (1/2), 4–21.

McFadden, L., Seidman, E., & Rappaport, J. (1992) A comparison of espoused theories of self and mutual help: Implications for mental health professionals. *Professional Psychology: Research and Practice, 23*, 515–520.

New Webster's Dictionary of the English Language (1981). Melrose Park, IL: Delair Pub.

Rogers, M. (1974). Instrumental and infra-resources: The bases of power. *American Journal of Sociology, 79*, 1418–1433.

Rappaport, J. (1977). *Community psychology: Values, research and action.* New York: Holt, Rinehart & Winston.

Rappaport, J. (1978, August). *Education, training and dealing with the contingent future.* Paper presented at the Annual Convention of the American Psychological Association, Toronto, Canada.

Rappaport, J. (1981). In praise of paradox: A social policy of empowerment over prevention. *American Journal of Community Psychology, 9*, 1–25.

Rappaport, J. (1985). The power of empowerment language. *Social Policy, 16*, 15–21.

Rappaport, J. (1987). Terms of empowerment/Examplars of prevention: Toward a theory for community psychology. *American Journal of Community Psychology, 15*, 117–148.

Rappaport, J. (1990). Research methods and the empowerment social agenda. In P. Tolan, C. Keys, F. Chertok & L. Jason (Eds.), *Researching community psychology: Integrating theories and methodologies.* (pp. 51–63). Washington DC: American Psychological Association.

Rappaport, J. (1992). The dilemma of primary prevention in mental health services: Rationalize the status quo or bite the hand that feeds you. *Journal of Community and Applied Social Psychology, 2*, 95–99.

Rappaport, J. (2000). Community narratives: Tales of terror and joy. *American Journal of Community Psychology, 28*, 1–23.

Rappaport, J. (2003, June). *Community psychology is not (Thank God) a science.* Paper presented at a Symposium, A. Wandersman (Chair),

"Science and community psychology" held at the 9th Biennial Meeting of the Society for Community Research and Action, Las Vegas, New Mexico.

Rappaport, J. (2004). On becoming a community psychologist: The intersection of autobiography and history. *Journal of Prevention and Intervention in the Community, 28,* 15–39.

Rappaport, J. (2005a). Why community psychology? A personal story. In G. Nelson & I. Prilleltensky (Eds.), *Community psychology: In pursuit of liberation and well-being* (pp. 41–43). London: Palgrave MacMillan.

Rappaport, J. (2005b). Community psychology is (Thank God) more than science. *American Journal of Community Psychology, 35,* 231–238.

Rappaport, J., Chinsky, J. M. & Cowen, E. L. (1971). Innovations in helping chronic patients: College students in a mental institution. New York: Academic Press.

Rappaport, J., Seidman, E. & Davidson, W. S. (1979). Demonstration research and manifest versus true adoption: The natural history of a research project to divert adolescents from the legal system. In R. F. Muñoz, L. R. Snowden, & J. G. Kelly (Eds.), *Social and psychological research in community settings.* (pp.101-144) San Francisco, CA: Jossey Bass.

Rappaport, J., Seidman, E., Toro, P. A., McFadden, L. S., Reischl, T. M., Roberts, L. J., et al. (1985). Collaborative research with a mutual help organization. *Social Policy, 15,* 12–24.

Rivera Ramos, E. (2001). *The legal construction of identity: The judicial and social legacy of American colonialism in Puerto Rico.* Washington, DC: American Psychological Association.

Ryan, W. (1971). *Blaming the victim.* New York: Random House.

Salzer, M. S., Rappaport, J. & Segre, L. (2001). Mental health professionals' support of self-help groups. *Journal of Community and Applied Social Psychology, 11,* 1–10.

Salzer, M. S., Rappaport, J. & Segre, L. (1999). Professional appraisal of professionally led and self-help groups. *American Journal of Orthopsychiatry, 69,* 536–540.

Seidman, E., Linney, J. A., Rappaport, J., Herzberger, S. L., Kramer, J., & Alden, L. (1979). Assesment of classroom behavior: A multi-attribute, multi-source apporach to instrument development and validation. *Journal of Educational Psychology, 4,* 451–464.

Seidman, E. & Rappaport, J. (1974). The educational pyramid: A paradigm for research, training and manpower utilization in community psychology. *American Journal of Community Psychology, 2,* 119–129.

Serrano-García, I. (1986). Why prevention? *The Community Psychologist*, *19*(2), 19.

Toro, P. A., Reischl, T.M., Zimmerman, M. A., Rappaport, J., Seidman, E., Luke, D. A. et al. (1988). Professionals in mutual help groups: Impact on social climate and member's behavior. *Journal of Consulting and Clinical Psychology*, *56*, 631–632.

12 Searching for OZ: Empowerment, Crossing Boundaries, and Telling Our Story

Julian Rappaport

Before Barack Obama took office as President of the United States of America, the United States and the world entered a deep financial crisis. As I write this it is obvious that both of these events (his election and the financial crisis) will have a profound impact on U.S. domestic and foreign policy for many years. It may well be that these events will also influence the course of social science in general and community psychology in particular for at least the next decade and probably considerably longer.

The economic crisis has reminded people that their individual behavior is not the sole factor in their success or failure. Social, political, and economic systems make a large contribution to individual well-being. Without denying individual responsibility, it is obvious that economic distress may not be the sole "fault" of one's own individual decisions. One's well-being may depend on the decisions of others and on the priorities and values that systems are designed to favor. Where one exists in a system and the "rules of the game" matter quite a lot.

As Murray and Adeline Levine (1970, 1992) have shown, the theories (and research and practices) of the social sciences and helping professions tend to be congruent with the contemporary socio-political climate. During conservative times, individual difficulties are more often attributed to personal characteristics. During progressive political times, environmental explanations and interventions are more abundant. Similarly, the dominant socio-political climate during the period of time in which one comes of age politically tends to sustain one's political disposition in the future. Those who grow up in an Obama era are likely to maintain different political sensibilities than those who grew up in the Reagan era.

For some years now, progressive, social justice-oriented, community psychology has been "laying low;" its adherents seemed to be hoping to survive without calling too much attention to their politics. Programs have survived (sometimes under new names), students have been trained, and communities have been engaged. Practitioners have learned creative ways to survive and contribute in lean times. There now will likely be a shift in priorities, not back to the origins of community psychology but forward to new opportunities. Once again, "the times, they are a changing." Once again, our time has come and we must be prepared to "seize the time." These words refer now to different opportunities than they did when they were first written, but they do refer to new opportunities. They call for us to offer a clear and compelling narrative about what we mean when we refer to *community psychology*. We need a narrative that can capture the imagination of a new generation of progressive scholars and practitioners who are responsive to the politically aware citizenry and the dreams and aspirations of ordinary citizens.

The Obama election has been called the "fruit of the civil rights movement." The absolute joy experienced by so many people all over the world is meaningful regardless of what this president accomplishes or does not accomplish in the future. Like his election, community psychology could not have come into being without the many progressive social movements that cleared the cluttered space of traditional biases and viewpoints. Community psychology has always been less a cause than an effect of the social forces that have transformed society in the last half-century. Nevertheless, community psychology was a considerable influence in changing the field of psychology as many of the concepts and ideas pioneered by the community psychology movement, including prevention, empowerment, and diversity, were adopted by others, with or without attribution.

Community psychology emerged somewhat audaciously in the powerful discontent of the 1960s and 1970s. It has survived in the 1980s and 1990s. It staggered into the 21st century alive and well. It is now ready to re-emerge, not exactly as it first appeared, but ready to take its place alongside disciplines peopled by other progressive practitioners, scholars, and researchers who have waited patiently for a change in the temper of the times. We have crossed many borders and are ready to un-self-consciously use multiple levels of analysis, multiple methods of research, and cross-disciplinary conceptual frameworks. The practice and pragmatics of social change is about to re-emerge in social science. Let us seize the time once again. It is important for us to recognize that there is a pent-up energy among people longing for social justice. Barack Obama's election has re-awakened our collective consciousness to demand more from ourselves than the selfishness of the immediate past. Once again it is fashionable to ask questions about community well-being and shared resources rather than to simply promote individual selfishness.

Community psychologists can contribute to this new spirit in the air if we are able to once again eschew the traditional biases of an essentially conservative social science that has characterized psychology as a discipline. Hopefully, we can avoid the trap that mainstream social psychology fell into when it traded its social justice origins for academic acceptance in the dominant culture of U.S. university psychology departments. Community psychologists need to be outrageous—not just with our politics but also with our methodology. We need to assert our capacity to learn from as many and all methods as we can master. To do so now would be consistent with our history, and to argue against a tendency to domesticate the field (i.e., to make it "fit in" to what others define as psychology) would be consistent with our legacy (Marchel & Owens, 2007).

In late 1976, after I sent the manuscript for *Community Psychology: Values, Research and Action* to my Editor at Holt, Rinehart, and Winston, I began to write the Preface. The book appeared in print in April of 1977. My idea had been to summarize the emerging field of community psychology by placing it within broad historical, disciplinary, intellectual, cultural, and political perspectives. I hoped that my analysis might provide both an organized way to think about the then somewhat chaotic field of community psychology (and community mental health) and a coherent roadmap for a different way to think about the psychology of human services and community intervention across social systems, not limited to mental health and including criminal justice, education, and training. My original subtitle was the search for new paradigms, but the editor thought that was too esoteric. It now sounds a bit hackneyed, and I am glad that he convinced me not to use that phrase in the title, although I did use it in the book

As I started to write the Preface, it became clear to me that the book ended in a place that had only begun to dawn in my consciousness. To capture some of that feeling, I wrote the preface using a variant of the *Wizard of OZ* story as a preceding title page vehicle to suggest that what I had learned writing the book, among other things, was that it is not always necessary to follow the yellow brick road (i.e., do things the prescribed way) and that the project of community psychology might be about learning to share our bricks and paint (tools, resources) while encouraging people to build their own roads and houses. I do not think that the word "empowerment" appears in the book, but that was the unnamed idea I carried away from writing it. As I reread the book on later occasions, I could see this was its implicit theme.

I first formally introduced the idea of empowerment to community psychology in my Presidential Address to the Division of Community Psychology of the American Psychological Association in 1980. That address was later published in the *American Journal of Community Psychology* (Rappaport, 1981). By then I had come to the conclusion that much of what passed for something new and exciting about how to think about human services and social change was more of the same well-meaning paternalism at best and social control at worst. In that paper, "In Praise of Paradox: A Social Policy of Empowerment Over Prevention," and several that followed, I began to make more explicit the underlying themes of the earlier book and their implications for both research and action. For the next several years, my empirical research continued using mostly quantitative analysis of group data, including my longitudinal work with self- and mutual-help organizations for people with serious problems in living. At some point, I had an epiphany. Working with the same people involved in a mutual-help organization over a period of several years, I realized that the presentation of this sort of data about them tended to keep the reader quite distant from the experiences of the research participants.

Although I had predicted in 1981 that "empowerment" might become a dominant concept (and that if so we should probably worry), I was nevertheless dismayed when the term was appropriated by both those with conservative political agendas and those with therapeutic ambitions decontextualized from political analysis or intention. I was, furthermore, surprised when some viewed empowerment as only an individual construct, rather than one that is, at its heart, communal, organizational, and contextual. It is less that empowerment in the sense that I had used the term become the dominant phenomenon of interest, and more that its language had been appropriated by some to describe agendas that are neither progressive nor community-based—or simply ignore social justice and social change altogether.

In an effort to solve both the problem of misuse of the empowerment agenda and the failure of quantitative methods to capture the most meaningful experiences of the real human beings in our research settings, I began to develop a narrative theoretical approach based on a social cognition perspective and a narrative methodology based on the insights of qualitative researchers (*see*, for example, Mankowski & Rappaport, 1995; Rappaport, 2000). I have found this approach to be useful for both understanding and action in multiple community settings.

I still believe that to embrace a community psychology perspective, one must take seriously social history and the values of cultural relativity, diversity, and the ecological viewpoint as I described them in my textbook more than 30 years ago. What this requires is a democratization of our discipline: an openness to evaluation criteria that are community-based, a methodology that is responsive to the styles and preferences of our target communities, and a commitment to work with, rather than do things to or for, the communities and individuals to whom we are committed. Expressed in more radical terms, one might conclude that community psychology includes, but is "more than," science (Rappaport, 2005).

Saying all this in the 21st century is not so provocative as it was in 1977, but although these words are more common today, their meaning for research and action often remains illusive. For community psychologists, these concepts must be more than words or ideas. They are what Sarason (1978) might call "ideas to live by." They are the ground on which a psychology of social justice walks. They are the linchpins between psychology as an intellectual discipline and psychology as a field of action with goals to foster a more just society. These ideas are not neutral. They are intentional, interventionist, and value-laden. They have implications for research as well as practice. They favor a multimethod, boundary-crossing approach to methods and disciplines—an idea expressed most consistently by Kelly (*see*, for example, Kelly, 2006).

This way of thinking suggests that we must be interdisciplinary conceptually but also methodologically. Literary and cultural criticism, historical analysis of documents, case studies and visual documentaries, and qualitative and quantitative sophistication are losing their more limited identification with particular disciplines, and community psychologists have much to gain by broadening the horizons of our acceptable methodology. If my ideas about community research and action have changed in the last three decades, they have become more open to more ways to understand and act in the social world.

My most recent view of community psychology and social change now includes the idea of community narratives, the ways in which people, settings (including organizations and institutions), and communities are understood by themselves and others in storied form. The basic idea is that all communities have a narrative about themselves. This narrative may be explicit or implicit, depending in part on how well organized the community is. Most members of a community learn the narrative and adopt its themes into their own personal life stories. But this is a two-way street with a mutual influence process. This mutual influence process is the mechanism by which individuals are influenced by their communities of membership and by which individuals change their communities. Although I have generally described and illustrated this process in several different contexts in the papers referenced above, the framework is applicable to many other of the research contexts and problems with which community psychology has been concerned.

One way for community psychologists to advance our interests and to engage in strengths-based social action is to apply this framework to our own community. We should be telling our story to as many people and in as many contexts as possible. If we work in government or for non-profit organizations, in psychology departments or in colleges of education, in schools of social work, in law schools, in schools of public health, in criminal justice or in legal settings, in grassroots neighborhood organizations or traditional mental health settings, we may use different words and even refer to ourselves using words other than "community psychology." What matters is that we remain faithful to the underlying values, goals, and intentions that have so often established us in settings as both insiders and outsiders, able to both advance and critique the many places where a progressive social and political agenda can benefit from a research-based scholarly analysis. The road to OZ may not be the path that is easiest or most acceptable to the powers that be. It must be the one that enables us to work, using whatever tools are available, in honest partnership with those who we hope will benefit from our research, practice, and scholarship. This is my story, and I am sticking to it.

References

Kelly, J. G. (2006). *Becoming ecological: An expedition into community psychology*. New York: Oxford University Press.

Levine, M. & Levine, A. (1970). *A social history of the helping professions*. New York: Appleton-Century-Crofts.

Levine, M. & Levine, A. (1992). *Helping children: A social history*. New York: Oxford University Press.

Mankowski, E. & Rappaport, J. (1995). Stories, identity, and the psychological sense of community. In R. S. Wyer, Jr. (Ed.) *Knowledge and memory: The real story*. Hillsdale, N.J.: Erlbaum.

Marchel, C. & Owens, S. (2007). Qualitative research in psychology: Could William James get a job? *History of Psychology, 10,* 301–324.

Rappaport, J. (1977). *Community Psychology: Values, research and action*. New York: Holt, Rinehart and Winston.

Rappaport, J. (1981). In praise of paradox: A social policy of empowerment over prevention. *American Journal of Community Psychology, 9,* 1–25.

Rappaport (2000). Community Narratives: Tales of Terror and Joy. *American Journal of Community Psychology, 28,* 1–24.

Rappaport (2005). Community psychology is (Thank God) more than science. *American Journal of Psychology, 35,* 231–238.

Sarason, S. B. (1978). The nature of problem solving in social action. *American Psychologist, 33,* 370–380.

INDEX